Computable Bodies

ADVANCES IN SEMIOTICS

Semiotics has complemented linguistics by expanding its scope beyond the phoneme and the sentence to include texts and discourse, and their rhetorical, performative, and ideological functions. It has brought into focus the multimodality of human communication. *Advances in Semiotics* publishes original works in the field demonstrating robust scholarship, intellectual creativity, and clarity of exposition. These works apply semiotic approaches to linguistics and nonverbal productions, social institutions and discourses, embodied cognition and communication, and the new virtual realities that have been ushered in by the Internet. It also is inclusive of publications in relevant domains such as socio-semiotics, evolutionary semiotics, game theory, cultural and literary studies, human-computer interactions, and the challenging new dimensions of human networking afforded by social websites.

Series Editor: Paul Bouissac is Professor Emeritus at the University of Toronto (Victoria College), Canada. He is a world renowned figure in semiotics and a pioneer of circus studies. He runs the SemiotiX Bulletin [www.semioticon.com/semiotix] which has a global readership.

Titles in the Series:

A Buddhist Theory of Semiotics, Fabio Rambelli

A Semiotics of Smiling, Marc Mehu

Introduction to Peircean Visual Semiotics, Tony Jappy

Semiotics of Drink and Drinking, Paul Manning

Semiotics of Happiness, Ashley Frawley

Semiotics of Religion, Robert Yelle

The Language of War Monuments, David Machin and Gill Abousnnouga

The Semiotics of Che Guevara, Maria-Carolina Cambre

The Semiotics of Clowns and Clowning, Paul Bouissac

The Visual Language of Comics, Neil Cohn

Computable Bodies

Instrumented life and the human somatic niche

JOSH BERSON

Bloomsbury Academic
An imprint of Bloomsbury Publishing Plc

B L O O M S B U R Y
LONDON • NEW DELHI • NEW YORK • SYDNEY

Bloomsbury Academic

An imprint of Bloomsbury Publishing Plc

50 Bedford Square	1385 Broadway
London	New York
WC1B 3DP	NY 10018
UK	USA

www.bloomsbury.com

BLOOMSBURY and the Diana logo are trademarks of Bloomsbury Publishing Plc

First published 2015

© Josh Berson, 2015

Josh Berson has asserted his right under the Copyright, Designs and Patents Act, 1988, to be identified as the Author of this work.

British Library Cataloguing-in-Publication Data
A catalogue record for this book is available from the British Library.

ISBN: HB: 978-1-4725-3273-2
PB: 978-1-4725-3034-9
ePDF: 978-1-4725-2762-2
ePub: 978-1-4725-2827-8

Library of Congress Cataloging-in-Publication Data
Berson, Josh.
Computable bodies: instrumented life and the human somatic niche/Josh Berson.
pages cm. – (Bloomsbury advances in Semiotics)
Includes bibliographical references and index.
ISBN 978-1-4725-3034-9 (paperback) – ISBN 978-1-4725-3273-2 (hb) –
ISBN 978-1-4725-2827-8 (epub) 1. Semiotics–Social aspects.
2. Semantics–Social aspects. 3. Intercultural communication–Social aspects.
4. Biolinguistics. 5. Anthropological linguistics. I. Title.
P99.4.S62B48 2015
302.2–dc23
2015010430

Typeset by Deanta Global Publishing Services, Chennai, India
Printed and bound in India

In memory of Riki Kuklick

Contents

Preface: Registers

Toward the end of winter in 2012 I broke my foot. This was a stress fracture, the cumulative effect of cyclic loading stress over a long season of running uphill on a treadmill three mornings a week. It had been a mild winter by Berlin standards, but the previous weeks had seen a cold snap, and I was scheduled to present a paper the following week, and my personal life had become needlessly baroque. It occurred to me that Friday morning, the second of March, that I should do something that required less concentration than running. When, at 39'12" I had to stop with an unusual pain in my right foot, I viewed it as an annoyance. My foot was swollen and tender but not especially painful. I taped it, took arnica, gave my paper, and went to Paris for a short break, where I hobbled around pretending my foot was improving and practiced at a favorite yoga studio. It was seventeen days before I was diagnosed with an MTII stress fracture (Figure Preface 1).

At the time, on top of running, I was lifting weights three days a week and practicing yoga just about every day. In the face of an absurdly cerebral professional life, I invested a lot of effort in staying active. Two years earlier, I had gone through a major depression, my second. When I recovered, I found that the cyclic dimension of my mood had become more pronounced and more episodic. The manic periods lasted weeks and took on an erotic cast, leaving me depleted and irritated in a way reminiscent of erogenous stimulation that has gone on too long. Vigorous movement kept all this in check. It was my main strategy for keeping sane. The nine-plus weeks I would spend on crutches felt like a gaping hole opening up before me.

This was, let's be clear, a minor injury. No one had any doubt I would recover completely. But having my capacity for movement frustrated provoked a deep anxiety in me. More than that: it provoked a deep uncertainty about who I was and how I manifested in the world. Eleven years of practicing and occasionally teaching yoga had primed me to appreciate how kinesthesis, the awareness we have of movement in our own bodies and others', shapes us as phenomenal and social beings. But twelve weeks of enforced attention to how I distributed my weight as I stood, walked, and reached made kinesthesis salient in a way few experiences could. It was when I broke my foot that I started to think about the relationship between movement and awareness in a rigorous way.

Specifically, I became aware of how central *body schema* is to how we experience ourselves as subjects, that is, as first-person presences—and as

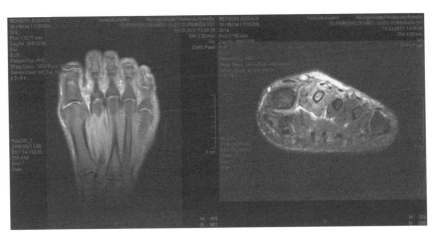

FIGURE PREFACE 1 Body as research instrument. *Author's MTII marrow reaction seventeen days post-trauma, March 2012.*

social presences. By body schema, I mean the ensemble of unconscious expectancies we use to calibrate the movements of our bodies against the proprioceptive, vestibular, visual, auditory, and tactile sensations elicited by that movement.[1] Over a lifetime of motor activity, we come to associate certain ways of holding and moving our bodies with distinct sensory profiles. These sensorimotor schemas provide a reference for current experience, allowing us to keep track of ourselves in space and gauge the intentions of other embodied presences moving through our perisomatic space. This last part, gauging the intentions of other moving beings and coordinating our movements with those of others to enact *shared* intentions, is something we are particularly good at. Ordinarily we don't even think about it.

Laid up at home watching my legs turn to jelly I started wondering what had been written about the relationship between kinesthesis and other dimensions of awareness—awareness of other people, say. I was surprised at how thin the literature seemed, and how little of it dealt with locomotion, with how we carry ourselves from place to place—let alone with the rhythmic alternation of activity and rest, alertness and distractedness, and, in some of us at least, euphoria and despair.

The dearth of commentary in the available literature on the rhythmic dimension of bodily movement particularly disturbed me. As I was learning anew, walking and many other kinds of movement demand an exquisite sense of rhythm. Those forms of movement that are distinctly human—dancing, making music, turn-taking in conversation—demand something more, the capacity to coordinate one's own movement rhythms with those of others.

Once I was tuned in to the role of motor rhythmicity in human sociality, I saw it everywhere. I noticed that the management of activity-rest rhythms had burst into public awareness as a focal point of self-care. Accelerometer bracelets, long used in research on bipolarism and sleep disorders, had been transformed into consumer accessories for tracking the quality of one's movement over the course of the day and that of one's sleep at night. Bright-light therapy, too, was migrating out of clinical settings and into the realm of personal enhancement. Timothy Ferriss' *The 4-Hour Body* had popularized polyphasic sleeping, whose practitioners dispense with a consolidated nighttime sleep episode in favor of a regime of precisely timed naps spaced over the 24-hour day.[2] Pop music had become indistinguishable from dance music as personal music devices made it possible to self-medicate at 180 beats per minute all day long.

I formulated three hypotheses. First, the management of activity-rest rhythms was newly salient as a dimension of self-care because the selective environment for human activity patterns was changing at an unprecedented pace. Urbanization and increasing mobility were contributing forces. But the decisive factor was the rise of pervasive computing. The volume of cues to social synchronization we take in over the course of the day is dramatically greater than even ten years ago, while the periodicity of these cues is dramatically lower—because they come to us from well beyond our perisomatic space. Reports on the role of circadian disentrainment in mood disorders, metabolic syndrome, and, possibly, the alarming growth of attention and arousal problems in kids, suggested the cognitive and somatic challenges of adapting to an environment in which we are always on, always, to use architect Rem Koolhaas's 1994 formulation, *in transit*.[3]

Second, the activist mobilizations taking form around the use of fine-grained behavioral time series data to tune the self were experimenting with a new way of experiencing first-person presence: the introduction of external sources of data about the body into somatosensory awareness. Building on primatologist cum philosopher Nicholas Humphrey's argument that sensation represents movement turned inward upon the central nervous system, I proposed that body-borne instrumentation might form the basis for new pathways of sensorimotor feedback.[4]

Third, as the body and its gestures become ever more intimately tied to instrumentation we experience a new entente between surveillance and self-awareness, a kind of dissociation or depersonalization in which it becomes difficult, then meaningless, to distinguish between seeing ourselves from within and seeing ourselves from without.

Instrumentation

This is a book about what happens to our bodily experience of the world as we become *instrumented*, that is, as we start to attach sensors to our bodies and our environment that generate time series data about our physiology and behavior. At this point, many readers will be subvocalizing *Quantified Self*. The Quantified Self, a social mobilization that originated in San Francisco in 2007, has become the public face of a heterogeneous set of efforts to figure out what it means to lead an instrumented life. The Quantified Self is a fascinating community and one characterized by an openness toward outsiders' interest in interpreting their work that makes working with the community a pleasure. This is not a book about the Quantified Self, but it is informed by my conversations with people in the Quantified Self community, predominantly in Europe, between 2012 and 2015.

The second phrase many readers will have in mind is *Big Data*. Big Data, of course, is all the rage, in particular when the data in question concern human behavior. Indeed, while this is not a book about Big Data in the strict sense, it *is* concerned with how the concept Data is tied to human behavior and, specifically, human bodies.

When we focus on data—how much of it we're producing, what it says about us, who has access to it—we lose track of the bodily intimacy of instrumentation. In focusing on *the instrumented life* I am stressing that whatever else computing is, it is a bodily phenomenon.

This sometimes gets lost. In fact, denying the somatic dimension of data has become a key device for marking out what is new about computing, how it differs from previous strategies for amplifying human movement. Generative art pioneer Casey Reas' formulation is exemplary: "Software is a tool for the mind. While the industrial revolution produced tools to augment the body, such as the steam engine and the automobile, the information revolution is producing tools to extend the intellect."[5]

This way of thinking invokes a shopworn view of the separability of mind and body that has no place in contemporary cognitive science—and offers no help thinking about the design challenges posed by the new volumes of human data we encounter today. Worse, it bears no correspondence to the experience of those people—all of us—who know, even when we can't put it in precise language, that pervasive computing is doing something to how we use our bodies.

Registers

In Berlin, where I lived when I wrote most of this book, one of my favorite things to do is to ride the U-Bahn, the metro. There is a quality of kinesthetic presence that is distinctive to the Berlin metro, an openness, a sense of the possibility of unbidden encounters that I find appealing. The vibe on the metro in Munich or Paris is different—people are more closed-off, inward-turned. These differences come across in how people hold their shoulders and hips, where they focus their gaze, the expressions they wear on their faces.

You don't have to be an anthropologist to pick up on the fact that people hold and move their bodies differently on public transport in different places, though the difference is clearest in direct comparison. How might we make these observations more rigorous? What kind of framework would prepare us for the possibility, say, of *instrumenting* trains and riders to figure out what, exactly, we're picking up on, what we mean when we talk about the *vibe* of a particular movement scenario?

You might start by looking at body coordination dynamics—things like spontaneous phase locking of hip sway, for instance when you and I are facing each other and without realizing it start to coordinate the timing of the minute adjustments we make to the position of our hips relative to our legs, so that we sway toward one another and then away from one another in a sustained rhythm.[6] We can imagine sensor montages to capture this kind of information in the field. But the vibe of a social situation, its kinesthetic ambiance, unfolds in a number of linked channels simultaneously, characterized, for participants in a given motoric community, by distinctive shared repertoires of gesture, coordination, and *trope* or deliberate violation of norms.

The problem is similar to one we encounter when we talk about language. You don't have to be a linguist to pick up on the fact, say, that the English spoken among teenagers in Los Angeles is different from that spoken by BBC presenters, or that when I conclude a lengthy technical argument with a sentence that starts, "All's I'm sayin is—" I'm invoking African American English to soften the technical rigor of what came before and reestablish empathy with listeners. We all *pick up* on these things. But to say exactly what we're picking up on is difficult.

Focusing on isolated coordination phenomena is like focusing on isolated phonological phenomena. Take final rhoticity—do you drop your *r*'s? Final rhoticity tells you *something* about the difference between English spoken in different parts of the world (or different social strata or age cohorts) but hardly everything. Similarly, looking at differences in the conditions under which people start to sway in time with one another on trains in Berlin and Paris would tell you *something* about how the kinesthetic vibe differs between the two places. But alongside measures for things like hip sway phase-locking propensity, we also need a theory of how variation in these measures coalesce into patterns.

The theory we need is that of registers. Again, let's start with language. You, and you, and I belong to a network of continuously evolving social formations defined by the shared enactment of speech registers, linked repertoires of gestural (above all vocal and manual), referential, and syntactic behavior. In enacting these shared registers, we enact our participation in various *speech communities*. All of us, at every moment of our waking and dreaming lives, are participating in multiple gestural-referential-syntactic communities.

After I broke my foot, I began to think of bodily movement as something we might apply register theory to. Language, after all, whether in the haptic, vocal, or glyphic (written) mode, is nothing more than a highly developed and conventionalized form of movement.

This is not a new idea, but it is one we need to take more seriously. As we'll discuss in Chapter 5, profound changes are underway in the human *somatic niche*, the dynamic coupling between habits of holding and moving the body and the spaces and structures we fashion to support these habits.

Change in the human somatic niche has been accelerating for a long time—some observers would say since the origin of agriculture, others since humans first used fire to shape wild biota.[7] What is different today is that habits of holding and moving the body learned early in life may not even support successful coping over the course of life, because the environment changes so quickly that it is no longer matched to habits learned early on. This is true in many domains of behavior. Instrumentation is among the main causes of this development.

We need a vocabulary to talk about rapid change in the human niche and the processes of acculturation—in the case of the somatic niche, *kinesthetic* acculturation—this change entails. The metro, the airplane, the classroom, the gym—these spaces all demand, and are conditioned by, distinct habits of movement and posture. Likewise spending most of one's day seated or sleeping at night in a dark, quiet environment in isolation from other bodies. These are things we have to learn, individually and collectively. Until we have a way to talk about how qualities of bodily presence become *enregistered* in a community and diffuse to other communities, it is difficult to see these qualities as historical phenomena. They appear to us as timeless facts of bodily life, and we are at loss to understand how things could be otherwise, or to formulate criteria for asking if things *should* be otherwise.

Registers give us a framework for looking at the evolution of behavior that is free of the static quality associated with "cultures." In speech or any other domain of behavior, we all use multiple registers with varying degrees of mastery. Not only that: we all *code-switch*, using the boundaries among registers to a variety of communicative ends, among them renegotiating social position.[8] Using registers to talk about movement returns us to movement's intrinsic semiotic character: movement is meaning-making. In Chapters 1 and 2 I argue that it is by gauging and responding to movement in the world that we enact our own presence as concentrated centers of sensorimotor awareness. Instrumentation serves to amplify communicative properties of movement that are there from the start.

Registers serve a second theoretical purpose: they focus our attention on *duration*. Enregistered repertoires of bodily movement are the key to how we gauge intentionality in others over time. The *over time* part is critical. This is something that does not come up in the literature on embodied cognition discussed in Chapter 2 because, as with the literature on body coordination dynamics, the empirical basis for the embodied cognition literature is laboratory centric. Laboratory settings allow us to draw out the role of body coordination in the formation of shared moods and intentions—social synchronization, or more precisely social *entrainment*, over epochs of a few seconds to a few minutes. But social entrainment also plays out over epochs of days and years. It is implicated in the formation of shared *dispositions* as well as moods and intentions, above all the disposition to regard things in our environment that move as we do as *moral conspecifics* possessed of a quality of aliveness and social presence like our own. Instrumentation is changing how we formulate judgments about the aliveness, intentionality, sentience, and personhood of the moving presences that populate our world. The content of these changes is something, after writing this book, I am just starting to get a grasp on. We return to this theme at the end of Chapter 8.

Experience

Before getting to the main discussion, I want to call attention to one other term that crops up a lot in this book, this time to acknowledge how problematic it is.

For more than a hundred years[9] the term *experience* has been central to a discursive tradition, phenomenology, that is defined by an insistence on taking bodily sensation seriously as a source of knowledge about the nature of the world. This is not a book of phenomenology. But it is concerned with changes in the qualities of bodily sensation we register in ourselves—which is to say it is concerned with bodily experience.

This is where my problems start. In a series of daring essays the historian of Japanese Buddhism Robert Sharf has pointed out just how value laden "experience" is:

> The problem with the term "experience" . . . is that it resists definition by design . . . the term is often used rhetorically to thwart the authority of the "objective" or the "empirical," and to valorize instead the subjective, the personal, the private.

> The category "experience" is, in essence, a mere placeholder that entails a substantive if indeterminate terminus for the relentless deferral of meaning.[10]

Sharf's immediate concern is with how experience has been invoked as a category of evidence to buttress claims for the efficacy of certain meditative techniques and the states they are said to induce, claims not open to empirical refutation. The refounding of Buddhist doctrine on experiential grounds was part of a broad effort to recuperate Buddhism as a distinctly modern, *scientific* form of spiritual practice, particularly in Japan following the Meiji reforms. The Buddhist modernist moment is still with us, with implications for how we understand such terms as *mindfulness*.[11] Sharf's critique gives me pause, aware, as I am, of how the public conversation about the effects of instrumentation on human awareness is shot through with talk of mindfulness—the instrumented life is robbing us of it, we can get it back with the help of techniques of focused awareness adapted from Buddhist monastic practice. The problem is not with the techniques themselves so much as with the rhetorical work, the political work we ask them to do. Again, this is something we'll return to in Chapter 8. For now, speaking as someone with more than ten years of daily practice at sitting meditation: we need to be more critical with terms like *mindfulness* and *experience*. May what follows offer a start.

Chapters 1 and 2 start with a question posed to me by an airplane seatmate as I was beginning to formulate this book: *What is a body?*—a deceptively simple question that offers a point of entrée into a discussion of how our social world is structured by movement. Chapters 3 and 4 continue with an exploration of the central role of human bodies and human sensory experience in shaping the category of knowledge we call *Data*. To understand the political implications of pervasive human data we first need a better understanding of the epistemological circumstances in which these data come to be. Chapter 5 builds on the first four chapters to offer the book's central theoretical intervention, *somatic niche construction*, alluded to above. Chapter 6 applies the somatic niche framework to what has become one of the most highly instrumented dimensions of human behavior, our rhythms of activity and rest. Chapter 7 branches out to registers of facial display, integrating recent developments in face recognition technology into a longer historical arc in which first socially marginalized others and now a much broader *we* have learned to present ourselves to the camera. Chapter 8 draws into the foreground events that have formed the backdrop to the writing of this book: my fieldwork in the Quantified Self and polyphasic sleeping communities and my role as creative and scientific director of a large-scale experiment, still taking form at this writing, in mapping patterns of alertness, mood, and sense of place, predominantly in London, and in making the research participants the central figures in the interpretive process. A postscript describes events at the Quantified Self Europe meeting in Amsterdam in May 2014, where I proposed that the focus of a meaningful instrumented life should be not the well-being of the self, but of the community.

Acknowledgments

To write a book that will be worth reading more than six months after it was published demands a certain amount of staring into space and taking long walks, preferably someplace remote and sere. This I did not have. This book was written in a year, more than half of it in a three-month sprint in the summer of 2014. What I did have was a humbling level of support.

First from my parents, whose confidence, since long before this book, has sustained me when my own has faltered.

Next from the doctors who have helped me through a series of injuries and chronic complaints and, in the process, guided me toward a deeper understanding of movement: Jun Mao in Philadelphia, Günther Malek in Vienna, and Oleg Surminski and Claudia Camps y Espinoza in Berlin. Claudia in particular has demonstrated, in all our conversations, a unique abiding withness, *selbst als mein Deutsch den Sinn verfehlt hat*.

Many years ago, in a long series of difficult conversations, Carol Ciacci challenged me to take up space in the world. It is fair to say I owe her my life. Around the same time, Alison West challenged me to attend to *how* I take up space. I hear their words in my head every morning and evening when I hit the proverbial mat.

This book originated as a side project when I was a fellow at the Rachel Carson Center for Environment and Society in Munich in 2012–13. The Center's directors, Christoph Mauch and Helmuth Trischler, encouraged my veering from the topic for which I had been granted the fellowship. I hope this book makes the case for a broader understanding of "the environment."

From Munich I shifted camp to Leipzig, where Daniel Margulies had invited me to "come hang out" with his group at the Max Planck Institute for Human Cognitive and Brain Sciences. At CBS, Natacha Mendes helped with everything from returning library books to securing institutional clearance to apply for a grant, though *help* does not really begin to cover the kind of support, intellectual and moral no less than logistical, Natacha provided.

At Bloomsbury, Gurdeep Mattu saw this project from pitch to contract to production in less time than it takes to get a journal article published. Andrew Wardell offered timely advice on manuscript preparation. Bloomsbury Advances in Semiotics series editor Paul Bouissac left me speechless with his comments on the proposal, and his friendship in the year since has been among the unexpected benefits of writing this book.

I wrote Chapters 1 through 4 as researcher (or, depending on my mood, anthropologist, scientist, artist, or epistemologist) in residence at LUSTlab in The Hague, a role LUSTlab director Dimi Nieuwenhuizen and I cooked up one June day with no idea what it might entail. Dimi's generosity and friendship, and that of everyone at LUST and LUSTlab, especially Dimi's partners, Thomas Castro and Jeroen Barendse, and studio manager Kaja Kusnirova, buffered me against the nausea of a book deadline that seemed, at the time, impossible. A grant from Jorian Schutz supported my time at LUSTlab.

In Berlin, Paul Brody and Carol Scherer offered me a home crowded with teenagers and trumpet riffs. It was there, improbably—with a three-week interlude up the street at David Rocks' pied-à-terre—that I wrote Chapters 5, 6, and 7 in a burst.

In London, Felicity Callard, Daniel Margulies, Jamie Wilkes, Claudia Hammond, Charles Fernyhough, Harriet Martin, and Kim Staines not to say everyone involved in bringing Hubbub into being, have my deep thanks. Felicity in particular has been unswerving in her determination to getting the various institutional partners to accept changes to customary grant administration practices needed to realize the Hub program's vision of introducing the energy of a design studio into the research process.

Many in the Quantified Self community, but especially Florian Schumacher in Munich, Max Gotzler in Berlin, and Ernesto Ramirez and Gary Wolf at QS Labs, have my humble thanks for the warmth and openness with which they received a skeptic.

In the polyphasic sleeping world, Puredoxyk has played Virgil to my stubbornly monophasic Dante, in the process expanding my understanding of what vigilance is.

This book grew out of a series of talks I gave starting in October 2012. Depending on the setting, the theme was "emerging ecologies of rhythmic time" or "circadian selfhood." These talks formed the basis for Chapter 6. I thank audiences at the Korea Advanced Institute of Science and Technology, Daejeon, the Centre de Recherches Interdisciplinaires, Paris, and the Haus der Kulturen der Welt, Berlin. IxDA Munich endured the first full-dress version, in February 2013, and I thank Sebastian Wendlandt and Rachel Simpson for organizing that evening. Moja Lees' invitation to present a follow-up talk at IDEO Munich gave me the chance to test material for what became Chapters 5 and 7. Extra thanks go to Buhm Soon Park at KAIST for his early encouragement. At the HKW in Berlin, Christoph Rosol and Katrin Klingan consistently found a place for this book's concerns in the Anthropocene Project. Part of Chapter 6 appeared as a chapter in the Project's three-volume valediction, *Grain Vapor Ray* (Klingan et al. 2015). A different part of Chapter 6 grew out of a workshop at Yellow Yoga in Berlin, and I thank Claudia Dietrich and Amanda Morelli for their indulgence.

For reality testing I have relied on a number of colleagues and friends, among them Sarnath Banerjee, Etienne Benson, Geof Bowker, Daniel Cermak-Sassenrath, Philip Cho, Raine Daston, Nélia Dias, Judith Gregory, Orit Halpern, Poul Holm, John Joseph, Lars Kirdan, Molly McCoy, Alex Pang, Susanne Plassmann, Jared Pool, Joanna Radin, Minna Ruckenstein, Dagmar Schäfer, David Sepkoski, Dimitris Stereonova, John Tresch, Anna Vallgårda, Fernando Vidal, and Hadas Weiss. Natasha Schüll, Rebeca Lemov, Dan Rosenberg, and Jamie Sherman, fellow observers of instrumented life, get credit for periodically reminding me of the point of this project. Whitney Erin Boesel deserves recognition for raising the specter of technological determinism. Vered Manasse asked the question that kicks off Chapter 1.

Laura and Marie-Laure Neulat gave me a place to stay in Paris when I was laying the groundwork for this book. Dora Vargha and João de la Rangel gave me a home in Berlin during my exile in Munich, and João continues to dazzle me with his insight into containerized logistics. Amanda Yiu and Paolo Zotti provided tea and shelter in Amsterdam all through the writing of the first half. E. Taylor improved my taste in trash music and gave me my first point of contact with polyphasic sleeping. Rahima Dosani renewed my faith. Rita Tishuk made me miss New York. More than once Katja Heuer kept me up all night. Jeremy Pine always seems to appear exactly when he is needed.

Lise Dobrin and Mark Turin offered advice on code-switching and alpaca therapy, what kind of dog to take to the airport, dictionaries, and how to get the Kathmandu zoo elephant to come to your birthday party.

Rohini Devasher deserves a public apology for my having had to defer our joint project, Zeitgeber/Filament.

Years ago, John Stilgoe suggested I might enjoy a life spent poking into things. I thank him for twenty years of conversations about the bodily encounter with the built environment.

Years later, Asif Agha took me on as a student under the most unpropitious circumstances imaginable. What I understand of register theory and its extension beyond language I owe to him. Along with the confidence to attempt any kind of theory of meaning.

I wrote the memo that led to the proposal that led to this book in May 2013, fresh from the Quantified Self Europe meeting in Amsterdam. The first thing I learned when I got back to Munich that Monday evening was that the previous day Riki Kuklick had died. Riki was my other, my first PhD supervisor. She was impossible and brilliant. Working with her demanded a kind of participant-observation: you simply had to be present, lest you miss something important. It drives me crazy not to be able to talk to her. This book is for her.

Elaine Kuffel, arbitrageur and pastry chef extraordinaire, sharer of whiskey and llama porn, sender of Peruvian potions, inventor of games with the

Danish language. Your friendship has made, if not all things possible, then the important ones.

Jessy Layne Tuddenham. You entered my life midway through the writing of this book, and it is no exaggeration to say the thing got finished on time mainly because your presence served as a reminder there were more important things to do. As I write, it is late December, the first sort-of clear day in Berlin in four weeks. You are eight time zones away, and I do not know what will happen when you return, and that is thrilling. I'm glad I fished your email out of the trash.

1

Bodies

Boundaries

At the gate, boarding delayed, I am paged. I have been looking out at the tarmac: turbid glare, 5:00 p.m., late July New York. It is always beach weather when you have to spend the afternoon sealed inside the airport.

At the counter, I am told I've made a mistake. *No, go sit back down, you haven't been called.*

I am certain that I have.

No, she insists, *maybe you* thought *you heard your name. Nobody called you.*

This touches a nerve. I am deaf in one ear, and my ability to hear speech in noise is nil. The whole world is like a cocktail party. An actual cocktail party, or, for that matter, a crowded departure gate, is a wall of noise.

Sir, sit down. Oh, wait, you were right. There are four or five people behind the counter, typing, writing, talking on handsets. Information is being shared. *You've been upgraded. Give me your boarding pass.*

Why? She shrugs. *Probably they oversold the main cabin. Enjoy your flight.*

Onboard, I am seated, then reseated so a couple can sit together. The seat feels strange, in some ways more restrictive than what I am used to. It lacks the chance affordances that allow me to feel comfortable the first hour of a flight—the space, through careful negotiation with seatmates, to sit half-lotus or, by propping one heel against the back of the seat in front, to brace myself and relieve my back.

You, the woman to my left says, *are the third person to occupy that seat.* We have not yet pushed back. My seatmate, it transpires, is also sitting up front by virtue of an upgrade. She accepts a hot towel, orders a glass of wine.

Is Berlin home? I ask. It is. She is, in fact, a Grinberg Method practitioner and senior Grinberg instructor for Berlin and the surrounding region. My eyes light up.

You know about Grinberg technique?

Just in the most general way: that it's a body-centered form of psychotherapy. I have a professional interest, I explain, in how people hold and move their bodies. I'd be curious to hear her views on how the way we move our bodies enters into how we . . . take form, come together, as social presences.

Well, she says. *What is a body?*

If one task of anthropology is to make the strange familiar and the familiar strange, there can be no other starting question than *What is a body?* To ask is to challenge one of the axial constituents of the tacit shared ground, the store of things we hold in common without ever having to acknowledge them, by which we make sense of the world—by which we get a handle on who the *we* is who is doing the sense-making. Our status as sign-using presences, as information-bearers, as points in space to which information flows, is contingent on our having and being bodies. It is when a gap opens up between having and being a body—through depersonalization or autoscopy, things we'll come back to, or through other forms of misrecognition of the boundary between self and nonself—that we start to ask questions. These are questions about what has gone wrong: Why do I (why does this individual) refuse to acknowledge my (her) body? Why does she acknowledge it but suggest it belongs to someone else? Why does she acknowledge it as her own but insist it is some*where* else, not at the point in space where she experiences visual, auditory, and tactile sensation but across the room, or here *and* there at the same time? Even when we are forced to ask these questions, the questions take for granted the existence of a body with definite properties of spatial extension, material composition, and identity over time, and a stable repertoire of physiological affordances. In ordinary experience, the question *What is a body?* does not make much sense.

Let's ask it anyway.

A body, I offered my seatmate, is an *awareness sink*, a concentrated center of boundary production. By awareness, I mean two things. First, the incipience, the potential emergence of a boundary, an interface, a distinction between self and nonself. I'm not proposing that this potential is present in all matter, simply that it is a gradient phenomenon, and certain configurations of matter and information express it more intensively than others. If you imagine a large urban agglomeration viewed from an airplane at night, you'd see a network of concentrated settlements, some nodes more sharply bounded, some more diffuse, varying in size and luminance, joined by roads and other media of conveyance. Scattered among the settlements would be other lit regions, perhaps lending the entire surface a faint illumination. But these would not be salient the way the nodal settlements were.

Salient. Awareness is a function not simply of the configuration of matter and information but of the perceptual salience of those configurations to an observer. This might seem to open up an infinite regress—awareness is the awareness of awareness etc.—but really it's no different from hearing a metrical structure in the rain: there are patterns of movement in the world, and on top of that we are primed to find patterns in the movement we experience. Sometimes these two phenomena resonate *in phase*, so that perceptual salience amplifies, makes more present, what is there. At other times our biases of perceptual salience mutes our experience of movement.[1] These tendencies with respect to perceptual salience are conditioned by evolution, very roughly, on three horizons: that of the species, that of the community, and that of the individual.

So bodies are awareness sinks, and awareness is the tendency to elicit a distinction between self and nonself. There is another side to this, another way of looking at it: awareness is a capacity to respond to change in the environment, in the nonself world. No, let's make it simpler: *awareness is responsiveness to change in the environment.* By *change*, I mean movement in the broadest sense, variation over time in the material configuration of the world. The world *as it presents to us*—so it could equally be that *we* are moving, and as we move we encounter new parts of space, which are different from the ones a second ago. By *respond*, I also mean movement, in a sense we'll clarify soon, movement initiated from within the body, the center of awareness, the *presence*. To say that a presence is responsive to the environment is to say that it expresses a characteristic pattern of motor activity in response to movement *in* the environment. In some interpretations, this responsiveness is all there is to goal-directedness, to intentionality.[2]

One more thing: responsiveness is responsiveness to *uncertainty*. Tuck this away. We'll come back to it later.

Configurationality

I have proposed that bodies, organismic bodies, represent *centers of responsiveness*, configurations of matter and information whose boundedness, whose stability of extension in space and time, is partly determined by how they *respond*, by how they push back against the world. This extension, this property of taking up space and time, is less well defined than we tend to imagine. Bodiliness, what I have been calling *presence*, is a gradient phenomenon. Its strength depends in large part on the degree to which it gives rise to an *interface*, a separation between the self and the nonself

characterized by a tendency on the part of the self to respond to movement in the world with a characteristic pattern of its own. By *movement* I
intend something broader than what we typically have in mind. Think of the
heliotropism of a plant, its growing toward a recurring source of sunlight, as
bearing a generic resemblance to how you yourself tilt your head to catch
the sun. Both express a quality of responsiveness, a plasticity in the interface between body and world that is guided by the body's ongoing probing
of the world. The timescales are different, and this makes a difference for the
physiological mechanisms that support the two kinds of responsiveness. But
the two phenomena share a coherence, a quality of self-organization or con-
figuredness, that distinguishes them from other kinds of movement, say that
of waves lapping a shore.

There is no reason for you to take any of this at face value. I've started
this way because I'm working up to a vision of bodies, specifically human
bodies, as *configurational* phenomena, constituted not simply by the material
substances found in them but by the principle of configuration by which those
substances are organized and continuously replaced.

A thought experiment: Take a body, a living thing, not one of those diffuse,
gradient, maybe cases I've been talking about, something clear-cut, a largish
animal, say. To underscore what follows, make sure it's a *sentient* animal.
We'll come back to what sentience is, but for now let's say a being with
enough awareness of its own boundedness, of the interface between self and
environment, to experience pain. (Pain, too, we'll come back to. Work with
me. We're building a house—a tree house, if you like—drawing the planks
from a platform we're already standing on. Trust your experience. Just think
of pain as you experience it.) It could be you, this experimental animal, or,
preferably, something or someone you have trouble experiencing empathy for.

Now. We're still working with the question posed by my seatmate, the body-
centered psychotherapist: *What is a body?* We are going to find out what a
body, what this body is. Take it by the scruff of the neck, or, if its body plan does
not include a suitably scruffy neck, anything you can get a good dangling grip on.

Imagine a big blender, something with a lot of torque, like a Pacojet but
scaled up so the body you're holding fits inside without forcing. If it helps,
image standing on a stepladder or observation deck.

Blend the body to a fine consistency. Now subject the result to centrifugation,
electrophoresis, and spectroscopy. There it is, you've got it, that's what this
body is, or was, at the moment of analysis. Of course, we have no better
understanding of what that body is, or was, than when we started. In fact,
we'd have learned a lot more by *playing* with this other for a few minutes and
taking in its pattern of responsiveness to our own movements.[3]

The violence in my thought experiment is deliberate. What I want to stress
is this: when we foreground matter at the expense of the information manifest

in the structure of assemblage through which that matter is configured, we do violence to somatic presence—and to *social* presence. The violence I have in mind is not just symbolic violence, discursive violence. It is also physical, threat-to-homeostasis violence and social, threat-to-web-of-relationships-that-sustains-us violence. The payoff for this discussion will not really come until the second half of the book, when we look at what it means to live in an environment shaped by computability. For now I want to focus on the configurational and processual character of bodily presence, specifically human presence, in its phenomenal—what-it-feels-like—and social—you-and-me, back-and-forth—dimensions. Three notes before we start.

First, I say *human presence* and not *human bodily presence*. Part of what I'm arguing is that human presence is a *kind of* bodily presence, that there is no dimension of human presence that is not, ultimately, bodily.

Second, a lot of what follows will focus on vertebrate nervous systems. We live in a time when neuroscience has a hegemonic position in the epistemology of the human—from all sides we are bombarded by cues to think of our will, our presence in the world, and our bodies as extensions of our brains. On top of that, nervous systems offer a relatively well-studied instance of the emergent behavior of systems constituted by rhythmic coupling of pulsatile signal emitters. When it comes to dynamic systems, brains are good to think with. Not long before I started writing this book I took up a position as a visiting researcher in a group that focuses on functional connectivity—coordinate activation of different parts of the cerebral cortex. This was a stimulating and congenial environment in which to write, above all because it forced me to hone my case for an alternate epistemology of the human, one in which brains play a componential role: we are not our brains, rather our brains instantiate and support patterns of rhythmic responsiveness that originate elsewhere, in the dyadic and polyadic encounters between and among bodies.[4] The final section of the following chapter and, more obliquely, the rest of the book, will make this case.

Third, when I refer to the phenomenal and social dimensions of human presence, really I'm just stressing that we can't set aside the social part when we're talking about what it feels like to be a body. In fact, I don't think we can draw a distinction of any kind between the phenomenal and the social. Phenomenal experience, first-person sensorimotor experience is itself determined by social experience. In a way, this whole book is about this process of *somatic acculturation*.

Ok. Configurationality. I want to start by quoting Bill Hillier, a theorist of urban form. I've borrowed the term *configurational* from Hillier's *Space Is the Machine* (1996/2007). "To enclose a space by a construction," Hillier proposes, "creates not only a physical distinction on the surface of the earth, but also a logical, or categoric distinction"—that is, construction imposes an information structure on matter.[5] It is this information structure, often more than the matter through which it is enacted, that determines the character of a built space, the character of the response it evokes in us. This information structure is social in character—the semantics and pragmatics of *inside* and *outside*, the range of things it is appropriate to do in the two kinds of space, are things that, tacitly or explicitly, we have to agree on. Configuration is not everything—there is a strong degree of *substrate specificity* to how we respond to a space, and the quality of the configuration itself is shaped by the substrate—certain materials lend themselves to certain forms of assembly more than others. But the relationship between substrate and configuration is loose enough that we can start to imagine configuration taking on a life of its own as a dimension of the presence, the *thereness*, of a body or a city or any other partly autonomous complex assemblage of matter and information.

When we ask what cities are, what other kinds of phenomena they resemble, Hillier continues, what we're asking, what we should be asking, is not what other things share the mineral and organic substrate we associate with built form but what other things share similar principles of configuration, even when the built space less resembles other phenomena that share a similar substrate, mineral and organic matter, say,[6] than phenomena that diverge in substrate but share a similar principle of configuration, even when the divergence is so stark as it to make it difficult to say what the substrate is. There exists, Hillier writes,

> a class of artefacts which are no less dramatic in their impact on human life [than physical artifacts], but which are also puzzling in themselves precisely because they are not objects, but, on the contrary, seem to take a primarily abstract form. Language is the paradigm case. Language seems to exist in an objective sense, since it lies outside individuals and belongs to a community. But we cannot find language in any region of space-time. Language seems real, but it lacks location.

Or rather, Hillier continues, it is not that language and other abstract social artifacts do not manifest in space-time but that "these space-time appearances are not the artefact itself, only its momentary and fragmentary realisations."

Built space too reflects the ongoing transitory social enactment of artifacts that exist strictly on the basis of convention, that is, artifacts whose presence in the world is given by the systematic articulation of referential (representational, information-bearing, meaning-generating) events to tangible substance. Systems of referential convention—*registers*—afford the principle by which an accumulation of physical traces is configured into a language or a body or a city. Cities, like languages, "are space-time manifestations of configurational ideas which also have an abstract form."[7]

The *ideas* in Hillier's formulation suggests intentionality—ideas are things we *have*. What about *principles* or *phenomena*? What if these phenomena are not simply manifested but actively *enacted* through an ongoing process of self-production? That is, let's move the intentionality out of the information structure and into the unfolding of that information structure. Now we have a formulation that suggests useful resemblances among built space, language, and bodies. These resemblances will serve as a ground for the rest of the book.

What has long distinguished cities from bodies or languages is that in the case of cities the tangible precipitate of the artifact-enacting process is a lot more durable, giving us a chance to inspect it at our leisure and form hypotheses about the relationships between the topologies of the social processes that make cities possible and those of the built artifacts that make them palpable. Can we imagine something comparable for language? For bodies? A remote sensing apparatus that would afford us a synoptic feed of the ensemble of fleeting (gestural, physiological) artifacts that make up the instantaneous activity of a (speech community, body)? The fact that today we *can* imagine such a thing reflects a shift in the relationship, between language and its material traces, between bodies and their material traces, that really has no precedent. The rest of this book is dedicated to exploring implications of this shift.

Let me stress, I am not proposing that built space, language, and bodies are self-enacting in the same way, or that built space and language express properties of awareness and responsiveness similar to those sketched above for bodies. This is a point on which my own view oscillates. At some moments I want to say that the qualities of persistence, identity, and distinctness, the *thingyness* (or, to use a more technical term, the *sortality*) of bodies, is of a different order to that of languages or cities. At other points in time I'm inclined to say that the persistence, identity, and distinctness of bodies, cities, and languages represent points on a continuum, or, better, attractors—energy minima, sinks, stable points—in a dynamic landscape. As the forces through which that landscape is constituted shift, so too will the locations of the attractors, so that particular bodies, or bodies as a category, will appear more or less thing-like. The tension between these two views—that (a) bodies are characterized by a distinctive kind of boundedness or (b) bodies simply occupy a place in the dynamic landscape where boundedness is *more* salient, but still a gradient phenomenon—is a central theme of this chapter and the next.

Let's start with the distinctive-kind-of-boundedness side: We can look at language or built form as a gel or foam that gets spread over space and time like butter on toast, and we can do the same for a *population* of bodies, but we have a hard time doing that for *a* body, and not just because we're conditioned to experience our bodies and those of others as having a distinctive quality of extension and integrity. The interface between self and nonself is not something simply given, it must be actively achieved, and it changes over time—but it is *there*, in fact, the ongoing regeneration of a boundary between body and world is constitutive of the principle of configuration that makes a body a body. This principle of configuration is known, after Maturana and Varela (1980) as *autopoiesis* (self-production), though we can imagine qualities of self-production (those of built space and language, say) that do not meet the criteria proposed for autopoietic systems. Autopoietic systems must meet three criteria:

1 They exchange things with the environment via a *semipermeable membrane*, made up of the same kind of building blocks as the system itself. This boundary must "enable you to discriminate between the inside and outside of the system in relation to its relevant components."

2 Component parts of the system are produced "by a network of reactions that take place within the boundary."

3 The boundary and reaction network "are interdependent: are the boundary components being produced by the internal network of reactions, and is that network regenerated by conditions due to the boundary itself? If yes, the system is autopoietic."[8]

I want to take issue with how we construe the "network of reactions" through which the body and its boundary are continuously regenerated.

Dynamism

So it is not just that we are configurational, defined by the information structure, the pattern of assemblage, by which our material substance, the stuff in the blender, is composed, but that the dimension of presence we can see in the blender, the substrate, is ephemeral, experiencing constant turnover. The pattern of assemblage changes too, but it's stable enough to afford us an experience of continuity over time. Let's focus for a bit on the ephemeral dimension, the dynamism, the turnover in our bodies—the network of reactions that underlies a body's ongoing self-enactment.

When we talk about the dynamism of the material substance we're made of, what we usually have in mind is *metabolic* dynamism: the ensemble of physical events that subtend the ordinary processes of growth, maintenance, and repair in an organism, things like the citric acid cycle, chromosome tran-scription and translation, and the ecosystem dynamics of the gut microbiome, whose role in metabolism and in the maintenance of a healthy inflammatory is just starting to come to light.[9]

I want to propose a different way of looking at the configurational character of bodies. The metabolic view is not wrong—it plays a key role in helping us appreciate how human action is implicated in the cycling of nutrients and toxins through the biosphere—but it is incomplete. There is another kind of change that is, if anything, more central to what I think my seatmate had in mind when she asked *What is a body?* That is movement, movement in the conventional sense, the macrokinetics of gesture and locomotion. We are configured, as bodies and as social presences, by how we move, above all by how we move *with* and *with respect to* one another. An understanding of sign-using (meaning-making, information-bearing) behavior must start with the coordination dynamics of bodily movement and the faculties of somesthesis and kinesthesis—body sensing and movement sensing—by which we resonate motorically and, through movement, enact shared moods, projects, beliefs, and dispositions.

What I am building toward is an answer to the question *What is a body?* in which the structure of assemblage, the pattern of dynamism through which we are configured and reconfigured as bodies, is continuous with the pattern of dynamism through which we are configured as dyads, crowds, communities, and societies. And not just communities and societies as these are manifest in the moment-to-moment recurring coordinate movements of individual bodies, but as they are manifest in the *social artifacts*, the *mediations*, through which we enact communities and societies over longer timeframes—that is, the social artifacts through which recurring patterns of coordinated movement coalesce into *registers*. Chief among these social artifacts are language and built space. If we knew how to look, we would see similar patterns of configuration in the recurring movements that define bodies, dyads, communities, cities, and languages.

To drive home the continuity of somatic presence with social presence we would do well to invert the figure-ground relationship implicit in the question *What is a body?* Put this way, the question presupposes that the body is the main thing we need to explain and that the social, everything that happens at the interface between bodies, is residue, something left over. So let's shift our attention one level out from the body to the dyad and see how far we can get explaining bodies in terms of dyads.

What is a dyad?

By *dyad,* I mean the quality of presence manifest in two individuals orienting their movements toward one another—or, no, we can do better, we can avoid embedding the individual in our definition of the dyad, we can say: a dyad is a quality of presence in which we observe

1   Two focal points of movement, two points in space where movement seems to originate and conclude or around which movement is centered;

2   A *crossing* in space in the arcs over which movements unfold and the vectors from focal point (e.g., my center of momentum) to that which is moving (my arm and hand as I gesture), so that my center of momentum is governed partly by movements originating with your body and vice versa.[10]

Is this enough? This is a capacious definition, for it imposes no constraints on the sources of movement, nor on the degree of parity in the influence the two centers of movement exert on one another. So we could think of the empathic bond you sometimes experience in the presence of an imposing tree as an expression of a kind of dyadism.

There's a way in which this makes sense: a tree can be a kind of social presence, we ascribe social presence to no end of other-than-animal others— trees, spaces, places, physiographic features, qualities of climate. But trees and other slower-moving social presences do not participate in the same kind of self-other behavioral contingency as that manifest, say, in a conversation. The time horizon over which a tree expresses *intentionality*, movement directed toward some end, is orders of magnitude greater than that over which we do. So, for instance, if I am a tree, and you cut off one of my limbs, I form a scar, or new growth, and in this way my movements get oriented to your body and become contingent on your movements. But this is a weak form of dynamism because it's too slow to generate a back-and-forth.[11] You cut off my limb and go away, and over the next couple of years I respond—but meanwhile the dyad has dissolved, because you're no longer present to respond in turn. So we should add a third condition,

3   The two foci of movement should be sources of intention-driven movement over roughly the same temporal horizon, or, better, they should overlap in the frequency spectra over which they express intentions through movement.

Consider conversation, a prime example of dyadism. Turn-taking behavior in conversation varies by language and setting, but the latency between two turns, the time between you stop speaking and I start speaking, is on the order of 200 ms. This entails a precise coupling between the articulatory kinetics of your speech instrument, be it manual or oral, and mine, a coupling mediated by our attunement each to the movements of the other. My diaphragm, jaws and tongue initiate the coordinated movements implicated in speaking *before* you have finished your turn. This is possible because I can hear, in the falling sonority (loudness, gain) of your speech, that you are moving toward a cadence.[12]

Let's take a less obvious example: someone sits down next to you on the train. You are reading, you do not look up, you never make eye contact or even see the person's body, you simply feel the presence of another's thigh against your own and shift your own body accordingly. Or: You lock gaze with someone, adjusting, without having to think about it, the position and bearing of your head and eyes to match hers as she does the same for yours.

All of these are examples of motor *entrainment*, the forming of a stable relationship of period, phase, and sometimes gain in the recurring energy peaks that define two or more sources of movement. Stability does not mean constancy: motor entrainment is a dynamic process of ongoing recalibration, often involving the trading of explicit signals, as, say, when musicians (or even two people cooperating to move a table) use head gestures to alert a partner to an upcoming change of tempo.[13]

This is where sociality begins.

Creatures of movement

We are creatures of movement. The *thereness* of the world, including our own bodies, arises from our capacity to anticipate how the flow of information to our senses would change if we altered our own position. Our attunement to sensorimotor coupling develops with our early explorations of the world. Motor activity entails two sets of nervous signals: efferent impulses to the muscles and an *efference copy* that gets compared to afferent, or sensory, impulses to determine whether a given sensory event reflects our own activity (reafference) or activity in the environment (exafference). In this way, movement makes salient the boundary between self and nonself.

Efference copy helps you know that it is you, not just the world, that is moving, but it does something more: it provides a basis for fine-grained predictions as to the likely outcomes of possible motor acts via offline—that is, simulated—motor activity. As we grow into our motor selves, we extend and refine our offline predictive faculty, developing an internal loop linking potential motor acts with sensory consequences. It is our ongoing exploration of the world *in cerebro* that lends the experience of reality its palpable quality. That chair, that building, that person, are there to the extent you can imagine— automatically, unconsciously—how they would present themselves if you shifted your stance.[14]

The body itself is a source of reafferent stimuli, as when you stretch and your arm swings into view. This is an example of *exteroceptive*, or body-external sensation. To this, we must add body-internal sensory processes: *interoception*, awareness of the physiological status of the body's tissues, proprioception, and vestibular sensation. Proprioceptive stretch receptors embedded in the muscles, tendons, and ligaments, together with balance and motion receptors in the vestibular apparatus of the inner ear, afford the basis for kinesthesia, the phenomenal experience of movement. Visual, auditory, vestibular, and proprioceptive signals come together in the temporoparietal junction, just past the inner ear on either side of the head. When the four systems agree on the body's position and orientation, somatic presence is coherent and action and perception originate from a single point in space. This spatial coherence is part of the basis for the reflexive experience of egocentric or first-person perspective. Disturbances in the temporoparietal junction are associated with *autoscopic phenomena*, including heautoscopy (bilocation, the feeling of being in two places at once) and out-of-body experiences.[15]

Living things, in particular sentient beings and above all our own kind, have a special quality of presence, a social presence. This too comes from movement. We are attuned to movement in the environment, we seek it out and imitate it covertly in our own bodies. When we observe patterns of movement that resemble our own, the observed movement triggers activity in the same neural circuits responsible for initiating the corresponding movement in our own bodies (so-called mirror system activity). In this way, we simulate observed nonself movement and form predictions as to what the other will do next. As with our predictions of the sensory consequences of possible self-movements, we are continuously comparing predicted movement to actually observed movement to refine our model of the other's behavior. We look for patterns of self-other motor contingency: does this (person, creature, thing) respond to my movements with a characteristic sequence of its own? We look for signs of intentionality: is this other's behavior oriented toward effecting specific environmental outcomes, as mine is? When we observe jerky or unpredictable movement in another, we feel unsettled. We project ourselves, again, automatically and unreflexively, into others' first-person perspectives and form hypotheses about what they know (e.g., what is visible from where they stand).[16]

Covert imitation represents overt imitation where actual movement has been inhibited by higher-order nervous function. The inhibition is never perfect, and we are prone to traces of overt imitation, giving rise to a pattern of motor resonance between interlocutors. Up to a point, overt imitation is prosocial: when a counterpart imitates you, you become more receptive to that other's behavior, so long as you are not too aware of the imitation. Even in simple neural network models that omit explicit simulation, motor resonance on its own induces a form of cooperation.[17]

The human faculty for imitative learning far outstrips that of any other animal. Imitative learning entails three things: intention inference (simulating others' behavior to form hypotheses as to what they are trying to achieve), motor emulation (reproducing others' motor behavior simply on the basis of distal—visual, auditory—sensation), and the inference of a causal linkage between behavior and goal. No other animal consistently combines goal inference and motor emulation in this way. Imitation, as much as language, is a characteristically human behavior and part of the basis of our ability to attribute mental states to others.[18]

Often we can infer another's intentions and social stance even in the absence of contextual cues, simply observing her movements. With reaching and grasping behavior, for instance, we make fine-grained discriminations of wrist velocity and grip aperture. We use these discriminations, generally without being able to explain what we're doing, to make predictions as to whether a particular action forms part of a cooperative act (taking something to give it to someone else), a competitive act (taking something preemptively), or an individual act (taking something to eat it in the absence of competitors).[19] The intentional valence (cooperative or competitive) is one dimension of the social information we register from the kinematics of others' movements. We also pick up on the qualities of arousal and potency (sense of agency) others express through movement—though, critically, *not* necessarily the *affective valence* of their moods, that is, whether they are experiencing a positive or negative mood.[20] Indeed, the fact that we simultaneously register topological-directional and affective dimensions of movement bears comparison to how we simultaneously discriminate topological and affective qualities of touch.[21] This cross-sensory or *metamodal* character of experience is something we'll come back to in Chapter 3.

At the base of social life, then, stands a shared experience of *kinesthetic empathy*, an ongoing choreography of movement and intention that binds sentient creatures together via palpable traces of copresence. We sense others' moving and respond in characteristic ways, as do they to our movements. Indeed, it is not just that nervous systems have evolved to respond to socially significant self-other motor contingency, but that the community is the evolutionary niche to which nervous systems are adapted.

Let's pause and look back over the country we've passed through. I have proposed that bodies are manifest not so much in the stuff found in them, the stuff we could separate with a blender, but in the pattern by which this stuff is configured. The configurational vision of bodily presence is not really controversial, but we tend to be restrictive in the kinds of dynamism we imagine to be implicated in the configuring, we tend to limit ourselves to metabolic or, a little broader, physiological dynamism. So I suggested we consider movement as an alternative.

Ok, stop. This demands just a little more justification before we move on, because the kinetics of gesture and locomotion do not, in fact, embody the same kind of turnover in the material composition of the body as do physiological kinetics, except insofar as the muscular, skeletal, nervous, synovial, cutaneous etc. phenomena implicated in bodily movement are themselves physiological. Puppets, for instance, experience movement but not physiological reconstitution. That suggests that movement is a pretty weak kind of configurational dynamism.

Three responses. First, a puppet's behavior differs from that of the social presences my seatmate had in mind when she asked *What is a body?* in that the puppet's behavior is not intention-driven. The ambiguous sociality of puppets and other automata, the fact that they exhibit a kind of pseudointentionality, agency in the absence of inner experience, is what makes them so compelling and disturbing—and politically productive.[22]

Second, I think we *do* have a tendency, many of us, today, to exclude movement from our prototype, our core understanding, of the human body— maybe *in contrast to* the bodies of other animals. Quick, think of a horse!—a leopard!—now a human being. Did you imagine the horse and leopard in motion but the human being supine, immobilized in the anatomical position, as if readied for dissection? Where this tendency to erase movement, to erase vitality, from our cognitive schema of the human body comes from has been a central question of the history of medicine over the past thirty years and more.[23]

Third, convincing you that motoricity really is what defines us, that our presence, to ourselves and others, arises from movement, that social presence is in fact a kind of *impingement*, the perturbance of one locus of movement by many others, is one half of the burden of the rest of this book. The other half of the burden is to show that that thinking of social presence as a phenomenon of movement can help us make sense of changes unfolding in our environment today, specifically, the emergence of a new form of movement, computation.

2

Rhythms

Frameworks

The last chapter got us thinking about bodies as configurational phenomena. Let's continue in that vein.

There are a number of conceptual frameworks we could use to think about the configurational dynamics of bodies. I have been guided by two in particular: first, an attitude in the philosophy of embodied cognition known as Enaction or Enactivism; second, an approach to the characterization of human movement and nervous activity in terms of the nonlinear dynamics of coupled oscillators—generators of a rhythmic energetic pulse—that, for convenience, we'll call Metastabilism.[1] There is a productive disjunction between these two camps. Enactivists and Metastabilists do not cite each other. The intuitions participants in the two discursive formations bring to the question of what is most interesting about human movement, what is deep, which phenomena offer the greatest explanatory leverage border on the mutually incompatible.

For the Enactivists, it is self-production, autopoiesis, that is deep. Autopoiesis, as we noted above, entails the ongoing regeneration of a semipermeable boundary between self and nonself. Intentionality and self-awareness emerge from autopoiesis, since a capacity to respond to environmental stimuli outside the boundary embodies a kind of awareness of the distinction between self and nonself. The capacity to seek out raw materials from outside the boundary and incorporate them into the self for the purposes of sustaining the boundary is itself a kind of intentionality.

For those who view movement in the body through the lens of the nonlinear dynamics of coupled oscillators, what is deep about movement, what invites us to make the leap from movement *in* the body to the motoric coming-into-being *of* the body, is its *scale-free* character. I have dubbed this side the Metastabilists after Kelso's emphasis on metastability, a condition in which patterns of coupling are neither chaotic nor stable but occupy, in succession, the neighborhoods of a range of attractor states without becoming stable in any of them.[2]

By *scale-free*, I mean the fact that so much is shared in the recurrence dynamics, the rhythms of information or *semiotic texture*, of the patterns of configuration that inform phenomena of presence and awareness across a wide range of scales and timescales: from the alternation of electrical spiking in different parts of the central nervous system to the intrinsic rhythms of motor readiness of muscles to the rhythmic swinging of trunk, head, limbs, and extremities in walking, dancing, or other modes of locomotion, to turn-taking in conversation or the synchronization of facial movements between infant and caregiver. These continue via slower forms of social entrainment, those playing out over periods of a day or a week or a year or the growth of a child from birth to social maturity and over the spaces given by a city or the network of places implicated in the production of a commodity—for concreteness imagine coffee or petroleum—or the planet as a whole. In this view, the boundedness of presences, their status as discrete awareness sinks or *bodies*, is a gradient phenomenon. *Oscillators*, sources of a rhythmic pulse (of energy, of information), may be compact in space, or they may be diffuse, sometimes superimposed on one another. *Attractors* or critical regions in phase space, that is, states where the energy required to maintain stable phase relationships across a population of oscillators is minimized, may be well defined or they may be "stretched" or "dirty." There is growing evidence that these "stretched" critical regions are central to the patterns of coupling characteristic of the central nervous system.[3] In the Metastabilist view of the world, the boundedness of a presence (awareness center, body) depends partly on the observer's frame of reference—how small does something have to be relative to you, and how fast does it have to be happening relative to your own faculties of sensory discrimination, for it to seem well defined in space and time?

None of this is precisely *excluded* by the Enactive view. In complex organisms, for instance, autopoiesis plays out over at least two scales, that of the cell and that of the organism, and at the organism level it involves not just the subsumption of the activities of individual cells and tissues but a nonhierarchical coupling between the organism's "own" cells and the commensals of its microbiome. But the gradient character of body boundaries is simply not salient in the Enactive view. For Enactivists, the *whereness* and substance specificity of self-aware presences is central.[4] This emphasis on whereness is useful: it keeps us mindful of what is specific, for our own experience, about somatic copresence, what changes as we start to experience ourselves and others through computational mediation.

But combining an Enactive view with a more explicitly information-theoretic view of presence as something manifest in the mutual impingement of coupled oscillators opens us up to a view of the body that is more radically—literally, *at the root*—social. Indeed, the social character of phenomenal experience has become something of a problem for embodied cognition theorists. Is there a meaningful kind of awareness to be attributed to the dyad? Is the *sentient city* more than a metaphor—or could it become so?[5] Is social cognition something that unfolds in the coordination dynamics of enminded bodies, or is it something that unfolds jointly in the individual participants in coordinate action?[6] What kind of responsiveness to the world exists in the dyad (community, city, network) that is not reducible to the responsiveness of its constituent bodies? By asking the question this way do we take for granted that it is the dyad (community, city, network) that is constituted by the individuals and not the reverse?

Rhythm

There is a third way of slicing the body-as-configuration. This one starts with the questions *Where does music come from? Why do we dance?*

When I broke my foot, as described in the Preface, and began to reacquaint myself with the world-making force of kinesthesis, the first thing I looked for, the first term I queried in the scientific citation indices, was *dance*. It felt like the obvious place to start. The thinness of the literature I turned up, and, specifically, the fact that so little of the phenomenology of dance was engaging with the exploding literature in embodied cognition, left me first nonplussed and then frustrated.[7] It took me about six months, long after I'd stopped using crutches, to realize why. Walking with crutches changes everything about the biomechanics of locomotion: gait, center of balance, the phase angle of propulsion relative to the planting of the intact foot, load dynamics on the intact foot. Initially I was most struck by the new information I was receiving about the work involved in the redistribution of one's weight in standing and reaching, the cascade of activity in the musculature of the neck, shoulders, thoracic spine, lumbar spine, and hips, guided by a coordinate set of visual, vestibular, and proprioceptive cues, that is implicated simply in shifting one's center of gravity to support a reaching-grasping gesture. The effort of reaching without toppling over, previously submerged in body schema, was now suddenly the object of ongoing and exhausting conscious control, something I had to think about constantly (how many times do you reach for something in the course of preparing a meal or doing the dishes?). Walking, by contrast, was simply tedious and physically exhausting but not all that interesting. I expected the crutches to rapidly become incorporated into my locomotive schema and was dismayed when that did not seem to be happening.

But in the fifth or sixth week of walking with crutches, after I'd been switched from a cast to the sturdier and more shock-absorbent suspension boot, something changed. Walking started to feel pleasurable again, still more effortful than with two intact feet but no longer so awkward or tedious: a recognizable expression of the urge to move, that urge amplified by six weeks and counting with no other vigorous exercise.

I had begun to internalize the distinct *rhythm* of walking with crutches. That rhythm, once learned, stayed with me long after my foot had healed. I found this out the following February, when a reinjury found me once more in an orthopedist's office. Uncertain whether my second metatarsal was again "kaputt," I began, the night before the appointment with the orthopedist, to make my peace with the possibility of going back on crutches. Walking home from the metro that evening, protecting the injured foot, I experienced a kind of kinesthetic memory unlike any other I've had, a constellation of coordinated preparatory activations that cascaded over the whole musculature of my body, rehearsing, I have to say with real *pleasure*, the rhythmic quality of walking with crutches.

These preparatory activations were not muscular contractions exactly, though they were contrac*tile*. My awareness of them was more proprioceptive—that is, arising from the sensation of muscle stretch—than tactile. What I was feeling, the individual pricks or contractile sensations, were evoked motor potentials—nervous potentials in the muscle, responsible for initiating muscle fiber contraction, instigated by a network of central nervous activity with a hub incorporating the premotor and supplementary motor areas, parts of the frontal cortex focally implicated in the planning and rehearsal of movement.

Until that moment when I began to imagine being back on crutches, I had never experienced coordinated muscle readiness in such a crystalline way. I think what lent this experience its unusual clarity, its kinesthetic saturation, is this: in contrast, say, to yoga postures, walking involves a relatively limited and repetitive sequence of motor activations, while in contrast, say, to intact walking or running, walking with crutches had remained, for me, a *marked* form of movement. It was always the contrasting figure, never the ground, it was both familiar and exceptional in a way that set it off from other ways of moving with a sensuous intensity that has stayed with me.

Rhythmic gating

We'll come back to walking in a minute. First I want to continue with motor rehearsal and the central nervous coordination of motor behavior, because even here there is a rhythmic element in play, a pulsatile quality to muscle contractile excitability known as *physiological tremor*. Physiological tremor is a *tactus*, a regular pulse, of 8–12 Hz (beats per second). The tremor is a pulse in the *gain* of muscle excitability—on the beat, the strength of the nervous potential required to instigate contraction is dramatically lower than off the beat. Repeated voluntary muscle flexion is limited to the rate given by physiological tremor, and the initiation of muscle contraction occurs at a characteristic phase angle to the peak excitability events of the tremor—that is, the initiation of movement *keeps time* with the tremor, with the onset of muscle contraction anticipating the beat.

From a functional perspective—that is, to speculate as to what evolutionary fitness advantage pulsatile excitability might confer over continuous excitability—pulsatility makes coordinated signaling more *computationally tractable* in three ways. First, it dramatically reduces the combinatorial dimensionality of coordination and sequencing. That is, if, in a 1,000 ms interval, there are just ten slots in which signals to contract can be scheduled, the number of possible combinations of simultaneous and sequential contraction signals is much lower than if, say, there were 100 or 1,000 slots. Second, and related, coarse-grained pulsatility reduces the combinatorial load of sensorimotor coupling, the calibration of motor activity to (especially reafferent) sensory information. Third, pulsatility serves to linearize peripheral response latencies, making it easier to plan for the fact that a signal dispatched to the toes will arrive a fraction of a second later than signals dispatched simultaneously to the shoulders. Pulsatility may confer one further, biomechanical advantage, facilitating the same kind of in phase additivity of impulse we use to overcome inertia in everyday life, as in pushing a swing.[8]

Ontogenetically, the intrinsic pulsatility of muscle fiber excitability originates in the muscles, "*before motoneurons have even made contact with the muscles they will later drive.*" At a later stage of development this muscle rhythmicity is transferred to the brainstem, where it is encoded in the cellular architecture and firing patterns of the inferior olivary nucleus. Critically, the inferior olive is characterized by *regenerative firing*, that is, the cells of this body depotentiate at a regular tactus even in the absence of any excitatory input. Each cell fires once or twice a second. As a population, they enact a tactus of 8–12 Hz, the same as that of intrinsic muscle excitability.[9]

So motor activity is intrinsically rhythmic, and this rhythmicity can bleed over into kinesthetic awareness, say, during highly marked forms of motor rehearsal or when we're engaged in a rhythmic activity that pushes up against the limit given by the intrinsic rate of excitability (think of an experienced tablaist).

There is more to be said about the rhythmic nature of nervous activity. I have referred to *criticality*, *metastability*, and *entrainment* in passing, and now I want to unpack these terms a bit more. Criticality refers, broadly, to a condition in which a system of potentials or signals exists in a boundary state between order and disorder. In highly ordered states, the rhythm, the pattern of recurrence, in the time series of signals arising from a population of emitters is regular. This does not mean it is simply, for example, an unadorned pulse like the ones we've been talking about. It could have a complex metrical structure reflecting the superposition of a number of rhythmic phenomena and complex interactions among emitters, but it will be stable, *predictable*. In a disordered state, the pattern of recurrence in a time series of pulses is statistically indistinguishable from random. Systems in a critical state exhibit both order and disorder, perhaps over different timescales, for example, episodes of phase alignment in a population of oscillators combined with high lability, or tendency toward sudden dissolution of one regime of phase alignment and the constitution of a new one. Criticality, it appears, is essential to the rhythmic organization of electrical activity in the central nervous system—and, no doubt, to a wide range of phenomena involving the mutual impingement of populations of oscillators distributed over a network, whether the network is manifest in a particular type of vertebrate cell or a transit system.

Metastability is a related phenomenon. It refers to systems that, rather than jumping from one stable regime to another, repeatedly approach conditions of stability without actually becoming stable. Imagine the end of a day-long walk through a landscape of rolling hills and basins. This is the phase space of a system of coupled oscillators. The light is falling and your feet are sore, and you are at pains, as you make your way back to shelter, to avoid the depressions, the low points in the landscape. These depressions are the stable states in phase space, the regions of predictable entrainment. You kind of skirt the edges of the basins without entering all the way into them. This is metastability.

Entrainment is comparatively straightforward. It refers to the degree to which a population of oscillators expresses a stable relationship of phase, period, or gain (power, volume, intensity)—the degree to which the relative timing of the signal emitted by the constituent oscillators is stable over time. This stable relationship need not be one of synchronization, though it can be, as in fireflies' flashing. It might be an antiphase relationship, as in turn-taking in conversation, or something more complex, as in making music or dancing. The signaling, the coordination, implicated in entrainment may be bidirectional, as in these examples, or it may run in just one direction—we entrain to the phase, period, and amplitude of daylight, but our behavior has no discernible corresponding influence on the earth's rotation and solar revolution.

I have been hinting that criticality, a kind of rhythmic edge play, is a central feature of what it means to be a sensorimotor presence and a social presence, a body and a person, and this criticality could be evident at every scale of organization of self-aware presence. Within the vertebrate central nervous system, the time-domain texture of oscillatory coupling is remarkably well conserved across a 17,000-fold range in brain volumes.[10] Brain electrical activity unfolds over ten classes of oscillation, with mean spiking frequencies ranging from less than one pulse a minute to more than 200 per second. Oscillations are *nested*, with the phase of slower bands, which reflect coordinated firing over greater distances, influencing the power of the faster, more localized oscillations. Cross-frequency coupling appears to be implicated in forms of awareness that demand simultaneous registration of rhythmically incident signals over a range of tempos—as in speech, where we are attending at once to phonemic, prosodic (pitch, stress, and volume), and syllabic events.[11]

Criticality, the tuning of oscillatory impingement to maintain a state that is neither multistable (alternating among a set of stable attractors) nor disordered, is implicated in metastability, the sustained superposition of tendencies toward synchronization and divergence. Criticality is also implicated in *avalanches*, sudden-onset episodes of elevated, coherent activity in a population of neurons. Avalanches reflect a high degree of *global lability* of synchronization, that is, a tendency toward sudden "massive coordinated changes" in the patterns of phase coupling in a population of oscillators.[12] In simulations and *in vitro* cell cultures, sustained avalanche activity emerges when excitability and inhibitory connectivity are balanced. This is also the state in which the system has maximal dynamic range, that is, it is sensitive to stimulation over the broadest range of stimulus intensity.

All of this must seem hopelessly abstract in a key respect: *where* are these oscillators, these recurring transient patterns of coordinated periodic alternation in signal intensity—rhythmic flashing? Where are they in the body, in the brain? The rhythmic geography of the intact nervous system is poor as yet, in part because functional magnetic resonance imaging, the technique most often used to visualize functional connectivity—patterns of coordinated activation that reliably co-occur when the body is put under characteristic cognitive demands ("Listen to the following sentence," say, or "Click the button corresponding to the location of the red square," or "Relax, hold still, focus on the cross") does not have the time-domain sensitivity to measure these oscillations. Nor in fact does it measure electrical activity at all but the blood oxygenation understood to *follow* periods of activation, as tissues that have participated in signal propagation seek nutrition to recover the stored energy depleted in firing. And of course these tasks are all highly stylized, contrived to be possible while the person whose brain activity is being measured lies in the bore of a magnet powerful enough to pull the keys out of your pocket and send them sailing across the room. It is not clear what relationship these contrived tasks bear to what we get up to as we move through the world.

Still, understanding the *metrical dynamics*, the hierarchical patterns of coupling and periodicity among large populations of oscillators inclined simultaneously toward synchronization and divergence, even in the absence of a detailed geography, does allow us to begin to imagine the metrical dynamics of bodily presence.

Synchrony, as one longtime observer of brain electrical activity notes, is a *relational* phenomenon. Whether the spikes generated by a population of oscillators are synchronous or not depends on the presence of a "reader," some further element that receives signals from the population in question and acts according to whether enough of these signals arrive within a *window of simultaneity*. In the case of cell assemblies in the central nervous system this window ranges from about 10–30 ms. It is the sum of excitatory and inhibitory activity at the synaptic interface between members of the cell assembly and the reader that occurs within that window that determines whether the reader itself will discharge. The reader, of course, is an oscillator too, so that its reading ("accrual") and output ("discharge") phases alternate, and of course all the constituents of the assembly are themselves readers in other assemblies. Over time, populations of oscillators that often pulse synchronously become *more likely* to pulse synchronously, giving rise to a pattern of recurring compositional instantiation, that is, a *syntax*.[13]

The rhythmic character of this syntax is given not just by the intrinsic pulsatile dynamics of neuronal accrual and discharge but by the rhythmic character of the body's exploration of the world—"the reader plays the initiating role" through a process of *saccadic priming*, the small movements of the sense organs—the darting of eyes, the twitching of whiskers, the flaring of nostrils in sniffing. These movements are setting the tactus, the basic rhythm, of sensory excitability, of the body's receptivity to information from the nonself world and its own substance.[14] It is the *rhythmic gating* of the fine-grained interplay between movement and sensation that provides the strongest case for the Enactive stance, that is, that awareness is a consequence, not a cause, of goal-directed movement.

But the rhythmic basis of sensorimotor contingency extends beyond the saccadic quality of exploratory motor activity in around the sense organs. It encompasses pattern generation involving the whole body, above all breathing and walking.[15]

Walking and exploring

So we are back to walking, that most ordinary expression of the body's will to exploration and self-regeneration. My own experience of locomotion frustrated, and of the reorganization of body schema entailed in accommodating that frustration, was transient and partial, and I would not presume to speak for, or do justice to the experience of, those who confront more profound and enduring forms of motoric dislocation.[16] But even this brief period of compromised movement was enough to unsettle me, to draw into awareness the fact that the ordinariness, the invisibility of walking is not something given to us, it is something achieved, something we learn—and this learning marks us in ways distinct from, though coordinate with, the recurrent act of walking itself.

Walking upright—not standing on the hind limbs but *walking*, taking the erect posture as the modal posture of balance and locomotion, is something of an evolutionary departure.[17] From a developmental perspective it presents novel challenges to proprioceptive learning, among them the ongoing recalibration of the musculature of the neck and upper back to keep the head erect. (These muscles, the sternocleidomastoids, scalenes, and upper trapezius, are where so many people whose work finds them immobilized and sitting for long stretches experience recurring tension—the draining of tonus from the musculature of the abdomen, lumbar spine, and thorax renders the body less present, leaving us cut off at the neck.) Learning to sustain verticality shapes our experience of the fine-grained push-pull of motoricity and sensation, of exteroception (visual, auditory, and cutaneous tactile sensation) and proprioception (posture and orientation cues provided by strain-responsive nerve endings embedded in the muscles and tendons and by the gravity-sensing vestibular apparatus of the inner ears[18]), of exafference (patterns of sensation arising from movement in the environment) and reafference (patterns of sensation arising from movements of the self). "The kinesthetic function," writes Olivier Gapenne, an observer of how visuopostural coordination develops in children, "mobilizes sensory organs with low spatial resolution and high temporal resolution"—peripheral vision, the fast mechanoreceptors of pressure touch sensation, to which we could add vestibular sensation. Locomotor kinesthesis is an apparatus of exploration exquisitely sensitive to simultaneity and seriality, and to patterns of recurrence in the seriality of events registers in different sensory modalities. In learning to hold ourselves upright we allow body schema to sink below the surface of that which registers to our attention, inviting "the progressive disappearance of consciousness of the lived body, *to be replaced by a consciousness of the environment.*"[19]

The interleaving of movement and sensation implicated in holding oneself up primes the body for the recurrence of synchronous cues across the sensory modalities and from all parts of the body. The intrinsic *periodicity* of kinesthetic reafference—the fact that locomotion entails a *gait cycle* that repeats—reverberates through the motoric responses through which we set ourselves in motion. The dominant spectral component of this intrinsic periodicity is a 2 beats/second tactus manifest, *inter alia*, in the vertical acceleration of the head as we walk. The 2 Hz frequency seems to be independent of age, height, and body mass (thought it could be conditioned by kinesthetic acculturation—the data supporting the finding of an intrinsic 2 Hz locomotor rhythm come from walkers from a fairly narrow range of social settings).[20]

Remarkably, given how central walking is to our encounters with the world—indeed, to the process by which a distinction between self and world becomes salient over the course of early childhood—we have but a vague understanding of how the cascading coordination of trunk, pelvic, limb, and head movements, stretch sensation, vestibular sensation, and vision and audition come together to enact and sustain the walking rhythm. Proprioceptive reafference from muscle-stretch and joint-load receptors plays a role in stimulating extensor contraction at a low level of central nervous integration, that is, via reflex arc, but locomotion cannot be simply something that emerges from spinal reflex phenomena distributed among the joints and appendages of the body. It is, rather, a product of *central pattern generation* in the spinal column, modulated by sensory integration (notably, in the temporoparietal junctions) and motor planning circuits.[21]

It is this motor reverberation that provides the *tactus*, the fundamental beat, for the social dimension of environmental exploration.[22] The approximately two beats per second linear acceleration of foot, hip, wrist, and head we experience in walking recur in a wide range of settings when we synchronize our movements to those of others—above all in music, where a pulse tempo of 120 beats per minute—two per second—has salience in a range of culturally distant stylistic contexts.

The human capacity for motor synchronization, and motor entrainment more generally, reflects both an ability to keep a steady beat independent of what others nearby are doing *and* an ability to copy the actions of others, adjusting the phase, period, and intensity of one's own gestures to match those of others. Indeed, entrainment entails *prediction*, since there is a certain latency between when the person next to you acts (clapping, bobbing her head) and when you become aware of that action. Just as in turn-taking in conversation, we need to start acting *before* we have sensory validation that we're in time with our neighbors.

This combination of a knack for keeping a steady beat and a knack for predictive entrainment is not uniquely human. It has evolved independently in fireflies and frogs, for instance, as a mechanism of signal amplification for mate attraction and collective defense respectively, and something similar is seen in the synchronized pant-hooting of bonobo chimpanzees. Far less common is the capacity to entrain motorically to an arbitrary beat (by bobbing one's head on the beat, say), or to pick out the underlying tactus from a metrically complex rhythm where not every pulse is sounded. Some parrots do this spontaneously, most famously YouTube sensation Snowball, a captive sulfur-crested cockatoo whose grooving to the Backstreet Boys has inspired a new wave of interest in the comparative ethology of pulse entrainment. An Asian elephant has been videoed spontaneously moving in time to the beat. A California sea lion, Ronan, trained by her human collaborators to bob in time to pulse trains at 80 and 120 beats per minute, independently extended her new skill to metrically complex music at a range of tempi, raising the possibility that finding the beat in a complex rhythm is a widespread but latent skill, rarely observed because few animals are given to expressing the beat through movement without prompting.[23]

Similar paradigms have met with no success in simians and other-than-human primates, with the equivocal exception of Ai, a veteran chimpanzee research participant who, having been taught to tap out a sequence of alternating keys on a piano-type keyboard, spontaneously aligned her tapping to an outside sound source—but only when the external pulse tempo was close to the tempo at which she tended to tap the keys in any case.[24]

Other-than-human animals, large gregarious vertebrates in particular, have had a central role in the process by which humans have become what they—we—are. Animals have shaped the spaces of human habitation and the contours of human selfhood. They were the source of many of our shared rubrics for interpreting movement in the nonself world, for distinguishing aliveness, intentionality, and moral agency—personhood. We'll have more to say about interspecies sociality in Chapter 5. But there is something unusual about the rhythmic dimension of human movement, something that lends specificity to the question *What is a* human *body?*

This exceptional rhythmicity grows out of our motor explorations of the world, but these motor explorations, in turn, are guided by species-specific faculties supporting the *social* enactment of movement. These include imitation in two partly distinct senses: (1) the imitation of intentional behavior, the tendency to observe others, infer the intended outcome of their efforts, and attempt to achieve a similar outcome, without necessarily copying the specific pattern of movement used by your model; (2) *motor resonance*, the overflow of activation in populations of bimodal neurons tuned both to the preparation or execution of movement and to the perception of the same type of movement, into overt movement. This bimodal pattern of activation is usually referred to as a *mirror* neuron system, but it supports something more than imitative mirroring, a more general capacity for complementary joint action.[25] It is the combination of these two dimensions of imitation that makes social learning possible.[26]

The emergence of complementarity and coordination from imitation does not require an explicit "theory of mind" on the part of the interactants. It simply demands that the participants in a dyad both be inclined toward the rhythmic pursuit of contact. This inclination comes out even in highly denatured forms of interaction, as, for instance, in a series of experiments in which two people are asked to manipulate avatars in a one-dimension virtual world, distinguishing when they've come into contact with their counterpart from when they've come into contact with their counterpart's shadow—an object, perceptually indistinguishable from the other participant's avatar, moving in parallel with the other's avatar at a fixed distance from it. People who play this game consistently register true interactions more often than shadow interactions even though they cannot tell, in a given encounter, whether they are faced with their counterpart's avatar or it shadow. This is possible because when the participants encounter one another, that is, when their avatars meet, they *both* respond with a kind of oscillatory exploratory behavior, first stepping back, and then reaching out again to see what they've encountered, creating a two-way coupling, a dyad. Awareness of individual bodies—the other in the experimental paradigm described above, the other *and the self* in real life—flows from the dyad to the individual.[27]

Indeed, it is the *desire* to enact coordinate patterns of movement—and, by extension, coordinate moods and dispositions—perhaps *more than* a unique capacity to pick out others' intentions from their actions, that underlies the uniquely human elaboration of recurrent habits of movement transmitted by social learning, that is, *culture*.[28] So we should revise my earlier statement: it is not that we are creatures of movement, it is that we are creatures of co-movement, of moving *with*.

We are not REPLs

At this point some readers may feel misled. These first two chapters have had little to say about instrumentation or computability or data or self-tracking. These topics are coming. But before we could talk about what happens as bodies become instrumented, we needed to have a working understanding of what we mean by *bodies*. This is particularly important because if there is a domain of knowledge today that rivals neuroscience in its hegemonic role in our understanding of who and what we are, it is information science. And between the two, when we talk about encounters between bodies and computers we are prone to a kind of analogic assimilation, treating bodies as if they worked something like how computers do—for example, that the quality of responsiveness exhibited by bodies is the same as that exhibited by computing systems.

This way of talking might seem to flow naturally from something I've suggested more than once in this chapter, that is, that patterns of dynamic coupling—mutual influence, cascading of activity, plasticity—recur across multiple scales, timescales, and substrates. We see functional connectivity in the brain and look for similar kinds of connectivity in our social networks, our cities, and our languages. Because the glue, the connectors, in these larger networks are often built out of computers, we sometimes imagine that the mind, and the person, must work in a way basically like how computers work. We smear out critical distinctions of scale, focusing, in our metaphors for how we work, on our day-to-day encounters with computers.

Most of the time we spend interacting with computers we're in an *event loop*. In an event loop, we have a software process monitoring an input/output bus for different kinds of events caused by the user or, today, another computer. These events trigger *callbacks* that cause the computer to respond. This pattern can be generalized over a network. Other than scanning for input events, the process responsible for managing the event loop does not do anything while it's waiting for an event. The event loop process is a passive recipient of input.

There's another term for this design pattern that comes from functional programming: the Read—Eval[uate]—Print Loop, or REPL. We sometimes speak as if we imagined ourselves to be REPLs: we receive input through our sense organs, process it in the central nervous system, and respond motorically. Read—Eval—Print.

Actually—this was one of the points of this chapter and the last—we don't work this way at all. The event loop or REPL metaphor treats the body as an interface, an input/output bus, and the central nervous system, or even just the brain, as the central logic unit. In this metaphor the body is literally *peripheral*.

But this is backward. It's not that the body exists to serve the brain. It's that the brain exists to serve the body. The central nervous system is an error prediction device.

If you're a tree or a jellyfish, most of the time your environment changes pretty slowly. The intensity of sunlight or the ambient temperature, these change over periods of hours or days, and for the most part without sudden jumps. You don't need a special-purpose organ to manage uncertainty in your environment over periods of hours or days. The ordinary epigenetic processes responsible for cell metabolism will do fine. And of course we use these processes too, for things that change over hours or days.[29]

But if you're moving around, you've got other problems. Once you start moving, your environment starts changing a lot more rapidly. The change in the environment is *reafferent*, not *exafferent*. In other words, it's change in the environment that is produced by your own movements. But it's still change, and you still have to have some way to manage it. For things that move around a lot, the epigenetic mechanisms are too slow. So we need a new way of responding to self-generated change in the environment. A way of responding to the unexpected. That's where brains come in. We are not passive scanners like event loops, waiting for input before they do any processing. We're constantly active, maintaining and constantly updating models of how the world works and seeking out *errors*, discrepancies between our models and what our senses are telling us.[30] The relationship between sensing and moving is one of Bayesian prediction—we are constantly updating our expectancies of how the sensory flow should change in response to self-generated movement, incorporating new mismatches, new errors, into future predictions. The small rhythmic movements of our sense organs are what allow us to be sensitive to information coming from the environment. The gain on our senses is pulsatile. When a rat twitches its whiskers, every twitch corresponds to a peak in the gain of sensitivity, an opportunity to record information from the environment.

So it's not that we have nervous systems, and the nervous system does cognition, and cognition means using the body to do things, to feel and move. It's just the opposite: We are bodies, and as bodies we feel and move, and we use our nervous systems to *coordinate* sensation and motion. Goal-directed movement is not the product of cognition. It is the source of cognition.

So what happens to cognition when we start to instrument new pathways between sensation and motion?

3

Modalities

Putting a face to the raster

It has taken me two weeks to write this sentence. There is something about Data—the big D is there to make it clear we're talking about Data as a type, the concept of Data, as opposed to particular instances of data—there is something about Data that defies redescription. Data, after all, is a phenomenon of abstraction, and if you're going to start a Monday morning in January—the sky clear after days of squalling rain, the bright cold air a welcome change from the damp of the previous two weeks—attempting to bring specificity to the quality of abstraction that distinguishes Data from cognate phenomena (event, occurrence, experience, activity, pattern, information, or evidence, to offer a non-exhaustive list), you might quickly find yourself reaching for metanarrational devices and a fifth glass of green tea laced with cayenne pepper. So let's try something different.

There we go (Figure 3.1). Nineteen sixty-nine: Data (big D) gets real. In fact, Data had been getting real for two hundred years at this point, and we'll come to that, but I start here because there is something haunting about seeing something familiar, especially a face and above all a human face, the face of a conspecific, emerge out of abstraction. Haunting is the word for it: this is a visitation, the improbable return of the familiar, the uncanny. Recognition. The processual character of this recognition, the coming-into-presence, is something we don't yet really have an idiom for talking about, though we have the vocabulary: resolution—the image (sound, sensation) resolves, comes into focus, becomes present.

The phenomenon of resolution I'm pointing to bears comparison to the *just-noticeable difference*, the becoming-present of a contrast between two sensations juxtaposed in space or time, and we have an idiom for talking about just-noticeable differences. The concept of the just-noticeable difference is central to how we talk about color, pitch, and other dimensions of

FIGURE 3.1 The face of data, 1969. *"Appearance of a 400 point representation of a woman's face as seen on the monitor oscilloscope,"* corresponding to the tactile representation provided by Bach y Rita's sensory substitution system (Bach y Rita et al. 1969, 963, Figure 2).

sensation, but it is not elastic enough to cover the recognition, the becoming-present, of complex *perceptual objects*. This second-order recognition we could call *just-legible presence*.[1] Just-legible presences have a distinct physiological signature—there is a characteristic ensemble of nervous events that accompany and compose awareness of a distinct *something*, a foreground against which the rest of the auditory, visual, tactile, or olfactory scene recedes into background.[2] This process of perceptual coalescence draws on the perceiver's experience, the history of events in which she became aware of some object. It unfolds in multiple dimensions, some less specifically sensuous, more concept-laden, than others—so, for instance, speech in a language you know is more intrinsically salient, has a lower threshold of perceptual legibility, than speech in general.

There is something distinctly pleasurable about the just-legible presence. Let's look at another, this one from 1992 (Figure 3.2).

These images come from reports describing a pair of *sensory substitution devices*, apparatuses for transducing, in these cases, visual information into other modalities so as to make it available to individuals who are blind. The first, from 1969, involves tactile-visual sensory substitution, in which the information captured by a video camera is encoded as vibration in an array of bristle-like actuators—Figure 3.1 above shows the vibrational tactile sensation from a single video frame translated back into the visual modality via an oscilloscope, an early type of computer display. In this version, the vibrotactor array was positioned across the user-participant's thoracic back. The user sat in a dentist's chair with the vibrotactor array affixed to the

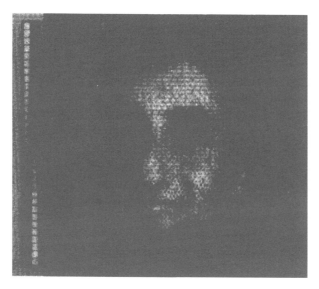

FIGURE 3.2 The just-legible presence, 1992. *"Spectrogram of a sound pattern for a human face" (Meijer 1992, 118, Figure 4).*

back support while the video camera was mounted on a jointed armature affixed to the base of the chair so the user could point it with her hand. Later iterations have used vibrotactor arrays placed on the surface of the tongue and a head-mounted camera.[3] The second image, from 1992, comes from an auditory-visual sensory substitution system developed at Philips Research Laboratories. In this system, visual information is encoded as sound, with frequency used to represent vertical position in the image, time used for horizontal position (the user hears—sees—we'll come back to what the user experiences—the left edge of the image first, the right edge 1,050 ms later), and volume for pixelwise brightness. More recent auditory-visual systems have taken a more sophisticated approach to signal transcoding, associating a characteristic sinusoidal function with each pixel of the video image or with overlapping receptive fields modeled on the retinal anatomy of the eye and exploiting binaurality (the fact that most hearing people hear with two ears simultaneously) to represent stereoscopy in the auditory modality.[4]

Part of what is fascinating about sensory substitution devices is how well they work—not just how low the threshold of the just-legible presence is, lower than we would expect given the sample rate, the resolution, of vision, audition, and tactile sensation as we commonly experience them, but how far beyond bare legibility we can go in these hybrid modalities. Ten hours of training with the simplest of the auditory-to-visual systems in use today, the one that simply maps the transverse axis into the time domain (Figure 3.2 above), is enough to allow users who have been blind since birth or early childhood to perceive facial expressions and letterforms, and, indeed, to instigate synaptic remodeling of the left fusiform gyrus, a part of the left ventral occipito-temporal cortex focally implicated both in the recognition of human faces and, in the literate, in visual word recognition.[5]

Users of tactile-visual sensory substitution devices report that they experience the sensation of the actuator array *in space*, where the camera is pointed, as well as on the surface of the skin or tongue. That is, the experience rapidly acquires a distinctly *distal* character similar to that of vision. The degree to which the experience becomes visual is correlated with the degree to which you are able to consistently match changes in the sensory experience with distinct patterns of movement, above all self-directed movement, in a manner similar to the pattern of sensorimotor contingency characteristic of vision.[6] Users of visual sensory substitution devices also rapidly learn to experience the scene made available by the tactile or auditory stream spatially, so that object size becomes a cue to distance from the self and the scene as a whole coheres as a representation of an environment with *depth* whose features vary in their distance from the self and each other.

Sensory substitution devices, and more particularly twice-transduced images of the type reproduced above, encapsulate much of what is essential about how somatic experience is folded into Data (type, concept) and data (instances, specimens, stuff). For one thing, images like these draw out just how easily we accommodate *sample aliasing*, the degradation of sensory experience when it is filtered through a raster, a rake or grating, of lower resolution than we are otherwise capable of processing. Perceiving ambiguous or degraded signals is effortful—think of the fatigue you feel after spending the evening at a loud party, where every conversation is degraded by ambient noise. But recognizing perceptual objects under sample aliasing can also be a source of pleasure—the instant of recognition is drawn out, so that we enter into it reflexively, observing a process of perceptual gathering-in that ordinarily remains below the threshold of awareness. And not just observing, but participating, applying willful creative effort to the gathering-in. Situations in which we must infer the presence of something from an ambiguous signal give us a chance to appreciate, as I stressed at the end of Chapter 2, that awareness is a phenomenon *of* movement, of ongoing exploration of the world.

There is something more going on here. Sensory substitution highlights how much of our experience plays out independent of the modality of sensation in which particular experiences are cast. Most of our sensory experience, in fact, exhibits this phenomenon. Usually it is referred to as amodality, but it's not that sensory experience is without modal quality. Let's call this the *metamodal* component of sensory experience.[7]

The metamodal component of experience is defined by recurring patterns of variation over time and space in the spectral composition and intensity of movements and stimuli, in the world and in our bodies. These patterns of variation are available to us in a number of different sensory modalities, and we can recognize them as the same across modalities, so that smoothness and roughness, or percussiveness and diffuseness, are meaningful in vision, audition, tactile sensation, and proprioception—the sensation of the movement and posture of one's body given by stretch receptors embedded in the muscles, tendons, and ligaments—and perhaps olfaction, taste, nociception (pain), and balance or graviception.[8]

For some dimensions of recurring variation in the energetic profile of perceptual experience we have reflexive access to the fact that the recurrence dynamics are the same across different senses. This reflexive access is encapsulated in *image schemas* such as *slippery—rough*. To get a sense of the heuristic value of these schemas, in particular for describing qualities of movement, consider Shigehisa Kuriyama's characterization of slippery and rough *mo* (crudely and imperfectly analogous to pulse) in classical Chinese medicine:

> The slippery *mo* "comes and goes in slippery flow, rolling rapidly, continuously forward" (*liuli zhanzhuan titiran*), says Wang Shuhe. The rough *mo* is the opposite: it is "thin and slow, its movement is difficult and dispersed, and sometimes it pauses, momentarily, before arriving"; one has the impression of flow made rough by resistance, struggling forward laboriously, instead of in a smooth, easy glide. "Like sawing bamboo," says the *Mojue*.[9]

Data, like the metamodal component of sensorimotor experience, is, at root, a phenomenon of *transducibility*, of the possibility of a signal's being made available in a number of different media of propagation. What sensory substitution makes clear is that transducibility is nothing new.

What is Data? What are data?

Are we any better positioned to talk about Data now that we've seen that signal transducibility is a basic fact of somatic experience and not something introduced into the world in the past two hundred years? The defining property of Data (type), as opposed to event, occurrence, experience, activity, pattern, information, or evidence, is a loosening of the relationship between a phenomenon and representations of selected characteristics of that phenomenon. Let's try this on:

Data are

1 *Encodings* of palpable impressions of change, difference, or variation—that is, of movement—in the world.

2 *Variation*: Over time, over space, or over the abstract space of concepts—data can be about other representations as well as the "world" in the narrow sense.

3 *Palpable*: Ultimately, via however many degrees of transduction and amplification, data exist by virtue of their availability to our senses.

4 Crucially, these encodings are *polymorphous* with respect to medium. This does not mean we can separate encodings from palpable marks or that data are ever "mediumless". But the coupling between pattern and representation is loose. What distinguishes data from signal is that with data we can imagine more-or-less unproblematic transductions from one medium to another.

5 *Traces*: Data are traces or readings of events in the world, not something inherent in those events. Data must be *generated*.

Computing is the creation, transduction, transmission, and algorithmic manipulation of data.

Data is defined by its *representational promiscuity*, its susceptibility to being made *present*, available to bodily apprehension, in a range of modalities and representational formats. Representational promiscuity is not new exactly, in that the metamodal character of sensory experience lends it an unexpected familiarity, an uncanniness—the idea that a face or any other object could become legible, legible in a way we would like to call *visual*, when we receive information about that object in the auditory or tactile modalities, is somehow less surprising when we experience it in our bodies than when we try to think about it. Representational promiscuity makes somatic sense.

Of course, just because something makes somatic sense does not mean that it is not at the same time new, or at least newly salient. We learn to use our bodies in new ways all the time, to experience the interface between body and world in new ways, and this learning unfolds at the level of the community no less than that of the individual. This is the context for the passage I quoted earlier from Kuriyama's *The Expressiveness of the Body and the Divergence of Greek and Chinese Medicine*: for the community he's describing, the recurrence dynamics of pulsatile pressure changes in the flow of blood through the arteries of the wrists, gauged by the pattern of tactile sensation experienced in the fingertips of a trained practitioner, have come to bear a quality of presence along the *slippery—rough* dimension. The image schema itself, the prototypical experiences of slipperiness and roughness, will vary according to the contexts in which one learns to discriminate slippery from rough, and these prototypes will change within the individual as she learns to make discriminations in a particular context, say, the quality of a patient's *mo*. It is an open question whether any specific image schema is universal in the sense that one could identify roughly comparable dimensions of metamodal sensory discrimination in just about any community.[10] That is, image schemas, along with the experiences of somesthetic and kinesthetic—body-sensing and movement-sensing—discrimination that underlie them, are phenomena of *enregisterment*: they are the products of a historically specific process in which chains of encounters among individuals give rise to social conventions for the interpretation and communication of experience.[11] Somesthesis and kinesthesis are subject to, are *products of* acculturation. And the unexpected familiarity of sensory substitution is partly a mark of the growing prominence of representational promiscuity in our lives.

Let us examine the shared history that has made Data such a central feature of our lives.[12]

Why is it so difficult to say what Data is? Why did we start with sensory substitution devices?

What I'm doing here, just to be clear, is constructing a theory of Data (the concept) that ties its elusive abstractness to something familiar to us from everyday sensory experience. The abstractness of Data, the source of the difficulty in saying what Data is, has two components. First is the surface lability or representational promiscuity of particular instances of data, the fact that data can become available to awareness in a number of different modalities. Sensory substitution devices illustrate this phenomenon. The images reproduced above are visual representations of something that is experienced by the users of the devices in question in something other than visual form, yet the experience is recognizably *the same* in that in all cases it has a coherence as the experience of a particular kind of perceptual object—the face of a conspecific. This coherence transcends the modality—or, to shift to an idiom more common in discussions of Data, the *medium*—of representation. Since we never experience data in the raw, as it were, but only through representations, it's difficult to put our finger on what the *something* under the changing representations is. Maybe we'd be better off trying not to think of data as something that exists *under* its representations. Perhaps we should imagine the *something*, the data itself, as a kind of intersection, that which endures over a network of possible transformations from one representation to another.

So lability of form, representational promiscuity, is part of what makes it so difficult to talk about Data. The other part is the fact that data can be about so many different kinds of phenomena, and the concept-domain of Data is vastly greater than that of everyday sensory experience. Data can refer to things at many orders removed, say, from the cutaneous tactile pressure of the mantel against the back of my arm as I turn away from the screen, hoping to see the next sentence written in the crease between wall and ceiling opposite. The number of words I've written this week, for instance, is not something available to bodily sensation, but it exemplifies a common kind of data.

I offer metamodality as a device for managing the difficulty these two facts—representational promiscuity and the scope and abstractness of Data—present for talking about Data and data *ontologically*, for talking about what they *consist in*. By becoming aware that something like what seems conceptually unmanageable about Data is familiar from our experience, say, of slipperiness, we can begin to find a way to talk about Data—and data—that is at once not too constrained by the characteristics of particular genres of data and at the same time not made too vague by an insistence on avoiding reference to the particularity of individual representations.

What does sensory substitution feel like?

The experience of interacting with the world through sensory substitution devices offers a good starting point for thinking about the experience of interacting with the world through streams of data. So let's continue with this theme another couple pages: What does sensory substitution *feel like?*

This is a difficult question, because redescription, in words or any other medium of symbolic gesture, is such a poor substitute for sensuous experience. Usually we can paper over the limits of redescription by optimistic appeal to the principle that others have experienced *something like* what we're trying to describe and that we participate in a shared set of rubrics for cashing out verbal descriptions into simulations' of others' experience. That is, we take for granted that your experience and mine are *commensurable*, and most of the time this serves us well. It is when we need to describe subtle *divergences* from shared experience, often for diagnostic purposes (of tinnitus, say, or interoceptive pain, pain in parts of the body, such as the intestines, that we don't generally think of as having touch) that we are moved to wonder whether there could be a significant divergence in the quality of your experience and mine. Even in anomalous cases such as chronic pain I can say, for instance of tinnitus, "Today it's like a kettle whistling three rooms away . . . like tape hiss . . . like a refrigerated display case . . . like knives being sharpened," and be confident you will be able to imagine what it sounds like to me, if not, perhaps, the affective dimension, the way it sometimes feels like being hunted, other times like a friend.[13]

Sensory substitution is more exotic.

The experience has been described as "acquired synesthesia". It entails a conjoined set of properties of the substituting (audition, touch) and substituted (vision) senses. Space, depth, and movement present in ways that strike us as visual. Consider these comments from long-term users of The vOICe, the auditory-for-visual sensory substitution system described earlier:

> **Interviewer:** If you look ahead at a dark object you would see the object through your eyes [via residual ocular vision] but you would also see something through the soundscape [via auditory-visual sensory substitution]. But would both be in the same space?

> **Respondent CC:** You are seeing with two different sets of eyes, because you see the blurry sort of dark version with my eyes and a very crisp clear, but not as entirely detailed as other people see it, but very detailed version with the camera of the phone.

On depth perception:

> **Respondent PF:** One day I was washing dishes and without thinking I grabbed the towel, washed my hands, and looked down into the sink to make sure the water had got out and I realised "Oh! I can see down. I can see depth."

On movement:

> **PF:** If I am just walking, it [the auditory-visual sensory substitution device] will see the images as if you would be walking. I don't see the second break anymore [i.e., the fact that each sonification lasts 1 second], it's like totally gone. . . . My mind no longer does that, it just sees the whole image. It just redraws the difference of the image, there is no time lag.

The same individual noted that riding a bike was different—the device could not keep up with her, lending her visual experience a quality we could compare to video frame drop.[14]

For CC, the user with residual ocular vision, the auditory information provided by the sensory substitution device is superimposed on the visual information provided by her eyes in a single, metamodal space. For both PF and CC (not quoted), movement no longer feels jerky, even though it takes a full second for the device to convey its sonification of the visual scene: *It* [my mind] *just redraws the difference of the image* [as opposed to whole image], *there is no time lag.*

The auditory impressions provided by the sensory substitution device allow a user to construct a model of what's going on that draws on past (visual, tactile) experiences not directly available from the device itself. In fact, we all do this kind of filling in. Sensory substitution simply casts it in sharp relief:

> **PF:** Now it has developed into what I perceive as color. . . . Over time my brain seems to have developed, and pulled out everything it can from the soundscape and then used my memory to color everything.[15]

But after three decades without ocular vision, there are many things in PF's sensory substitution-enhanced world that lack this kind of surface property—microwaves, computers. These things appear in her visual field as "line drawings".[16]

This sounds a lot like what happens in 3D scene rendering for computer-generated imagery. First you draw a wireframe—a set of vertices together with a path connecting them, and, if necessary, logic specifying how to interpolate additional vertices to generate a surface tessellation. Then you map a texture to that surface tessellation, adjusting the color values of the texture to simulate the reflectance properties of different kinds of materials (the diffuse light scattering of rough surfaces, the uniformity of polished surfaces, the subsurface scattering of waxy and matte glossy surfaces).

It would be too simple to say that Data is what you get when you strip sensory experience of its modal specificity and its motor exploratory dimension, that is, the schematized expectancies for how our impression of the world should change as we move that make us something other than read-eval-print loops. But sensory substitution gives us a way to start bounding Data, to say where it ends. Lately I've been asking children—this works well with kids of around ten—*If you could invent a new sensory modality, what would it be? How would you instrument it?*

Surveillance ecosystems

By now I hope it is clear that I'm less concerned with Data as it is usually presented, that is, as a force for good or ill in our lives as consumers, patients, or citizens, than with Data as an *evolutionary force*, something that is reshaping the interface between body and world, along with the conceptual matrix of Body and World, in a profound way, a way that it is difficult to grasp with the usual tools of historical and anthropological contextualization. This is not to say that Data stands outside history, or that it has arrived, to invoke a famous trope of the anthropology of colonization, like a ship on the horizon.[17] Data is an artifact, a product of culture, with all the arbitrariness—the *contingency*, as historians of science like to say—that that entails. So while Chapter 5 starts to rough in a theory of the role of Data in the cultural and biological evolution of life on earth, and above all of humans and our commensals and cohabitants, this chapter and the next look at how Data came to have the shape it does—a distinctly *somatocentric* shape.

Sensory substitution got us started looking at Data's somatocentricism. Before we continue I want to pause to survey some of the many forms that data takes, and the many things it takes for its object, its referent. Of course I have an agenda: to draw out how much of the data in the world, and how much of the data-generating activity underway today, is oriented toward human physiology and behavior. Indeed, in 2009 the chief technology officer of a leading digital storage vendor forecast that within ten years 90 percent of the world's data would come from personal sensors—things like accelerometers, photoplethymsographs, pulse oximeters, galvanic skin resistance sensors, point-of-view cameras, or the four or five modalties of location signaling afforded by mobile phone handsets.[18] And data from personal sensors does not begin to exhaust the part of the total corpus of data, let's call it the *Datome*, that is in some fashion about human bodies or human behavior.

Are we warranted in thinking of these many streams of sensing, of data generation (for data is never there waiting to be collected—it is created by the act of sensing) as instances of surveillance that together enact a *surveillance ecosystem*? At the outset it may seem polemic to label as surveillance things like wearing an accelerometer bracelet to track one's rhythms of activity and rest. Surveillance connotes something imposed from without, often, at least initially, without our awareness, often without our consent, or with consent given with queasy reluctance. Consenting to surveillance has become a big part of the tacit compact we enact with the apparatuses of credit, communication, and transport that lubricate the grooves of our day-to-day lives.[19] Surveillance is menacing. Often it is a form of violence in itself, as when it is used to intimidate or humiliate—or to facilitate execution, as in drone warfare. Even when it is not itself intended as a form of violence, it carries the seeds of control, of the modification of behavior, of *discipline*.[20]

But discipline comes from within as well as from without. There is the discipline you impose on your own body, be it through habits of diet, or exercise, or sleep, or all those practices that come under the heading of *bodywork*—disciplines of posture and movement, of slowing down coordinated movements that have become automatic—breathing, running, stretching, lifting, speaking—taking them apart, reassembling them under close inspection. And there is, of course, the discipline imposed by others—

parents, teachers, Facebook, the social and technological coagulates, some more fluid, some more crystalline, that impose limits on what and how we eat, how we dress, how and when we move, where we go, whom we encounter, what we say. Our days are saturated with discipline. Sometimes discipline imposed from within represents the internalization of codes of comportment imposed, initially, by others, but it's not always so straightforward. Often when we say of someone, "She's so disciplined," what we're saying is that she has *rejected* the codes of comportment given by her social environment.

I'm playing with the slippage between two uses of *discipline*, an everyday or focal usage—the discipline of getting up at four every morning to meditate—and a usage that is more inclusive in the range of phenomena it refers to but more specialized in the range of situations where it's an appropriate characterization of those phenomena, where it makes sense to call these things instances of discipline. This second usage is a *technical* (anthropological, say) usage: the discipline of the everyday limits on what we eat and wear, how we move, and so on, limits imposed by social circumstance. Outside settings where this technical usage has the status of a shared convention, it sounds off, it jars, it is *marked*. But this markedness serves a purpose: it opens us up to the possibility that the distance between the everyday and the technical usage is not so great, that there is something about the social constraints on our behavior—being disciplined *by* some combination of social cues more and less coercive—that is similar to the focal kind of discipline—being disciplined *simpliciter*. Both are imposed, both carry the trace, or the threat, of *force*.

So it is with surveillance. I'm proposing an extended sense of surveillance, encompassing patterns of data generation we impose on ourselves and those imposed for purposes other than the kinds of social control we tend to associate with surveillance, knowing how marked, how borderline dishonest, this usage will sound to most readers. I'm doing this (1) because I think it won't be long before we have no trouble understanding these things—self-tracking, sentiment analysis—as continuous with surveillance in its focal sense, and (2) to emphasize the trend I referred to in the preface as a "new entente between surveillance and self-awareness". Self-awareness in the sense of knowing how many steps one takes in a day is not the same thing as self-awareness in the more intimate sense, the awareness generated by the ongoing comparison of sensory experience to the expectancies encoded in body schema—our baseline for gauging cutaneous sensation, interoception, arousal, and so on, the kind of awareness we looked at in Chapters 1 and 2 and just now with sensory substitution. But again, as with the two kinds of surveillance, the two kinds of self-awareness, that mediated by strings of symbols and that mediated by body schema, are not so far apart.

The "new entente" I'm pointing to, the new intimacy of surveillance, bears comparison to what the philosopher Gilles Deleuze, around 1990, despairingly called the *societies of control*. For Deleuze, the societies of control represented a successor to the *disciplinary societies* that Foucault had proposed as a template for making sense of the encroachment of state power on bodily comportment over the preceding two hundred years. Control society emerges from a "crisis in relation to all the environments of enclosure," by which Deleuze has in mind both the physical spaces of socially salient forms of enclosure—"prison, hospital, factory, school, family"—and the enclosures in the abstract space of knowledge erected by the disciplines (medicine, law, architecture, security—to which, today, we could add interaction design).[21] There is one enclosure that remains intact in the transition from disciplinary to control society, that separating an *us* from a *them*. For Deleuze the problem of the societies of control is the problem of developing novel tactics in the struggle for liberation from control imposed by a narrow class of hegemons, no longer principally agents of the state but recognizably sinister in their motives—and strangely aligned in their interests, as if capitalism were a magnetic field that oriented its subjects, hegemon and oppressed alike, along a common axis.

Here I'm concerned with a different kind of shift, a softening of the boundary between sensing from without and sensing from within, a softening of the interface between body and world. So I want to set aside our conventions for what comes under the heading *surveillance*—set aside metadata collection and packet sniffing, the covert weakening of encryption algorithms, drones, even symmetric or participatory forms of surveillance like stalking your ex on social media.[22] The question of how to minimize surveillance, by states or any other kind of actor, of what role, if any, surveillance in the focal sense has in societies predicated on respect for the individual and the collective, freedom of movement, and equality of opportunity, is one of the big questions of our time. But the politics of instrumentation run deeper. Taking instrumentation seriously will lead us, in Chapters 7 and 8, back to an emancipatory critique of surveillance, but one better prepared to say why we should be unnerved, and excited, by the proliferation of instruments of self-tracking—and by the social mobilizations that have formed around them.

Smart everything?

In a 2013 review of ambient sensor technology, the authors, energy policy researchers, offer a list of the "capabilities enabled by information and communication technology" that reads in part:

1 Near-zero marginal cost of reproduction and distribution

. . .

9 Access to information 24 hours a day

10 Universal searching

11 Easier and more widespread public access to technical information

12 Dematerialization of products and services

13 Improving measurement and verification of processes

14 Improving the speed and accuracy of analysis

15 Enabling more rapid institutional change[23]

Let's focus for a minute on dematerialization. Dematerialization encompasses not just the size and mass of sensing elements but how much energy they consume to perform a given unit of computation and the strategies used to channel energy to computing elements.[24] This last dimension has become an area of active research, since sensors that can meet their energetic needs by harvesting energy from the environment, in the form of light, vibration, heat, radiofrequency emissions, or, say, piezoelectric discharge from coated textiles, are freed of the need to rely on external sources of power. As computing elements become energetically autonomous it becomes more feasible to organize them in *mesh networks*, the nodes of which "not only manage their own communications but also act as relays for other nodes in the network."[25] Mesh networks in turn give rise to *nanogrids*, networks that are self-organizing not only as instruments of information transfer but of energy transfer.

Of course, dematerialization does not mean cost-free. "[T]he electricity used by embedded sensors and computing controls in appliances and industrial applications is almost impossible in practice to estimate because the needed data are closely held proprietary secrets of many different companies" (so much for capabilities nos. 11, 13, and 15).[26] Similar difficulties confront efforts to estimate the power consumed by data centers (where the servers live) and to conduct lifecycle assessment of electronics components. Nor is the "use phase" the only part of a computing element's lifecycle where the material facts of power consumption obtrude on the zero marginal cost and dematerialization of pervasive sensing. The recovery of solder, rare earths, and other high-value metal substances from discarded printed circuit boards— accomplished with "coal grills, propane torches, [and] kerosene burners" in unvented workshops across the less affluent world, notably China and Ghana, is one demonstration of the enduring materiality of dematerialized products and services. Often when we talk about dematerialization what we're talking about is shunting the problem of material disposal to some part of the world where we don't have to see it.[27]

The scenario sketched by Koomey and colleagues, in which arrays of partly autonomous sensing devices, deployed in arbitrary configurations over the environment (attached to elements of built structure or infrastructure, such as buildings, roads, or the power grid, or to our bodies, or not attached to any one feature of the world but periodically or continuously in motion), deriving power from the environment or the behavior of their hosts, finding other devices nearby and forming transient networks with them for the propagation of data and power, relaying data downstream to more powerful fixed repositories where it can be aggregated with data from other sensors, other networks, matched by time and location, recoded in uniform high-level representations, subjected to pattern analysis, archived, and recirculated—everything, that is, we can imagine about the imminent future of machine sensing, the Internet of Things, the Internet of Spaces, however you want to call it—represents the outcome of a technological, social, and cultural unfolding, a series of concurrent and overlapping *instrumentation transitions*.

The earliest uses of fine-grained time series data to describe variation in animal physiology date to the 1770s. By the 1870s, self-observation was becoming a standard practice in laboratory physiology, above all in studies of nutrition, metabolism, and starvation. After 1900, these were joined by experiments in sleep deprivation, rest-activity cycle inversion, and extended exposure to constant light and constant dark. The 1920s saw the advent of noninvasive direct recording of central nervous activity with the invention of electroencephalography.[28] But it was not until the 1970s that the automated recording of physiological time series data, and above all data on variation in *mood*, began to seep out of the laboratory and clinic.

A number of overlapping transitions in instrumentation are necessary to get us from the invention of the thermometer to contemporary uses of ambient and wearable sensing devices. These include

1   *Automation* of data-recording.

2   *Portability* of the recording apparatus.

3   *Noninvasiveness* of the recording apparatus (partly correlated with portability).

4   *Continuous transcription* of data to a remote repository from which it's widely available, so that data from any number of observation series, spread over time and space and made with different recording equipment, can be combined into big-N datasets.

5   In fact, we can add as a partly separate item that data must become *indifferent* to device of origin, that is, we need uniform high-level *interface definition languages* for describing data.

6   *Ubiquity* of the computing power to aggregate and analyze data from a single series of observations, so that recording, storage, and transmission start to merge.

7   To these we could add *computational tractability*, that is, the wide availability of algorithms for the rapid solution of data classification and statistical inverse problems.

Each of these transitions engenders a change in how we know our bodies and those of other moving presences and in how we experience the flow of matter, energy, and information across the interfaces that bind self, other, and environment.[29] In the next chapter we start by looking at traces of these transitions visible in the present before roughing in a history of how data became a constant presence in our lives.

4

Data

Cultures of data

In the last chapter I argued that how we think about data is strongly conditioned by a phenomenon of abstraction of experience from sensory modality that is fundamental to how we make sense of the world. In this chapter we continue with a look at how bodily activity, in turn, forms the basis for so much of what we call data.

To start, a pair of obvious cases. Genomics and neuroscience are arenas where casual inspection (a glance at news reports, say, or at the proliferation of online journals dedicated to promoting data-driven science) would suggest that the shift to what some have called a new paradigm for science— "data-driven," "hypothesis-free," or "discovery" science, science that starts not with *a priori* research questions but with a large body of data ripe for pattern recognition[1]—is, if not fully achieved, then at least assured. I want to unwork our assumptions about the kind of sophistication, statistical, computational, and epistemological, researchers in these sciences bring to working with data. I'm going to do it by unpacking anxieties these researchers express to one another in professional communication. Three things to keep in mind in what follows:

First, data, contrary to the word's Latin etymology ("that which is given"), is never given, nor even collected. It is *achieved*.

Second, the effort expended to achieve data—including the work entailed in making data promiscuous, making it *sharable*—has a lot to do with the creation of a *social environment* in which actors (individuals, institutions) subscribe to shared expectations about what kinds of information they are trying to communicate through data and under what conditions different actors should be granted access to data maintained in particular repositories. That is, the effort expended to achieve data has a lot to do with fostering an appropriate *data culture*. Labor of a more technical kind—the formulation of metadata ontologies and file formats, the deployment of specialized high-bandwidth transmission infrastructure, the hashing out of institutional roles for maintaining the above—unfolds in parallel with the cultural labor. But this technical labor is itself saturated with culture, with a web of shared values and practices transmitted by social learning and, by turns, bolstered and vitiated by fluctuating gradients of status and prestige among the actors concerned, as anyone who has ever sat on a standards committee would affirm. A well-designed technical architecture is not enough to bring a culture of data into being—that requires an effort all its own.

Third, *data is a form of capital*, and sharing and hoarding data are economic and *political* acts. In the sciences these play out, initially, in the *economies of authorship and attribution* that form the basis for researchers' credibility among their peers. But because scientific credibility is essential to career advancement and, indissociably, to winning research funding, economies of attribution quickly spill over into the "real" economy, the economy in the everyday sense. As human behavior has become ever more focal as an object of data generation, these two economies have started to fuse. For those with an interest in moving a particular technique of data generation out of the lab and into the consumer wellness sphere, scientific credibility, underwritten by the exclusive access to data that makes authorship possible, forms part of the basis for credibility with investors in capital markets. The growing liquidity of human data has both fostered the conditions for and been abetted by a new genre of private actor oriented toward the commercial exploitation of data of a sort that would once have been collected strictly in clinical or research settings: the *human data startup*. These companies form one part of a broader emerging field of commercial *personalized medicine*. The personal genetic testing vendor 23andMe is the best-known instance, but it has its counterparts in cognitive performance—the San Francisco–based Lumosity—and in activity/movement classification, something we'll return to later in this chapter and in Chapter 4.[2]

We have grown accustomed to reports of the sequencing of genomes (of individuals, of species) and of the association of gene sequences (coding regions, promoters) with (1) distinct phenotypes, for instance susceptibility to specific diseases and (2) the flow of information across genetic clades, whether by common descent or horizontal gene transfer. High-throughput sequencing techniques have made possible the sequencing of *metagenomes* encompassing the genetic information of whole populations or ecosystems (above all, the prokaryotic ecosystems comprising the human microbiome[3]) sampled directly from their environment. If any part of the science of bodies, above all human bodies, has been reduced to the algebraic manipulation of data, it would seem to be genomics.

In fact, the turn from genetics to genomics, from the gene to units of analysis orders of larger magnitude, has proceeded in a halting and uneven fashion. A 2012 article on the interpretation of next-generation sequencing data expresses concern that "the capacity to generate the data greatly outpaces our ability to analyze it," or even to store it in a way that it can be shared among research groups. "Any future progress within the life sciences acutely depends on the *democratization of biomedical computation*." Among the most basic problems created by unequal access both to computing power and to the expertise to use it is the fact that there are no standards for how long a hosted data repository will be available, nor are there agreed-upon procedures for insulating data repository maintenance from changes in the host's funding. Other problems include a failure to integrate data visualization into analysis and "*lax standards of computational reproducibility*."

> Replication of computational experiments requires access to input data sets, source code or binaries of exact versions of software used to carry out the initial analysis (this includes all helper scripts that are used to convert formats, groom data, and so on) and knowing all parameter settings exactly as they were used. In our experience, publications rarely provide such a level of detail, making biomedical computational analyses almost irreproducible.[4]

The problems of data-driven genomics go beyond a failure of knowledge transfer for data management and analytic workflow. Sometimes the appropriate tools are not even available. One of the features of high-throughput sequencing techniques is that they're prone to generating data with errors, that is, ambiguities of reading (multiple sequencing runs over the same source material yield variant apparent base-pair sequences) and alignment (matching up of base-pair subsequences in readings of a locus or loci in the genome or metagenome that correspond to different versions of a single sequence, either across individuals in a population or at loci that have been reduplicated within a genome over the course of evolution). The output of high-throughput techniques also includes artifacts of the sequencing process, including duplicate sequences and sequences appearing out of order. This does *not* mean something is wrong with the sequencing techniques. Error is a universal feature of data generation. But you'd like to know *how much* error a dataset contains and reduce the rate of error where you can. You'd also like to know when variant readings and alignments represent variants in the population and when they represent error. To reduce the degree of error, ideally you'd calibrate the high-throughput data against datasets generated by lower-throughput methods that yield lower rates of error. But producing these calibration datasets takes time and expertise. If you're working with human genetic material, or material from popular model organisms, that's not a problem—auxiliary datasets are readily available. Otherwise, you're faced with the task of working around the role these auxiliary datasets play in the recalibration and realignment toolchains, something that "may be too complex for most researchers, who choose to use more straightforward approaches, potentially sacrificing the quality of their results."[5]

Just how quickly the capacity to generate data has outstripped the capacity to use it is made clear by the case of the 1000 Genomes Project, considered a model of data management workflow in the genomics community:

> The initial plan for the 1000 Genomes Project was to collect 2 × whole genome coverage for 1,000 individuals, representing ~6 giga–base pairs of sequence per individual and ~6 tera–base pairs (Tbp) of sequence in total. Increasing sequencing capacity led to repeated revisions of these plans to the current project scale of collecting low-coverage, ~4 × whole-genome and ~20 × whole-exome sequence for ~2,500 individuals plus high-coverage, ~40 × whole-genome sequence for 500 individuals in total (~25-fold increase in sequence generation over original estimates). In fact, the 1000 Genomes Pilot Project collected 5 Tbp of sequence data, resulting in 38,000 files and over 12 terabytes of data being available to the community. In March 2012 the still-growing project resources include more than 260 terabytes of data in more than 250,000 publicly accessible files.[6]

To support the sharing of data on this scale among the sequencing and analysis centers—more than thirty lab groups in all across multiple continents—required specialized file-transfer technology that diverges from the standard network stack used for most Internet traffic. And the technical and methodological challenges of managing high-throughput sequencing data do not include the difficulties of securing shared data against the identifiability of individual study participants. This requires an additional layer of metadata to specify relationships among participants, submitters (i.e., research teams sending data to shared repositories), and others (principally researchers) seeking to access that data later on.[7]

The rise of genome-wide association studies has complicated efforts to set guidelines for data sharing. In genome-wide association studies, variants for a large number of loci in the genome are assessed for individual participants against a phenotype (i.e., expressed traits). Genome-wide association studies present new problems of identifiability and privacy, since they offer more data points by which to triangulate a participant's identity,[8] and these data are sometimes linked to phenotypes—say, for disease susceptibilities—that could, if widely known, compromise an individual's social and economic standing. But identifiability is just part of the problem.

Genome-wide studies are valuable for understanding the genetic component of complex phenotypes, in particular, relative susceptibility or immunity to diseases like malaria and HIV. But the communities where these high-value traits are found—often poor or formerly colonized communities, or simply culturally distant from those most medical researchers come from—often subscribe to an ethos of access to bodily substances and a view of the relationship between bodily substances and the data generated from them that is at odds with that taken for granted by genetic epidemiologists and their institutional patrons. This makes it difficult to get informed consent from donor-participants. *"The potential uses and benefits of data often extend far beyond the original purpose specified in the consent form"*—Should future researchers be prevented from using these data if the donor communities have not expressed their consent to the uses these new researchers have in mind? Should repositories be required to obtain consent for requests for access to data that do not involve the collection of new genetic material? What about researchers *from* the less-affluent communities essential to genetic epidemiology? Should they receive early access to data releases out of consideration for the fact that they are at a disadvantage, vis-à-vis their colleagues from more affluent places, at building the cultural capital necessary to advance their careers?[9]

The conflicts that arise from the preparation, maintenance, and sharing of human genomic data are remarkably similar to those that have arisen over the preparation, maintenance, and sharing of human tissue samples. As my colleague Joanna Radin discovered when she set out to write a history of anthropological tissue collecting, blood and other tissue samples sit in freezers for *decades*, sometimes forgotten. When word got out that Joanna was retracing the journeys tissue samples had made from field to freezer, and had a synoptic picture of the indigenous tissue archive, she found herself asked to track down sought-after samples and broker their transfer to new labs that wanted them. Source communities have generally been horrified to learn about what they see as a cavalier attitude on the part of researchers to the bodily substance of their kin.[10]

Data, I proposed in the last chapter, is distinguished by its representational promiscuity. In the language of Chapter 1, data is configuration extracted from substrate, pattern without medium. Or this is what we often say. But the representational promiscuity, the metamodal quality of data, is not the same as being free of attachment to the material world, especially when the medium from which the data were extracted is one of biological consubstantiality. Blood, milk, semen, skin, saliva—these substances have a stickiness, they stick to what they touch and they stick us to one another. They leave a residue, a web of adhesions, long after they have been transformed into strings of symbols.

Genomics faces one further, insurmountable problem with data. No matter how much data genomicists collect, no matter how much care they take with their data, they are constrained by the aleatory, single-trial nature of the evolutionary process: for any given set of observations of the change in gene sequences over time, evolution has happened just once. "Consequently, even with perfect knowledge of the state of populations, based on a single outcome of the process, there will be considerable uncertainty in any attempt to estimate population genetic structure and the underlying evolutionary processes" that gave rise to that structure.[11]

You could be forgiven for wondering how the science-data interface could be in such disarray in genomics if not for the fact that, by comparison with neuroscience, genomics looks like a model of rigor, transparency, and the seamless integration of data generation, analysis, visualization, and circulation. In neuroscience—and here I am writing not from the journal literature but from my own experience working with neuroscientists to make data sharing an integral part of the brain imaging workflow—we see all the problems we saw in genomics, along with others given by the economics of data creation particular to brain imaging. There are the technical problems of grooming or cleaning up the data. Just as gene sequence data as it comes out of the sequencer is useless until it has been stripped of duplicates, resorted, realigned, and recalibrated, so brain image series, as they come out of the magnet bore, are not fit to be analyzed until slice sequences have been realigned, images have been "defaced" (stripped of personal characteristics from the participant's skull and face), slices have been reconstituted into a volumetric representation, and the brains of different participants have been conformed to one of a handful of standard atlases—for brains vary in the relative volume of different topographic features. Finally, for functional scans (those measuring blood flow following brain activity) the anatomical location and cytoarchitectonic properties of voxels (volume elements, "3D pixels") in the parts of the brain to be analyzed must be verified by lining slices up against corresponding slices from an anatomical scan of the same individual.

This laborious process of "pipelining" all comes *before* the analysis—before any evidence can be put forward to show, say, that activation in one region of the brain is consistently associated with activation in some other region of the brain under certain conditions (when the person being scanned is lying in the magnet bore at rest, say, or watching a movie, or having her foot touched with a feather[12]). But in another sense, pipelining is part of the analysis, because it entails a large number of decisions about whether, how, and in what sequence to conduct the data grooming procedures sketched above. At each stage in the pipeline, researchers have a number of options—choices of algorithm for denoising, slice alignment, and voxel smoothing, parameters for estimating the statistical model (i.e., the distribution of results to be expected if the experiment were run a large number of times), strategies of activation thresholding (ways of deciding how much activity a voxel must show to be considered meaningfully active at a given point in time). These choices give researchers considerable flexibility in analyzing and interpreting a single set of scanner data, yielding, in one estimate, close to 7,000 possible pipelines, some of which yield widely divergent concurrent activation maps. This is sometimes known as the *vibration* of detected effects.[13]

In some cases a single pipeline design may yield divergent results depending on choice of software, or even on *which version* of a particular suite of software is used.

On top of all this, complex or physically demanding experimental setups inevitably yield a proportion of data that cannot be used: because the participant could not hold her head perfectly still for the image acquisition,[14] or the interaction between participant and experimental apparatus diverged from the investigators' script in some unforeseen way. All this adds up to more time in the scanner suite, which is at a premium—scanners are expensive and must be staffed with technicians to assist investigators, and institutes and departments that have a scanner of their own try to keep it booked at full capacity.

It is partly because it is so expensive to create data that researchers are disinclined to share their data. Brain imaging scientists, like most of us, most of the time, operate in a *labor economy*, that is, they—we—take for granted that we create things of value by applying our labor to the raw materials provided by nature or others. To recoup your investment of time and effort, you need to convert the value locked up in the data you've created into some more liquid form. In science, that more liquid capital is the credibility that comes from publicizing one's analyses in respected outlets—journals, mainly, along with conferences and talks. To share your data with other researchers before you've had a chance to convert it into cultural capital through publication would be like giving away food you had grown at your own expense. This is especially true for researchers early in their careers.

So researchers hoard their data until they have had a chance to publish analyses of it. But since it takes so much time and effort to prepare a brain imaging series, the upshot is that most published studies in the neuroscience literature may be severely underpowered. That is, for want of data from a wider range of participants they may have a relatively low chance of identifying a *true effect*, of rejecting the null hypothesis from the evidence.[15]

There is another way to look at the creation of value: through the lens of an *exchange* economy. In an exchange economy, value resides not in the goods produced by one's labor but in the relationships enacted by sharing those goods. Anthropologists like to invoke the Western Pacific when they talk about exchange economies, and with good reason: this is a part of the world where networks to support the long-distance exchange of ceremonial goods for the purpose of reaffirming relationships have been particularly salient and where people have been especially articulate about how value is created by giving things away and allowing them to return in altered form.[16] But we see something similar in open-source software communities.[17]

Once we start to see the central question of data management as a question not of technique but of culture—*How might we get people to change their view of the world so they see themselves as operating in an exchange economy rather than or alongside a labor economy?*—we start to see that data itself is a phenomenon less of instrumentation than of culture. If we ask, *Was a particular data culture shaped by technical constraints on the production and dissemination of data, or has that data culture shaped how the techne of data has grown up in this particular discipline?* the answer is generally *Both.* Neuroscience faces certain technical constraints on data sharing—the expense of making brain images, the size and complexity of the storage assets, the files, themselves—but it is also possible that neuroscience attracts people who, for whatever reasons of background or personality, have, until recently, been less receptive to the exchange model of credibility. Genomics, on the other hand, prides itself on a "culture of openness" that dates, in actors' own telling, to an early hope that gene sequencing would yield rapid "translational" advances—advances in medical care. Genomicists and population geneticists have had to make their protocols for sharing data *less* open so as to start to include source communities as stakeholders in the research process. But despite their preference for wide access to data sets, genomicists have not figured out a way to credit researchers for making data available.[18]

Human displacement

For all the confusion I've described for genomics and neuroscience, these are more or less mature fields when it comes to data management. The real frontier, the growth market, as it were, for human data is human *behavior.* This takes a bunch of forms. We don't have time to more than scratch the surface of the current scene—and anything I put down here could be hopelessly dated by the time you read this. That's why in a couple of pages we'll turn to history, the only sure way to get traction with a subject like data. But let's at least see what we're up against, the breadth of methods and outlooks being brought to bear on the question *What does all this data we generate say about us as people, as social beings?*[19]

That evasive "being brought to bear" (*By whom?*) is deliberate. The rise of data-driven research paradigms in the science of human behavior—that is, approaches to the investigation of human behavior that start not with anecdotal observations of how people act but with large datasets generated by people's actions—has instigated a shift in the authority to bear witness to human action—away from people socialized in disciplines that concern themselves specifically with making sense of human beings and toward people socialized in disciplines defined by a concern with eliciting statistical patterns in large datasets.[20] We have already seen how the failure of statistical and computational sophistication to travel *within* a discipline has been a source of tension in genomics. The same thing is happening in neuroscience, where the diffusion of pattern classification techniques has been made possible mainly by the diffusion of software toolkits that make it possible to implement more sophisticated pattern classifiers without having a deep theoretical understanding of how they work.[21] The unevenness of data expertise in genomics and neuroscience pales in comparison to what is happening in linguistics, where researchers with little domain expertise—little experience working with *language*—have succeeded in publishing papers in high-profile venues using techniques unfamiliar to most linguists.[22] Cultural evolution presents an even more fraught case: when a population geneticist points to patterns in the change in word frequencies over time and calls his method "culturomics," without including any semantics theorists or linguistic anthropologists on the paper, it marks a shift in who is authorized to comment on the relationship between word usage and the cultural salience of the concepts included in that word's referential prototype.[23]

The most basic form of data-driven social science—basic in the sense of making few assumptions about the underlying motives for human action and the relationships between intention and its visible effects—targets patterns of human displacement, that is, how we move around, as measured by proxies including the movements of bank notes, mobile phone handsets, and transit cards.[24]

It remains unclear what, exactly, these data can tell us. What human mobility researchers are mainly looking for from person location data are *scaling laws* for human displacement, relationships of the form $P(r) \alpha r^{-(1 + \beta)}$, governing the probability that an individual travels a distance r within some fixed time period. The greater the value of β, the steeper the falloff in the probability distribution, that is, the lower the probability of finding displacements greater than some arbitrary r. So far, the results of this research have not been all that deep, showing, essentially, that most people, most of the time, travel short distances but some people regularly make longer trips.[25]

Mobile behavior tracking

Moving up the scale of social intimacy from anonymous displacement tracking we come to forms of mobile tracking of behavior in which individual participants' identities are expressly incorporated into the *sensing ontology*, the pattern of categories that define the data to be achieved by mobile sensing. In studies of human displacement, researchers are concerned with attributing a series of actions to an individual so they can distinguish between patterns of behavior that hold at the level of the individual and patterns of behavior that hold at the level of the population.[26] This demands a relatively weak form of identifiability—you need to associate instances of an individual's activity (making or receiving a call, say) with other instances of that same individual's activity over time, but you are not concerned with associating these instances with other aspects of the individual's behavior or other properties of her social identity, for example, name, consumption habits, social network, or political views.[27] But in mobile behavior tracking, sometimes referred to, problematically, as "reality mining,"[28] participants generally know in advance that their movements and communicative gestures are being tracked, and their personal identities, as embodied in facts about where they live, where they work, and whom they associate with, are incorporated into the study. The point of the exercise is to form a synoptic view of how our relationships to places, people, and other dimensions of our social lives figure in routine displacement and communication—where we go, when and whom we see or talk to—and to form inferences about the nature of our relationships. The stress is on *routine*.

Raw tracking data ("Person *P* was at Location *L* at Time *T* in close proximity with Person *Q*") tell us little. Tracking data become useful when we extract patterns from series of events over time and label these events in ways that are meaningful for the people being tracked, that is, "*Most days*, Person *P* is at Location *P*-Home with Person *P*-Partner at 8am and at Location *P*-Work with Person *P*-Coworker at 11am . . ." By looking at how often different tracking events co-occur within a given time period (usually a day) we can come up with statements of the form *Most days* or *Often* or *Sometimes*, that is, sets of co-occurring events that account for as much of the day-to-day variance in people's behavior, individual and collective, as possible. Pentland and colleagues have called these statements *eigenbehaviors*.[29] Linear combinations of an individual's eigenbehaviors offer an approximation of that individual's behavior over time. Linear combinations of collective eigenbehaviors should allow us to predict the behavior of a population appropriately matched to that from which the eigenbehaviors were collected.[30]

It turns out most people's behavior is highly routine—we go to work at around the same time on the same days of the week and see the same people at the same places. We have a pretty clear sense how to decompose everyday life into constituent dimensions and what the salient categories are for each. For instance, if Location is a dimension of interest, major categories might include Home, Work, and maybe Favorite Post-work Hangout. So in the everyday world it takes just a handful of eigenbehaviors to approximate people's activity rhythms—perhaps one for "typical weekday," one for "typical weekend day" and so on.

Of course, there's always the chance we don't know what the salient dimensions of our behavior are, let alone the key categories within these dimensions. Reality mining, as it has been practiced, demands a high degree of *ontological commitment*: you need to have firm convictions about what kinds of things there are in the world (say, *places, events, relationships*) and what properties these things can have (*home, meeting, friend*). Disciplines are defined in part by a shared epistemic stance, a complex of attitudes toward ontological commitment. It would be oversimplifying to say, for instance, "Computer scientists are way at the positivist end of the spectrum, anthropologists way at the skeptical end"—there are domains in which anthropologists would be far more likely to take the nature of the world for granted than computer scientists. Human behavior is not one of them.[31]

Attitudes toward ontological commitment shape not just study design but the interpretation of data. Proponents of reality mining stress the method's superior precision and recall over self-report—sensor data embody a "ground truth" about where participants were and with whom. This has encouraged overconfidence in judging participants' dispositions (e.g., which recurring encounters represent friendships), even in the face of participants' own accounts ("You say this person is an acquaintance, but based on our data about how frequently you're in contact, we know she's a friend.").[32]

Sentiment analysis

Initially I thought a discussion of sentiment analysis would form the denoue-ment of this chapter. The concept is captivating in its boldness and simplicity—a remote sensing apparatus for human mood. As we shall see in Chapter 7, there have lately been other proposals to instrument inner states.

Sentiment analysis is the inference of affective valence—happiness—from large textual corpora, these days mainly postings to social media. A case in point is the Hedonometer, a project of the Computational Story Lab at the University of Vermont.[33] The Hedonometer uses affect valence ratings for the 50,000 most commonly occurring word-like fragments in postings to Twitter in the United States to calculate the valence of whole tweets—and from these to build heat maps and timelines showing how patterns of happiness, as reflected in Twitter, unfold in space and time.

The Hedonometer and like-minded projects draw conceptual inspiration and a sheen of social urgency from the growing literature on the economics of subjective well-being.[34] Hedonometrics is rife with methodological problems: demographic skew in Twitter,[35] mismatch between the pool of word valence raters and Twitter users in different places[36]—and the fact that word meanings, affective or otherwise, are generally not linear compositional in the way we often like to imagine.

In June 2014, it transpired that Facebook's Data Science team had conducted an experiment in "massive-scale emotional contagion" by manipulating the sentiment of users' News Feeds.[37] The authors contended that they had shown that "affective states are contagious" in the absence of direct interaction and nonverbal cues, but of course all they showed was a trend in the valence of individuals' status updates, operationalized as a word-level feature, in the same direction as the manipulation to their News Feeds. They did not show that this trend reflected a trend in how participants experienced the world. In fact, the term *participants* is misleading, since the investigators neglected to seek consent from the people whose News Feeds they manipulated.

Actigraphy: From subjects to users

In 1982, Thomas Wehr and colleagues at the U.S. National Institute of Mental Health described a novel approach to monitoring mood cycles in individuals with what today we'd call Type II or rapid-cycling bipolarism.[38] Fifteen individuals who had been hospitalized for rapid alternation between episodes of mania and depression were fitted with "a small, self-contained, electronic instrument worn on the nondominant wrist."[39] The instrument in question, the object of a U.S. patent granted the same year under the description "Activity Monitor for Ambulatory Subjects," used a piezoelectric element mounted so that one end was free to deflect in response to movements of the limb to which the bracelet was affixed. The voltage generated by this deflection was then amplified by a factor of a thousand and passed through a thresholding circuit. If the signal was above the threshold, the deflection registered as movement. That is, within the sampling interval, the device had a *binary* dynamic range— either the wearer was moving or she was not. Additional deflections within a single sampling interval were not registered—"only one threshold crossing is needed during the [single count interval] to produce a pulse." The device had twelve bits of storage for each "standard time interval" or movement *epoch*. Thus 4,096 pulses—movement/no-movement events—could be registered per epoch. The epoch itself was fifteen minutes long, giving a "single count interval" of 0.22 s or a sample rate of approximately 4.5 Hz. At the end of each epoch, the twelve-bit movement counter was truncated to an eight-bit storage word, giving a nominal dynamic range 256 grades of movement for the fifteen-minute epoch.[40]

In Chapter 4 we'll return to Wehr et al.'s "48-hour Sleep–Wake Cycles in Manic-Depressive Illness" and put it in the context of how arousal rhythms have become a focal object of self-care. Here, as in our discussion of genomics and brain imaging, I'm concerned with how much work—how many decisions—goes into turning bodily movement into data. The device described above, for all the care taken, in its design, to ensure that its dynamic range would not be saturated by agitated movement, offers a remarkably coarse approximation of the quality of a body's movement, and one that is biased toward particular *kinds* of movement—walking, say, or other forms of movement that involve a recurring swinging motion of the distal arm. It was less invasive than point-light techniques, then coming into vogue for studies of human gait and movement perception,[41] which in any case would not be appropriate for ambient measurement. But it was still kind of invasive for a device intended for something like 200 days' continuous use, since it had enough memory to store data for just two and a half days' worth of fifteen-minute epochs. Every two days, participants had to have their data uploaded to a PDP-11. So in 1982, we do not yet see the continuous transcription that is a key feature of how we think about activity tracking today—data collection is not yet *ambient*.[42]

Nor, with this early bracelet design, do we see any automated classification of activity into socially salient categories. In the decades since, research on bracelet actigraphy data has unfolded in two directions. First, a lot of effort has been expended to validate bracelet actigraphy as an alternative to less portable, more invasive approaches to estimating sleep time and sleep architecture—what proportion of time a sleeper spends in different phases of sleep, from light sleep to slow-wave to rapid-eye-movement sleep.[43] More recently, accelerometers, in bracelets and other form factors, have been adapted to the ambient instrumentation of wakeful movement, giving rise to a new vein of research on machine classification of movement from accelerometer data.

It is practically impossible, at this stage, to write a history of how machine classification techniques have been applied to the statistical inverse problem presented by accelerometer data—that is, What does a particular series of pulse-sampled movement events *refer back to*, what was this animal most likely *doing*, what was the quality of her (its) arousal? What do these data tell us about this animal's affective disposition or *mood*? The reason we can't say much about the algorithms used to address these questions, less still about how those algorithms were developed, the experimental protocol and *training data*—Did the study involve 20 participants or 2,000 or 20,000? Athletes, individuals with motor disturbances, people seeking to lose weight? How old were they? What was the gender distribution? Where did they live, and what mix of activities did they typically experience in a day? What was the starting point for classification—were participants given a list of activities to perform while wearing the device, or was their accelerometer data first analyzed to identify distinct patterns, which were then compared to participants' activity logs to see which recurrence patterns correspond to which socially salient activities?—is the same as the reason we cannot estimate the life cycle energetic costs of distributed sensors: *so much of the information in question is proprietary.*[44] As the research community liaison at one major player in the activity tracking space informed me when we spoke about the needs of a mobile experience sampling study I was designing, "*We will never*" provide third parties—that is, my research group—with access to raw accelerometer data. "*That's proprietary.*" Like every other vendor in this space, my interlocutor's was eager to have its device accepted as a proxy for polysomnography for sleep architecture classification, and they were conducting validation studies to this end. They had no plans to publish the results of this research.

It is not that consumers do not recognize the decisions that go into the design of an algorithm, and the design of experiments to train those algorithms, for what they are: statements about *values.* Participants in the Quantified Self talk about the difference between a "Fitbit step" and a "Nike Fuel step" (the consensus is that the latter is significantly more energetically demanding). But even technically sophisticated human data activists are limited in their capacity to compel device vendors to make these decisions public—let alone give consumers input into the design of training experiments or parameterize their algorithms so as to let users experiment, say, with different thresholds for what counts as a running as opposed to a walking footstrike—or even to swap in an entirely different classification algorithm.

Of course, it is not just algorithms that are subject to this kind of enclosure. As behavior transcription becomes ambient, or at least invisible—when we no longer have to come in to the lab to upload our data, when we no longer have to explicitly connect monitoring devices to something we recognize as a node in the network, when the grid itself is, as Koomey and colleagues say, *everything*—something else drops out of view: the technical-institutional assemblages in which the data we create through our movements are subsumed.

When I first started lecturing on this topic I spoke of a *migration* of activity tracking out of the psychiatric clinic and into the realm of consumer wellness. This felt like a good way to drive home to my audience, mainly interaction designers, how intimate the data in question are. But now that formulation feels tendentious and static. It presupposes an epistemic landscape populated by a collection of rival technical-institutional assemblages, rival *dispositifs*, to use Foucault's term, engaged in border skirmishes and territorial negotiations—a human data continent on which actors with different kinds of relationships to capital, different cultures of evidence, and different economies of credit and credibility compete for public recognition as arbiters of how movement configures human presence. Ok, individuals may adopt the personae given by these competing dispositifs with a certain strategic flexibility, now standing on the tech start-up side, now on the medical research side. But even this is too schematic. What is happening is less a migration of the power to classify from one technical-institutional apparatus to another than a dissolution of all these apparatuses in favor of a kind of epistemic self-fashioning at the institutional level. The warlords are no longer styles of reasoning-with-data but individual organizations whose power to arbitrate the meaning of data is tied less to public acceptance of a style of reasoning than to brand goodwill.

Don't get me wrong, I'm not proclaiming the death of the state or the disciplines. But when a company like Jawbone becomes the repository for data about the motor activity of thousands of identifiable individuals—along with users' food logs and data about how different users respond to different kinds of behavior cues—it assumes a role as a value-making force, shaping users' understanding of what kinds of movements are *good* movements and what kinds of social relationships are conducive to good movement.[45] This value-shaping role is more or less unidirectional, for the device vendors themselves are not all that responsive to signals from other actors in the community save venture capitalists and the capital markets. As instrumentation of this kind becomes common, and then pervasive, the community of those subject to its value-giving signals expands, and the signals themselves become less and less salient. This, of course, is what so much interaction design aspires to: that the interface should melt away, that the instrument should present itself to the user as an array of *affordances*, modes of potential use that appear immanent in the instrument.[46]

As with discipline, so with surveillance. Assurances of the form *You own your data* are meaningless, for two reasons. First, the data themselves are inert without access to an appropriate decoder, and the decoders, again, are proprietary. So much for mediumlessness. Second, Data is a distinctly *nonrival* kind of property—just because *you* retain access to your data doesn't prevent the device vendor from selling it to others.[47] As data diffuse through the surveillance ecosystem, the chain—more like a web—of custody by which particular event recordings came to be in the possession of particular entities, commercial or otherwise, evaporates, as does the role played by these event recordings in the tuning of classifiers, for movement or any other dimension of behavior.[48] The surveillance enacted through ambient somatic instrumentation is not, *pace* Deleuze, *pace* Baumann and Lyon, a rhizome or a liquid. It is a plasma.

5

Niches

In the last two chapters we saw that Data, the category, emerged from the instrumentation of bodies. Bodies, human bodies, have shaped the epistemology, the how-we-know, of data and computability. In this chapter we look at the causal arrow running in the other direction: How is computability shaping bodies—human bodies and the other-than-human bodies we share our living space with along—with our sense of what a body is?

This seems like a basic question—*Now that computing is everywhere, how is it changing our bodies, how we experience them, how we recognize bodily qualities of presence in the world around us?*—but it's a question that is not getting the attention it warrants. I don't want to dwell on the reasons why, save to point to the deep imprint, in the North Atlantic—roughly, Europe and its offshoots—world, of a strain of metaphysics usually referred to as Cartesianism. This view, which posits an antagonism between mental and physical phenomena, runs like a red seam through twentieth-century "Analytic" philosophy, which in turn played a central role in shaping computing as a discipline.

Mind-matter dualism is not uniquely North Atlantic, but in comparative perspective, that is, taking a broad sample of communities over the course of what little we know of human history, the appeal of dualisms—between matter and mind, spirit, or soul, between nature and culture—has been limited.[1] Nonetheless, philosopher of science Ian Hacking has argued, neo-Cartesianism "is bound to win in the end."[2] By this he means we are experiencing a delamination of personal identity from bodily substance in which genetic material, tissues, organs, and moods—the last understood as artifacts of brain function and not, say, as products of history and circumstance *in conjunction with* bodily dispositions—come to be seen as so many parts to be swapped out as warranted.

I'm not sure Hacking is right, though that's not because I'm optimistic that large numbers of people will spontaneously be moved, say, to see awareness and meaning-making as intrinsic properties of bodily movement. What I do see is a growing everyday appreciation of the fact that our own animate presence, and that of other moving things in our environment, is the product of a confluence of intention-guided impulses that could, in some cases, originate from distinct points in time and space. It's not that our bodies are in parts while our minds are whole. It is, rather, that our presence, our *bodily* presence, is distributed in novel configurations.

If anything, precisely because, as Hacking points out, we have come to understand them as apparatuses, as constituents of a technological and social *dispositif* that enmeshes us from before we are born, we are aware of bodies in ways, and to a degree, that never used to be the case. This is not to say we inhabit our senses more deeply, a point I'll come back to in a minute. But as individuals and collectives we devote considerable energy to the management of bodily substance and bodily presence. This is not new, but it is newly widespread. Physical culture—by which I mean things like exercise, the regimentation of diet, and the adoption of technical practices of movement, breathing, and hygiene—is a distinctly modern phenomenon, born of distinctly modern anxieties about race, climate, and bodily economy. These anxieties grew out of the entwined histories of physiological instrumentation, discussed in the last chapter, and (mainly European) colonial expansion.[3]

Physical culture, as a register of shared experience, is new, but the ritual cultivation and decoration of bodies is a universal feature of human society.[4] Bodily cultivation, in turn, is just one dimension of a broader coarticulation of community and environment. It is this broader phenomenon, *niche construction*, that I want to look at in this chapter. Specifically, I want to make the case for a *somatic*, that is, bodily dimension of niche construction and to explore how somatic niche construction might offer a frame of reference for thinking about the co-lamination of bodies and instrumentation.

Niche construction

The Niche Construction Hypothesis is so straightforward that you will wonder why it is referred to as a hypothesis and not, say, a perspective, or even simply a fact. We are accustomed to talking about evolution as a process of the reification—the fixing, the making real, the transformation of that which was implicit, transient, and partial into something manifest, ongoing, and total—of environment in the appearance and behavior, the phenotype, of the community and the individual. Evolution is simply conditioned change. It unfolds through a number of *semiotic chains*, material ensembles for the transfer of information from environment to body—the conditioning impulse—and then from body to body—the reification of that impulse in the community. We associate different semiotic chains with evolution over different temporal and demographic horizons: genome and species, social learning and community (cultural evolution), and the mesh of events, encounters, and acts of movement that make up the developmental trajectory of the individual.

Usually, when we talk about the semiotic chains underlying evolution, we talk as if the conditioning impulse were transmitted in just one direction, from environment to body. Of course we know that this is not the case, certainly at the level of the community and the individual—we fashion our cities, say, or our social networks, and these fashion us (collective, individual) in turn. The conditioning impulse runs both ways, between community or individual and the social and material environment that sustains that community or individual.

At the level of the species or higher-order taxons—biological units of information that coalesce and dissolve, roughly, over periods distinctly longer than the community—we tend to lose sight of the fact that the community shapes its conditioning environment. We talk as if the population of living things, whether composed of a single kind or a configuration of many kinds, a *biome*, were the passive plaything of its environment. Again, we know that's not the case, but natural selection, as a conceptual device, does not provide the affordances necessary to keep the mutualism between community and environment in the foreground when we create mental pictures of the evolutionary process. Niche construction offers a corrective, foregrounding the *co*-ness, the *both*ness, the bidirectionality of conditioning impulses between body/community and environment.[5]

Candidate exemplars of niche construction in humans include adult lactase persistence in communities that rely on fresh dairy products—those of northern Europe, western Asia, and northern and eastern Africa—and sickle-cell heterozygy in communities that took form in places where malaria is endemic—equatorial West Africa and its trans-Atlantic descendants.[6] Lactase persistence is a physiological trait, transmitted through the genome, the conditioning impulse for which arose from the *community*'s having organized its subsistence around livelong consumption of fresh dairy. Sickle-cell heterozygy represents a community-level adaptation, again, transmitted through the genome, the conditioning impulse for which points back to the fact that same wet, low-lying areas that make good breeding grounds for malaria-bearing mosquitoes are also well suited for the cultivation of a reliable, energy-dense food source, the underground storage organs of yams. In both cases it was the community that initiated the semiotic chain (by orienting livestock production toward fresh dairy, by clearing forested land for yam cultivation).[7]

More expansively and more controversially, the archaeologist Helen Leach has proposed that a broad constellation of morphological and behavioral characteristics common to descendants of communities that practice, or practiced, food production—farmers, herders—bear comparison to traits observed in domesticated animals when these are contrasted to wild animals of common origin. These include gracility, that is, the attenuation of bony structure, docility, and neotany, the persistence of features of early development in mature individuals—of which lactase persistence is an example. Humans, Leach argues, have essentially domesticated themselves, a fact reified not just in socially enregistered preferences for sedentism and sleeping indoors but in genetic predispositions to look, and maybe act, in ways consistent with prolonged high-density cohabitation.[8]

Ok. So far we've been treating niche construction as an undifferentiated phenomenon. Now let's imagine it as a cord composed of a number of distinct filaments braided together and see if we can tease apart some of those filaments. If we slice the cord crosswise we'll see the cut ends of a bunch of filaments bundled together. We can imagine a number of ways this bundle of cut ends might look. One way we might unbraid niche construction, implicit in the discussion up to this point, is by drawing a distinction in the material character of the semiotic chain through which a particular coupling between community (or body) and environment is enacted. So, for instance, we could distinguish among morphological, physiological, and behavioral traits. Another strategy of unbraiding would be to focus on salient—salient *to us*—dimensions of the social presences whose evolved relationship with their environment we're trying to characterize. Any kind of salience could do—say, an organ system that's particularly important to us. So we could talk about the evolutionary feedback between the nonself world and the skin and connective tissue as *integumentary* niche construction. And we could ask which filaments lie directly against the integumentary when we slice open the niche construction cord.

This kind of *polyadic* way of looking at niche construction has proved helpful for becoming attuned to the mutually constitutive conditioning impulses that give rise to sophisticated behavior. These include our capacity to manipulate objects at a distance using tools whose affordances bear a markedly indirect relationship to the movements of our body (think of piloting a drone) and the fact that we readily assimilate the task of assigning the features of our world to different categories to that of assigning features of the visible and audible world to different points in space—that is, that conceptualization feels like a form of spatial scene analysis.[9]

Now let's imagine that one of the filaments in the niche construction braid is the *somatic* filament, that is, it stands for everything having to do with the experience of our bodies as (porously) bounded participants in an ongoing enaction of social and phenomenal presence instigated by movement—all the stuff from Chapters 1 and 2. Excluded would be things that do not bear closely enough on the reflexive contingency between movement and sensation. So locomotion and gesture are in, along with biomechanical phenomena like wear and tear on the body's joints and the sensations, painful and otherwise, that accompany that wear, while things like metabolism and neural oscillations are out except insofar as they generate interoceptive sensations that we take into account as we move.

What delineating a somatic dimension of niche construction gives us is a way to draw together those aspects of bodily experience that we'd be inclined to include under the rubric *the cognitive* with those aspects we would be disinclined to call cognitive—and thus liable to ignore when we ask how computability is changing what it means to be human. Recall from Chapter 2: *nervous systems have evolved to mediate the body-world interface under conditions when that interface tends to change too quickly for other semiotic chains to keep up.* Generally this is when bodies are in motion. That is, nervous systems support movement, not the other way around. To speak as if the changes in our environment today concern the mind *as opposed to* the body, to ignore the bodily dimension of instrumentation, is to treat bodies as mediators of mind-world interaction. This encourages us to shear off everything about being a body that does not fit comfortably in our understanding of what minds are.

Some of the things we talked about in Chapters 1 and 2 would be equally at home under the sign of cognitive niche construction. Body schema, for instance. In light of what we've said about the bodily enaction of feeling and thinking, we could find a way to fit body schema in the category of the cognitive without too much forcing.

But what about joint wear? Where should the interoceptively and socially salient patterns of repetitive stress and inflammation in a body's connective tissues engendered by the habits of posture and movement demanded by different environments and different ways of life (squatting or sitting; bending at the waist or at the knee, walking barefoot or shod, grasping overhand or underhand) get braided into our theory of niche construction? Biomechanics and kinematics are no less intimately implicated in what it means to be us than, say, memory and awareness. What about differential qualities of sensory attunement? Is the fact that people who go barefoot most of their lives have greater tactile sensitivity—finer modulus of discrimination, perhaps greater dynamic range—on the plantar surface of the foot a *cognitive* fact? You could cast walking barefoot as a form of "training" comparable to music training and do all the usual brain imaging studies to see if there is relatively greater cortical volume dedicated to receiving tactile sensation from the plantar surface of the foot in those who go barefoot.[10] What you would learn from these studies would be no closer to a mythical "ground truth" about the nature of bodily life than what you'd learn by putting the integrated bodily experience—encompassing things like joint wear on an equal footing with things we think of as unfolding principally in the central nervous system—at the center of your theory of knowledge.

Besides which, it just makes no sense to use lab studies to ask questions about how the feedback loop between community (or body) and environment is changing. We'll talk about this more in the next chapter when we look at sleep and vigilance. Here, consider just one example of how the problem of *ecological validity*, the meaningfulness of laboratory data for interpreting events in the world, obtrudes itself—actually, fails to obtrude itself—in the cognitive science of pervasive media exposure:

> How can scientists break down the various components of "technology" and study their effects on brain development and function in a controlled manner? In a creative new study, Christakis and colleagues debut a possible solution—a mouse model of "overstimulation," meant to recapitulate the effects of excessive television viewing in early childhood.
>
> In this study, speakers playing sounds from children's TV shows were mounted above mouse cages and LED lights of varying colors and intensities were shone in accordance with the audio. This overstimulation paradigm was applied to mice developing from postnatal day 10 to postnatal day 52, for 6 hours every night. Later, starting at postnatal day 62, behavioral and cognitive assessments were conducted. The elevated plus maze, light dark latency, and open field tests revealed that overstimulated mice were generally more active and less anxious/more likely to take risks than controls, whereas the Barnes maze and novel object recognition tests suggested that overstimulated mice had diminished short-term memory and learning difficulties.
>
> This new mouse model powerfully illustrates the detrimental effects of audio-visual overstimulation during youth. However, the study also raises a number of questions, most fundamental of which is the definition of over-stimulation itself. What constitutes a mouse version of too much television? Because there is no clear consensus on this phenomenon, even in humans, it is challenging to establish the validity of a mouse model. Nevertheless, one can begin by considering the "construct validity" (strength of manipulation used to mimic the human condition) and "face validity" (resemblance of resulting phenotypes to key attributes of the human condition), as set forth by researchers evaluating mouse models of psychiatric illness.[11]

It is time for a more anthropological approach.

Impedance

In fact to start we need to gather together a number of strands within anthropology, none of which, up till now, has had much to say about the environment brought into being by the computing revolution.

Within evolutionary anthropology and allied aspects of archaeology, the past twenty-five years have seen a kind of "cognitive turn," a reorientation of research priorities and methodological outlook toward the question of how human beings became, not anatomically but *behaviorally* modern. This question presents problems of evidence and interpretation: What should we look for in the archaeological record to form inferences about whether a particular population of hominins living a million years ago, or even 50,000 years ago, thought, felt, or acted as we do? What does "as we do" mean? That they used language characterized by the recursive recombination of recurring partial features in the gestural (vocal, haptic), lexical (word-like units of form imbued with meaning), and grammatical dimensions? That they were about as good as we are at learning new skills by observing others and practicing? That they had the same powers of chronesthesis or mental time travel, the recombination of episodic memories to create imaginative scenarios? That they danced and sang and could keep a beat? Should we draw up a checklist of behavior patterns that form an exhaustive definition of behavioral modernity—the necessary and sufficient conditions of *like us*? If we draw up this list on the basis of evidence from one part of the world, does it make sense to apply it in other parts of the world where material circumstances (climate, physiography, flora and fauna, access to particular kinds of raw materials for tool-making) make it unlikely you're going to observe the same patterns of behavior—or that evidence of these behaviors will have been preserved in the archaeological record in the same way?[12]

Alas, the vigorous discussion of these points within anthropology has had virtually no impact on cognitive science, nor on public conversations about how plastic our habits of thought and action might be over various time horizons and what implications new developments in our environment could hold for how we behave or whether we survive. For evolutionary anthropologists, a feeling of marginalization is palpable: "Despite 20 years of concerted attention, paleoanthropology has established little of substance concerning the evolution of the modern mind, if by substance we mean conclusions that would be of interest and use to scholars of human cognition." "The disciplines producing primary data in paleoanthropology scarcely reach out to a broader picture and are often bypassed by writers in other disciplines."[13]

So we have a kind of *impedance mismatch*, an impasse in the flow of information, between the anthropology of the evolved interface among body, community, and world and the (lab-based) science of the central nervous system. The one struggles with profound questions of method, along with frustration about the fact that its message is not getting across, either to colleagues in other disciplines or to broader publics.[14] The other is up against the limits of its methodological and epistemological baseline, the controlled model environment. Neither has much to say about niche construction in the present day.

Medical anthropology, meanwhile, has cooled its ardor for the body, once the focus of its ethnographic and interpretive energies. This getting away from bodies is a positive thing. It reflects an awareness that the experience of the body as a bounded entity distinct from other bodies is a historically conditioned and partly defeasible condition, one that does not hold to the same degree in all times and places.[15] If you start by focusing on individual bodies, you'll have a difficult time making the salience of the individual body one of the things you track as it varies from place to place and over time. Over the past thirty-five years it has become common, in public conversation and public policy, to identify a wide range of social phenomena—wealth and poverty, stillness and anxiety, risk tolerance, addiction, fitness and debility—with the thriving or failure to thrive of individual bodies.[16] Releasing its grip on the body has allowed medical anthropology to focus on the *social dimensions of affect*, something that has proved essential to developing a nuanced understanding of the economic precarity that has engulfed so many people since before the financial crisis of 2008.[17]

But if, as I've been arguing, bodies remain the central fact of what it means to be a self-aware presence in the world, and if a complex of novel social and technological unfoldings is putting pressure on our enregistered strategies of bodily life, then we need something new, an anthropology of the somatic niche, to help us make sense of these pressures. This book offers an initial gesture toward such a creature.

Why put niche construction at the center?

Niche constructions offers two strengths as a framing device for an anthropology of somatic unfolding: it is political and it is evolutionary in the broad sense.

When I say niche construction is political, I mean that the process of shaping the environment is a process of reifying *value schemas*, in the case of somatic niche construction, value schemas for how to hold and move our bodies. Niche construction is political in a second way too, in that it both enacts and reifies social inequalities. We don't all share the same values about what is a good way to develop and exercise our bodily faculties, nor do we share the same capacities to shape the world to support those values. This will become more concrete in the next chapter, when we talk about vigilance management, but for now: What looks like mania to you might feel like flourishing to me, and what looks like too much sleep to me might feel like too little to you. This is political because as one set of preferences with respect to sleep or any other dimension of bodily life gets encoded in the persistent features of shared living space it becomes more difficult to act on desires that conflict with those niche-hegemonic preferences. When some people exercise a stronger capacity than others to shape the shared environment to support a somatic repertoire that feels good (pleasurable, virtuous, sustainable) to *them*, habits of movement, posture, and self-display become sources of power and objects of conflict. Again, we'll see concrete examples in the chapters ahead—rhythms of activity and rest, habits of facial display.

The evolutionary angle we've already mentioned. Despite thirty-five years of theorizing and a spate of recent popularizing works,[18] evolution is not well developed as a framework for making sense of conditioned change in enregistered repertoires of behavior and technology—that is, culture. In part this reflects ideological tensions within anthropology.[19] But a rigorous application of evolutionary theory to socially transmitted patterns of action also presents deep problems of method. There is no way to draw a bright line between homoplasy or convergent evolution—similar adaptations to similar conditioning impulses— and homology—shared innovation transmitted from a common ancestor. For that matter there is no ready-made discrete unit of transmission.[20] Above all, there is the difficulty of operationalizing the transmission mechanism, social learning. Most cultural evolution studies to date rely on crude cartoon depictions of how people acquire new skills and habits by observing others.

Here I want to set aside these concerns in favor of an overview of (1) the faculties by which we enact an interface between self and nonself aspects of the world, and (2) the big changes currently unfolding in our somatic niche, that is, the novel impulses conditioning our apparatus of body-world interface-making. Not all of these faculties and impulses get their due in the chapters that follow. But by drawing them all together we can provide a thicker context for the arguments in the second half of the book.

Six faculties of interface-making

What makes us human? If anthropology has a foundational assumption, an epistemological line in the sand beyond which the practices and dispositions attested of anthropologists would not hang together as the makings of a discipline, it is that humanity exists, that it represents a coherent object of inquiry, that there is a repertoire of social and somatic phenomena common to human communities and distinctly—which is not to say uniquely—human. Much of it we share, in varying degrees, with other animals and other aspects of the world. Following the tendency of our discussion up to this point, we could call this common fund of experience the *somatic unity* of humanity.[21]

So what can we say about the content of this somatic unity?

Most people, asked some version of this question, would start with language, and it is true, symbolic communication with some kind of recursive syntactic structure and a double articulation linking gestural and grammatical syntax is common to all modern humans (though the nature of syntax, down to the role that recursion plays and whether all languages make use of segments comparable to words, remains contested[22]). Beads—artifacts with symbolic significance—have been attested in the archaeological record at over 100 ka (100,000 years before the present), and from 60 ka they become widespread.[23] So, symbolic communication, sign use, semiosis—that is part of what makes us us.

There is *tool use*, increasingly understood as a conditioning factor for the emergence of language. The *chaîne opératoire*, the sequence of steps implicated in the production of even basic hand implements, from the procurement of raw materials to the fashioning of rough blanks to the refinement of active surfaces (scoops, blades, the load-bearing surfaces of baskets), entails a syntactic faculty, a capacity to decompose a task into parts and subparts and to grasp the creative process as one of recombinant subassembly.[24] Archaeological evidence of blanks (for hand axes, say) prepared en masse for later refinement suggests the presence of such a faculty of subassembly. We see this kind of planning in debris assemblages from Neanderthal sites in Europe at 250 ka, in Africa and Asia perhaps earlier.[25] The use of raw materials not found in the immediate vicinity of a camp site, meanwhile, suggests a faculty for symbolic binding, an ability to associate places, substances, and artifacts with activities—tool fabrication, tool use, the enjoyment of food, shelter, and the presence of others—over many stages, many degrees of referential redirection.

There is rhythmicality, encompassing meter perception and entrainment, which we discussed in Chapter 2 and will return to in the next chapter. Language, tool use, and rhythm perception are three domains of social-somatic presence where *syntax* is central to what makes the human forms of these behaviors distinct. By syntax, I mean a system of rules for the recombination of recurring actions to form complex expressions that are both novel and at the same time recognizably the products of a shared register. Part of what makes syntax fecund is that it provides the resources for its transformation by means of innovations, expressions that depart, whether by design or error, from the existing repertoire of enregistered combinations. The rules a syntax is composed of are gradient and defeasible, but they are no less rule-like for admitting a certain flexibility of application.[26] The recombination entailed in syntax includes simultaneity—two or more movements, articulations, gestures, performed together—as well as seriality, and it may involve the coordination of movement among multiple actors, multiple bodies. Copresence is syntactic, after a fashion.

There is more: memory, *episodic* memory, our memories of things that have happened to us, the kind of memory that includes sensory detail, this too is uniquely elaborated in humans, and that elaboration is syntactic. We could say something similar of procedural and semantic memory, the kind of memory embodied in learned motor sequences and the kind of memory manifest in the acquisition and recall of facts. In fact, the recombinability of all three types of memory is entailed in what we've said about tool use and language. With episodic memory it's less obvious: we like to think of our event memories as coherent wholes.

But: there are episodes that are slow to fade from my memory—the feeling of relief and openness that flowed through my body, riding in the cab of a truck, on the road from the Rwandan frontier to Isaka, Tanzania, June 2001. The scent of eucalypt woodsmoke in the air as I stared up at unfamiliar constellations, 4:00 a.m. on a cold winter morning in Pemberton, Western Australia, June 1997. There is a lover whose scent I pray never leaves me. These details are emphatically episodic, tied to the ensemble of sensory, motoric, and social circumstances in which they first impressed themselves on me. Yet in all three cases I can imagine the scene in question transformed, details swapped with those of other scenes or conjured from a sediment of scenic details that I no longer associate with any particular event, so often have I experienced roughly comparable versions of them. So: imagination, "mental time travel," the capacity to generate possible futures and possible alternate pasts by recombining elements of what we have experienced—this too is distinctive of how humans enact an interface between body and world.[27]

Finally, *imitation.* We are not the only cultured animal, the only animal that acquires behavior by social transmission. Livestock protection dogs learn their craft by shadowing more experienced dogs. A wild colony of Japanese macaques, provided with potatoes, quickly developed a habit of washing them in the ocean surf that spread by observation.[28] A population of orangutans in Borneo exhibits something like what we might call a rape culture.[29] Imitation involves both the replication of observed patterns of movement and the inference of distal intentions on the part of the one you're observing. Both aspects of imitation depend in turn on an ability to take the other's perspective, to project one's first-person presence out into the world, to dissociate from the point in space occupied by one's own body. Imitation also entails an ability to attribute statuses to potential models for imitation—to form value judgments about who would be a good person (or dyad or collective or institution) to imitate. We tend to be ambivalent about imitation, but it is not to be trifled with. At every scale, from the way we entrain the sway of our body to that of the person standing opposite us on the morning train to how we become socialized as members of a profession—as dancers, designers, anthropologists, farmers—imitation is the animus that keeps culture unfolding.

So far, while the phenomena we've been discussing are clearly somatic, they are also undeniably cognitive. That is part of the point: there is no way to separate the two, to speak as if the "cognitive-discursive" and the "physiological-phenomenal" were separate levels of experience, a material base supporting a symbolic superstructure.[30] But just as clearly there is a different way I could have written the previous section, emphasizing the biomechanical, kinematic, and psychophysical dimensions of tool use, language, memory, and imitation, the comparative anatomy of manual and oral articulatory faculties, the physiological specificity of human olfaction. In part it is my own biases on display here, in part the biases written into the available literature. What does it mean, say, to smell as a human? The question encompasses facts about the rhythmic characteristics of human sniffing behavior[31] and the chemoreceptors of the olfactory bulb—and these may vary with environment and training. But it also encompasses facts about the anatomy of sensory integration and the affective appraisal of multimodal sensory ensembles.[32] To smell or do anything else, as a human or any other kind of living thing is to participate in a multidirectional causal network in which nervous, endocrine, and biomechanical constituents of behavior—to say nothing of development, socialization, and fleeting dispositions—are so finely interwoven as to render efforts to separate them an exercise in epistemic purification, in the disregarding of some evidence on the basis of how that evidence feels, how it fits with your values.

Still. Let us take just one example of how we construct our niche where what jumps out at us is the biomechanical angle: bipedalism. Again, we could choose to ratchet up the emphasis on the central nervous system in our account, focus, as we did in Chapter 2, on bipedalism as an expression of central pattern generation, as a prime to the 2 bps pulse so common in music, as a factor in the developmental trajectory of verticality and the binding together of visual, auditory, proprioceptive, and vestibular sensations. Or, we could look at bipedalism as a phenomenon of hip flexion and metatarsal loading. Literature is scarce on the ground, and as always we need to bear in mind that science does not happen in a political vacuum. It is only in the past five years, for example, that biomechanicists have accepted what any woman could have confirmed, that the (statistically, on average) wider female pelvis does not leave women locomotorically disadvantaged vis-à-vis men. Perhaps more surprising, recent evidence suggests that plantigrade bipedalism, together with dancing the most distinctively human quality of motor behavior, emerged before hominins took form as a distinct clade. Walking erect was a conservative behavior. So much for innovation.[33]

One last trait, one last challenge to the reification of cognitive and somatic: *flexibility*, "behavioral plasticity," the capacity to adjust our habits of posture and movement—and tactile perception and digestion—to meet changing environmental circumstances. Flexibility is also *versatility*, the maintenance of a larger repertoire of behavior in reserve, to be called into regular use according to season or circumstance. Meat-eating is a prime example of adaptive versatility in humans. Depending on what is available and what we have been conditioned to prefer we can subsist on a wide range of diets, including those that feature no meat and those that consist largely of meat.[34] Here is a case where behavioral flexibility starts in a part of us that is emblematically chthonic, material, somatic (and, given the role of gut microflora in facilitating digestion, a part of us that undermines the apparent singularity of the body[35])—even though meat-eating was implicated in key developments in the evolution of human energetics.[36] More broadly, behavioral flexibility represents the extension of other-than-genetic strategies of responding to change in the environment to horizons longer than the 24-hour day. It is the colonization of somatic evolution by culture.

Writing this section has troubled me, because I am aware that it will be read as a statement of human superiority to other kinds of presence, other moving things. That is the last thing I intend. To be honest, as I look out across the room where I am sitting, I would much prefer it were filled with llamas than other human beings. This is a minority view, but I mention it to stress that my point in the preceding has been not to say humans represent a superior vehicle for the reconfiguration of the world, but simply that human strategies of niche construction are unique in the extent to which they rely on semiotic resources. The emergence of data as a salient dimension of human presence in the world is an expression of this human proclivity for manipulating symbols.

Big changes

So we construct our niche, and it constructs us in turn. Now let's look at that second direction—the conditioning signals flowing from our inhabited environment to us.

Urbanicity and the intensification of land use. Do we know urbanicity, the condition of being urban, when we see it? By 1938 sociologist Louis Wirth had characterized it as a thing not of the concentration of human and human companion zoomass but of the density of communications and transport networks bringing these animal bodies into sustained contact.[37] This view resonates with the perspective many people take today.[38] But let's pause for a minute to look at the fine-grained texture of urbanization. We tend to imagine urbanization as a phenomenon of dense urban agglomerations of unprecedented size. These do exist—Tokyo, Mexico City, Karachi. The fact that today large urban centers are growing fastest in lower-income regions is historically unprecedented, though rates of urbanization do seem to correlate with rates of economic growth.[39] But focusing on megacities, or imagining them as uniformly dense in the way the centers of older kinds of cities sometimes appear to be, obscures a broader trend of land use intensification in which peri-urban areas are getting drawn into new rhythms of recurring social synchronization that warrant an expanded understanding of the term *urban*. That is, it is an urban *tempo* that is expanding most rapidly.[40]

Added to this is the fact that human settlement is not the only form of human-driven land-use intensification. Urbanization is one aspect of a broader phenomenon of the emergence and growth of a range of *anthropogenic biomes* or *anthromes* that differ markedly from the forms of terrestrial surface transformations made possible, say, by agriculture and herding.[41]

Mobility. It is twenty years since architect Rem Koolhaas identified the airport as the modal built structure of the future.[42] But as with urbanization we miss the significance of what Koolhaas called the "in-transit condition" if we focus exclusively on iconic forms of urban megastructure like the international airport or the containerized shipping port. In a broader sense, mobility encompasses the growing circulation of goods, credit, labor, people, knowledge, and beliefs—a montage of circulation that is growing in its volume and speed and in the median displacement that things experience in their transit from production through consumption to disposal. But the in-transit condition means something more than the growth in the volume and speed at which people, materials, and signs circulate. It includes as well as syntacticization of the circulatory process, so that each step in the chain of value marked by the movement of a body or thing is less constrained by the steps that came before. In this way our displacements become recurring partial expressions available for recombination—which is to say they become combinatoric or computational in nature even as they are supported by multiplying layers of computational infrastructure.

Speed. How should we measure social acceleration? When people comment, with apprehension or satisfaction or a mixture of the two, that the world seems to be moving faster, what kinds of observations are they capturing, and could we make these observations more precise? In the North Atlantic world, complaints about the acceleration of everyday life and the decline time for reflection date back 200 years or more.[43] The sense that the horizon of novelty, the space of time we have in which to incorporate new things into our worldview, is contracting was a product, at first, of the colonial enterprise. Plants and animals, textiles and pigments, medicines and stimulants, cosmetics and techniques of body modification, skin colors and hair textures, to say nothing of languages and customs, models of labor organization cooperative and coercive, financial instruments, and strategies for making a living, trickled, then flooded in at both ends of the colonial exchange. Rupture, a transformation of circumstances and values that demanded a reconfiguration of habits, somatic and otherwise, within the adult lifetime of the individual, itself became a conditioning impulse of the human niche, a tendency that was intensified, in Europe, by the era of political revolutions that followed.[44]

I do not wish to say there is nothing new, that the technologies of the past generation or two, pervasive instrumentation in particular, do not mark some essential change in how we experience rupture. I do not wish to say that the thematization of speed in social theory, as "dromology" or "narrative collapse," is simply so much breathless presentism.[45] The past forty years or so has seen at least three new developments in the experience, collective and individual, of the time course of social change. One is what the anthropologist Jane Guyer has described as an evacuation of the near future and the near past in favor of a constant sense of punctuation, of impending rupture.[46] Second, the metrical structure of the human *zeitgeber environment* has changed markedly. Anxiety about the corrosive effects of a "twenty-four-hour society" appears starting in the 1980s, but much of this change has happened just in the past ten or fifteen years. *Zeitgeber*, a German neologism, "time giver," refers to the signals by which we maintain, or fail to maintain, a consistent rhythm of activity over the course of the day and align our activity rhythms with environmental phenomena such as daylight and with the rhythms of others. We will discuss the zeitgeber environment at greater length in the next chapter.

Third, the world has become a lot more *precarious*—or rather, precarity has become a feature of everyday life for people across a broader range of incomes and wealth levels.[47] Precarity is not simply a function of speed, whether of market activity or any other dimension of social life. But it is tied to actors' differing capacities to respond to rapid change in the market-influenced structuring conditions of household and community economic resilience. Precarity is less a lability in one's own circumstances than a rigidity or stasis, an inability to meet lability with lability. We can see this in the events that catalyzed precarity's new salience in anthropology, Hurricane Katrina and its aftermath. Vincanne Adams and colleagues, in their account of the struggles of Katrina survivors from the Lower Ninth Ward of New Orleans, stress the suspension of life trajectory experienced by those displaced by the storm—the years spent living in disaster response trailers, the sense of occupying a time of out of time.[48] This feeling of suspension, of hanging outside the accelerating unfolding of the social fabric—of social acceleration, in combination with mobility and precarity, as a kind of *punctuated stasis*—is common to many contemporary refugee situations.[49]

Species relations. A different direction, a different dimension of the newly combinatorial (syntactic, computational) character of our world: changes in the relationships that bind humans to other living things. There is, on the one hand, the *livestock transition*, a dramatic intensification in how humans raise gregarious terrestrial vertebrates for food, a concentration of other-than-human zoomass in "landless" (i.e., non–pasture-based) forms of enclosure supported by processed feedstocks (often animal-based) and human food waste. The shift to landless livestock production takes two forms. One, most readers will be aware of: feedlots and concentrated animal feeding operations, that is, factory farms. But there is another side to livestock intensification: household keeping of poultry and swine as a hedge against volatility in food prices, something that is unfolding across the emerging urban periphery. All of this has been coupled with dramatic if uneven increases in animal consumption.[50] At the same time we've experienced an unworking of safe assumptions about the categorical nature of species boundaries, stimulated by the production of genetic chimerae.[51]

The pursuit of mobile prey was an integral part of the complex of changes that gave rise to the faculties we looked at in the last section—tool use, symbol manipulation. Animals were the screen on which humans first projected their budding interiority, and our relationships with other large animals continue to provide a focal site, perhaps the focal site, for making and remaking a *social ontology of animacy*, a shared understanding of what is alive, what is intentional, what is a person. Keep this question in mind: *How is our experience of movement, in our bodies, in the world, conditioned by our encounters with other-than-human presences?* More and more of those moving presences are not animals but something else, in many cases the products of data, of instrumentation.

Climate change. Climate change could present a far deeper challenge to how we construct our niche, somatic and otherwise, than instrumentation. Earlier, in Chapter 3, I mentioned in passing the difficulty of gauging the energetic demands of instrumentation. The design ethnographer Jan Chipchase writes, in a related vein, of the *viscosity of data*, the material constraints on its production and transmission.[52] Today, as I write, I am sitting in a *Frühstückscafé* in Berlin. It is the fourth week of July. For a week, the weather was distinctly monsoonal. Now it is simply hot, and the pencil sinks a little deeper into the paper. I cannot do justice to this other viscosity, the viscosity of everything that is not data—the air, the water, our bodies before they are instrumented. We know the feeling of moving through air thick with heat and aerosols, the lethargy of a damp heat. That this has an effect on how we hold, move, and display our bodies no one would doubt. How this kind of viscosity articulates with that of data—how climate change is implicated in instrumentation and *vice versa*—is a question I cannot yet answer.

Instrumentation. Urbanicity, mobility, speed: an intensification of the flux of matter and information between self and nonself, among social formations, across species boundaries. One way to look at what is unfolding here is as a contraction and rasterization of the *modulus of recombinability* of the signals that pass between community/body and environment. Computing has increased the speed at which we disclose ourselves and others through movement and the volume of impulses we send and receive. It has also made the impulses themselves more fractional, more susceptible of recombination and coarticulation—and of disarticulation. Instrumentation gives us new ways to combine gestures but also new opportunities to pull them apart, to shear them off, to present ourselves in a narrower range of channels—or, as with sensory substitution devices, to recode impulses in a new modality. The truncated and translated modality of presence-at-a-distance is as central as speed or volume to what is new about how we disclose ourselves through instrumentation.

Speed, volume, recombinability, the transformation of sensory information into a new kind of modally promiscuous substance, *data*—these are the basic characteristics of computing. When these become pervasive features of the apparatus that binds us to the world, two things happen.

On the one hand we start to experience a novel kind of connectedness, that is, our bodies are exposed, as noted above, to a dramatically higher volume of entrainment cues—cues to the phase resetting of our senses, to the synchronization of our activities with others outside our perisomatic space. On the other hand we start to experience a new kind of instrumentation, that is, the attachment of measurement, sensing, or data-generating capacity to arbitrary features of the world, above all our bodies.

Connectedness and instrumentation are mutually implicated. More and more, the streams of data that bind us to the world originate with the continuous monitoring of behavior, our own and that of others. Instrumentation, in turn, as discussed in Chapters 3 and 4, is increasingly focused on human behavior, so that surveillance and self-awareness are being drawn into a new entente. Together, connectedness and instrumentation are giving rise to a novel dimension of somatic experience: we are becoming computable, susceptible of decomposition and recombination in the faculties of movement and sensing by which we create and negotiate the world.

The computability of human movement poses a challenge for our strategies of niche construction as they have developed up to this point in what historian

Dipesh Chakrabarty has called our "species history."[53] Chakrabarty's formulation comes from a discussion of climate change, but the challenge posed by instrumentation might be just as deep. For if climate change strikes us where we live, instrumentation strikes us in our skin, upsetting long-enregistered conventions about the *modal dimensionality of copresence*, the way different modes of sensory and motor presence coalesce into stable composites. When the coupling among modes of presence becomes labile, interesting things happen. Within the body, for instance, as discussed in Chapter 1, a loosening of the coupling among visual, auditory, proprioceptive, and vestibular graviceptive cues is implicated in out-of-body experiences and other forms of autoscopy ("self-seeing") and depersonalization. This decoupling or delamination, this parallax sensation in how we experience the flow of information to and from the body, offers a starting point for case studies in the construction of an instrumented somatic niche in the two chapters that follow.

6

Clocks

Sleep. Dreaming. Trance

An early sketch for this chapter appeared in an edited volume, and at one point the editors of that volume asked me for a couple sentences summarizing what I'd given them. Without thinking I wrote ". . . the ways that mobility, precarity, hypervigilance, and the continuous pulse of zeitgebers through the devices and apparatuses that frame our movements engender novel modes of self-presentation—desynchronized, polyrhythmic, creatures neither of day nor night but of some new temporality whose totems come from electronic dance music." I looked at what had appeared on the screen. *Where*, I wondered, *did* that *come from?*

When people ask me what this book is about, I usually start with the stuff about sleep. This book grew out of a talk I started giving in November 2012. Depending on the setting I called it "Emerging Ecologies of Time" or "Circadian Selves." It never failed to strike a chord. Everyone, it seemed, had a story about disturbed sleep, sleep frustrated, the pursuit of sleep, the negotiation of sleep with a partner.

There is no domain of somatic life where we have so thoroughly erased the recent past as sleep—where we are so thoroughly erasing it anew. With sleep in particular we take for granted features of our somatic niche that are historically and cross-culturally anomalous, not to say, once you start thinking about it, bizarre.

For a start, imagine yourself sleeping. Close your eyes and form a clear picture: your sleeping body, seen from a third-person perspective. Now: *How many other people were there in the space with you where you were sleeping?* If you said, none, or one, or even perhaps two, one of whom was an infant, you are part of the anomaly. We have come to experience sleep as an asocial behavior, the province of isolated bodies floating in a semiotic vacuum. Sleep has become the most perfect expression of liberal virtue: *something we do without help from others.*

Now: Picture yourself sleeping again. This time imagine you are watching a video played back at 4 hours to the minute, so that a whole night's sleep unfolds over a couple minutes. What is the rhythmicity of your sleep like? How often are you getting up, and for how long? How is your body moving while you sleep? If there are others present, are your movements and waking episodes synchronized or syncopated?

Again, if the scene you've imagined is one in which you sleep in long, uninterrupted stretches, more or less immobile and undisturbed, or perhaps *segmented*, to use historian Roger Ekirch's term, into two or more periods with brief intervals of wakefulness in between, you are participating a historical anomaly, or, perhaps we should say, a historical *inflection*, a profound, widespread, and potentially lasting transformation in the human somatic niche.

For Ekirch, this transformation begins in northern Europe sometime in the second-third of the eighteenth century.[1] Segmented sleep, what sleep medicine researchers would call *biphasic* sleep—sleep in two intervals of about 4 hours, the first starting just after nightfall, with an hour or two of wakefulness in between—represents, in Ekirch's history, the starting point, a biosocial default that has been obscured, over the past ten generations, by the technological reconfiguration of inhabited space. The endpoint is *monophasic* sleep, the consolidated nighttime sleep episode we take for granted. Ekirch's hypothesis has been corroborated in sleep laboratory studies designed to simulate a 14-hour scotoperiod (the complement of photoperiod). Under these conditions, a biphasic pattern "exactly the same" as that described by Ekirch was observed, suggesting that the emergence of the consolidated nighttime sleep episode, along with an "apparent decline in the seasonality of human reproduction," reflects the "clamping" of the photo/scotoperiod zeitgeber to its "summer mode."[2]

But the somatic niche of somnolence, both in eighteenth-century Europe—especially the social strata where we have a solid base of written records—and in sleep laboratories, is exceptional to start with. To the best of our sharply limited knowledge, sleep, in most human-centered communities over most of our history as a distinct kind of animal, has been not so much segmented as *punctuated*, a state of being loosely woven over the night, and day, with gaps filled by other states of being, active wakefulness just one among them.[3]

Sleep presents a methodological challenge for archaeology. It is rare to encounter bedding in archaeological debris assemblages from transient campsites, even those that were used over and over again, when the debris was created by mobile communities lacking elaborated fibercraft technology. This applies to practically any assemblage from prior to the onset of livestock domestication and sedentary agriculture some 12,000 years ago.[4] In nonherding mobile assemblages, bedding, or what archaeologists interpret as bedding, tends to be composed of layers of compacted grasses. So first there's the problem of finding these grass pallets, which are subject to a sharp equifinality curve, that is, they tend to decay to the point of archaeological invisibility faster than mineralized materials (lithics, bone, horn). Second is the problem of determining that these compacted cakes of grass do not simply represent the outcome of underwater sedimentation or a grass roof compacted into the floor of a settlement by subsequent occupations but were *fashioned* as pallets. Sometimes what is missing proves as significant as what is present—combustion by-products (charcoal, soot), particularly in carefully laid out hearths, in the absence of the debris typically associated with the preparation and consumption of food, suggests space reserved for sleeping and resting. To date these findings tell us little about the spatial, let alone temporal configuration of sleeping bodies.[5]

Earlier reports on the habits of mobile foragers, those of colonial explorers and those of professional anthropologists up to around 1950, refer frequently to the leisurely pace of subsistence activities, a tendency toward daytime napping, and an attitude some observers glossed as "laziness." These reports also, and a fixation, as anthropologist Marshall Sahlins summarized the literature in his landmark essay, "The Original Affluent Society," "on eating with gusto and digesting at leisure." These reports led Sahlins to comment, nervously and in an Marxian mode, "It is as if the superstructures of these societies had been eroded, leaving only the bare subsistence rock,

> and since production itself is readily accomplished, the people have plenty of time to perch there and talk about it. I must raise the possibility that the ethnography of hunters and gatherers is largely a record of incomplete cultures. Fragile cycles of ritual and exchange may have disappeared without a trace, lost in the earliest stages of colonialism,[6]

rendering the analogy from ethnographic evidence to historical fact even more tenuous than ordinary interpretive caution would suggest. Not to say more susceptible to projection on the part of ethnographers inclined to take their own sleeping behavior as an evolutionary baseline.

Of course, maintaining enregistered habits of sleeping can itself serve as part of a strategy of social recuperation in communities marked by colonialism. Here, as so often, Australia offers an object lesson in resilience and adaptation. The archives of the branches of the Australian government responsible for "native welfare" bear witness to administrators' frustration, over decades, at Indigenous Australians' seemingly inexplicable resistance to sleeping indoors, in households organized around a heterosexual couple and their children and dependents. Today, in settlements such as Yuendumu, in the Northern Territory, houses serve as places to store bedding, which, when it is time to sleep, is dragged outside and arranged in rows to facilitate collective defense, for example, against the aggressive camp dogs that are prone to attack younger sleepers.[7]

Among the clearest picture we have of punctuated sleep comes from horticultural and agricultural communities in southeastern Asia, where intact traditions of collective dwelling have it made possible for anthropologists to experience cosleeping in the course of fieldwork. Hollan's description from his time living in a Toraja community on Sulawesi from 1980 to 1983, is exemplary:

> Co-sleepers often huddled together closely, sharing blankets and covers for warmth and for the comfort and security of bodily contact. This close contact with one's sleeping partners along with the continuous awareness of other housemates and domestic animals that the permeable walls both afforded and could not prevent, meant that sleep in Toraja was always punctuated. One could not help but be aware of others as they turned in their sleep, slipped out of the house to urinate, mumbled or talked during dreams and nightmares, or chatted when unable to sleep or when a dream had awakened them.

Indeed, when they first arrived Hollan and his partner set up a household for themselves, only to find that "our neighbors wanted to take turns sleeping with us, fearing that we would become cold and 'lonely'," not to mention at the mercy of burglars.[8] The comparatively impoverished sleep environments most readers will be familiar with may, if anything, be too hygienic, "plac[ing] high, sustained burdens on the development of sleep–wake regulation systems and, in turn, contribut[ing] to contemporary sleep problems and disorders."[9]

So the picture of sleep offered by sleep medicine turns out to be premised on an outlier somatic niche. Even so, it is barely adequate to the task of making sense of the changes to the organization of our rhythms of activity and rest—the reconfiguration of perisomatic space, the delamination of sensorimotor modes of copresence—that we associate with urbanicity, mobility, and instrumentation. Even with the confines of noncollective, nonpunctuated sleep—I am defining our niche by its divergence from the patterns discussed above—we do not even know, for instance, how much sleep children at different stages of development "need" to stay alert, to learn, to develop as bodies and as social presences.[10] We know, for instance, that healthy sleep is essential for the maintenance of robust glucose tolerance and other dimensions of metabolism, and that the time children spend in bed at night has declined by about a minute a year over the past hundred years.[11] We have less of a fix on what healthy sleep *is*. Is it sleep that unfolds in a single nighttime episode or broken into two segments? Sleep that encompasses an orderly progression from light sleep to slow-wave sleep to REM sleep? Sleep in which we experience the tactile-motoric presence of others, rehearses the body kinematics of cosleepers in our own somnolent movements, perhaps in our dreams?

I am not the first to suggest that the physiology, no to say phenomenology, of our dreams is conditioned by our somatic niche, specifically by the spatial configuration of our bodies in sleep and the rhythmic architecture of states of arousal and sleep-wake transitions over the course of a night, a day, a season, or some longer period. In the days when it was frowned upon for anthropologists to do their own fieldwork, it was a staple of theorizing on the origins of religion that for primitive peoples the boundary between dreaming and waking life is more porous than for us moderns—that in setting where the time, space, and sociality of sleep is less firmly demarcated from those of waking, the world as it is experienced in dreams is prone to bleed over into real life, imbuing the everyday practicalities of subsistence with an oneiric quality that makes it easy to imagine one has witnessed animals talking, human beings flying, and all the other tropes of animism and shamanic trance. But in recent years it has become clear that segmented and punctuated sleep might foster an environment in which we are more likely to recall our dreams, and to share them with others, "since one is more likely to be roused during and immediately after dreaming" and to have an audience at hand to receive a report of your dream.[12]

In settings like the one Hollan describes, the social life of dreams is not limited to whispered conversations between cosleepers. The anthropologist Michael Dove, describing events among the Dayak of Borneo in the 1930s, notes how a dream, shared and retold, can become a vehicle for the shared representations by which a community enacts a kind of collective introspection. In the case at hand, the dream was of a rubber tree that is discovered to be hiding, in its bole, rice that had gone missing. The dream of rice-eating rubber, Dove argues, gave form to a shared anxiety about the danger the rubber trade posed to local food security.[13]

Sleep needs

Let's come back to the question of sleep needs. If sleep *architecture* is plastic—if we can transition among punctuated, segmented, and consolidated sleep strategies—and, as we'll see in a minute, if some of us can intervene more radically in our sleep rhythms, dispensing altogether with sleep episodes longer than twenty minutes—could sleep *needs* be plastic too?

A couple paragraphs back I mentioned in passing a recent meta-analysis of nightly time in bed among children and adolescents over a 100-year period.

The same authors looked at sleep recommendations and found a parallel trend: expert recommendations for children's and adolescents' sleep needs declined at the same rate as observed time in bed, approximately a minute a year, with sleep recommendations consistently exceeding actual time in bed by some thirty-seven minutes.[14] This is just one in a slowly unfolding series of studies that have led sleep medicine researchers to abandon the quest for simple formulas, based, say, on age and sex, for specifying optimal sleep duration— that is, a volume of sleep that would ensure optimal metabolic and cognitive function and, in children, optimal growth. Short sleep—4 or 5 hours or night, say—does seem to consistently lead to decreased vigilance and impaired glucose tolerance in laboratory settings. But of course, laboratories provide a poor approximation to sleep in the wild. A proper "somnotypology," an ontology of the self-selected strategies of sleep found in the community at large, would need to consider a much broader range of variation in sleep habits than that encompassed in chronotype, the morningness-eveningness scales used since the 1970s to classify individuals' rest-activity preferences by time of day.[15] It would, in fact, have to consider the social totality of our rhythms of vigilance and rest, the ensemble of adaptations by which we shape our environment to fit our (plastic, though not limitlessly so) bodily needs and shape our strategies of bodily care—of the self and others—to environment exigency.[16]

Then of course there's my friend Puredoxyk,[17] who argues that we can get by on about two hours of sleep in twenty-four, if we distribute it strategically:

Josh: You know, Pd, there's been this rash of studies lately using forced desynchrony protocols, you know, keeping people on, like, twenty-eight-hour activity–rest cycles, so they separate participants' social behavior rhythms from circadian time.[18] And these studies are showing that even a few days of internal desynchrony, or even just truncated sleep without internal desynchrony, causes all kinds of changes in the metabolic transcriptome.[19] And some of these changes look a lot like what you see in metabolic syndrome—

Puredoxyk: *In the lab! In the lab!*

J: —not to mention all the studies showing that short sleep causes cognitive impair—

Pd: Of course! I'm going to go to my grave saying this. Of course that's what these studies show. *Because these people [the participants] aren't transitioned.* Look, that first week, when you're transitioning to a polyphasic schedule, you go through all the same stuff. How your body responds to food is all messed up, and you're tired. And then it stops. The problem with these studies is that they're done in lab settings, and the people in these studies aren't given a chance to adapt to a new schedule.

J: Ok, of course you're right. I mean, I'd be the first to say that the ecological validity in these studies leaves something to be desired. That was part of what got me interested in chronobiology. We've talked about this, I was reading up on motor entrainment, firefly flashing and bonobo pant-hooting, and music and dance and turn-taking in conversation. And it took me a while to get my search terms right, because when you just look for "entrainment" you get much more stuff about circadian entrainment than motor entrainment. And at first I thought, *This is so not what I want.* But then I got into it, because some of it is just so crazy, the experimental protocols, with the isocaloric meals and continuous bedrest and they even admit that a lot of it is nonsense, because a lot of the lab work in chronobio has been done with model organisms, and you can't get data relevant to humans from rodent models because rodents, and cats too, are innately polyphasic, plus they're nocturnal, so the zeitgebers are inverted.

The newer work, the new clinical stuff, is much more careful. Still, you're right. No one's done a study of polyphasic sleeping in the wild. Even Stampi and the NATO people, they were focused on tours of, like, two weeks, enough for going back and forth across the Atlantic or continuous operations during a bombing campaign.[20]

Pd: It's beyond that. Reducing your sleep time safely is not something that just happens. Sticking to a polyphasic schedule takes discipline and planning. Even for me, even now it's hard work. Do I feel better sleeping polyphasically? Yes. But it's not the sort of benefit that is just going to spontaneously appear in a lab experiment.[21]

Puredoxyk practices polyphasic sleeping, which is to say that she has mostly given up on the idea of a consolidated nighttime sleep episode in favor of a regimen of naps, each about twenty minutes, spaced over the 24-hour day. Actually she's experimented with multiple regimens, ranging from the "core-free" Uberman, with six naps spaced precisely at 4-hour intervals, through a series of progressively less restrictive Everymans, which substitute an early morning core sleep for some of the naps.

Uberman (no umlaut) was Puredoxyk's original polyphasic schedule. She chose the formula on intuition, guided by a vague awareness that Leonardo da Vinci had slept in fifteen-minute naps. By luck, it turned out to be the best of the formulas she later tried, providing her with even, sustained alertness over the day. It remains her reference scenario for a rigorous, sustainable approach to sleeping polyphasically. On Uberman, one takes six naps of fifteen to twenty-five minutes each (optimal nap length varies from person to person, but once you've found your nap length you stick with it for all naps) spaced evenly over the 24-hour day. The timing of naps is key. "Asymmetric" core-free schedules, that is, those in which the time between naps varies over the course of the day in the absence of a "core sleep" of 90–270 minutes (i.e., one to three full slow-wave—REM sleep cycles), are considerably more challenging, both to transition to and to maintain. The basic formula is that one twenty-minute nap can replace one ninety-minute sleep cycle.[22]

It is safe to say that Pd is a respected figure, if not a legend, in the polyphasic sleeping world, though for her, polyphasic sleeping represents just a minor aspect of an effort to be vigilant. She'd much rather talk about taiji.

At the time of this writing, late 2014, Puredoxyk has been sleeping polyphasically, off and mostly on, for the past fifteen years. She and I have been talking since before I started thinking rigorously about sleep—more precisely, rhythms of vigilance and rest—as a dimension of somatic niche construction. Polyphasic sleeping offers a useful boundary object, a manageable field of evidence for asking about the tensions and pressures that arise where two registers, two regimes of socially coherent practice, meet. Polyphasic sleeping straddles the boundary between two registers of sleep-wake practice. It adopts the technical lexicon of a sleep medicine predicated on consolidated sleep and uses that lexicon to open up a new register, one that depends on affordances common to modern medicine and modern urban space—precise chronometry, precise control of artificial illumination, convenient access to stimulants and sedatives in a range of modalities, above all pharmacological—but directs these affordances to novel ends. Polyphasic sleeping is not segmented, nor is it punctuated. Nor, despite Puredoxky's emphasis on adherence to one's nap schedule—on the more rigorous schedules, nap durations must be timed to the minute and nap spacing to within fifteen minutes—is polyphasic sleeping in any way machinic.[23] To sustain it demands sustained attention to one's bodily state and a spirit of experimentation. It is, in the end, a lot of work:

> **Josh:** This came up on one of the polyphasic discussion lists just the other day: "I have a deadline, I have some play in my schedule, I've been meaning to try polyphasic anyway, could I transition partway, just to give me the extra working hours I need for this project?" Do you get this a lot?

> **Puredoxyk:** I do. That's a really common question. I compare it, sloppily but validly I think, to "I don't have time to eat healthily; maybe if I switched to being vegan real quick it'd be easier?" Kind of, if you don't have time to do it the easy way, why would doing it a harder way fix that?

> **J:** Ok, after thirteen-plus years as a strict vegan, I can appreciate what you mean.

But it is not just that polyphasic sleeping itself straddles the boundary between two registers of sleep-wake practice. The crystallization of a community, a social movement, around polyphasic sleeping is symptomatic of a shift in the *economy of vigilance*, the rhythmic flow of attention, arousal, and alertness through our bodies and through the dyadic and collective configurations of movement by which we enact our social world. The shift I'm pointing to is something more than simply a globalization of liberal sleep habits, it's also something like a partial disintegration of those habits. We are, you could say, becoming chronoplastic. That is, the relationship between the passage of time and the rhythmic alternation of our states of vigilance and quiescence is becoming more labile.

This lability, this chronoplasticity, embodies a coarticulation of somatic repertoire and living space of the sort we looked at in the last chapter. Mobility, in the sense we used it there, is implicated. For if it is not quite true, as Pico Iyer writes, that jet lag is "a deeply foreign country. . . . A place that no human had ever been until forty or so years ago"—for what of shift workers, who first caught the attention of nutrition physiologists in the 1880s?[24] What of the many traditions of using sleep deprivation to induce altered states of consciousness?—then it is certainly the case that recurring high-speed transmeridian travel has become a salient feature of the somatic niche of a large and growing part of the population, and with it the complex of phenomena we call jet lag.

Lighting is implicated, though in ways it is difficult to explore even in the field. We are becoming indoor creatures. Midday sunlight affords an ambient illuminance on the order of 100,000 lux, an overcast sky 20,000. Indoor lighting typically provides less than 1,000. (I think of the perpetual twilight of the international airport—even in the best designed airports, Zürich, say, or Incheon or Copenhagen, even at midday on a bright clear day with a fresh coat of snow on the ground, the airport is suffused with a just-noticeable luminosity.)

Posture is implicated too. One posture in particular, *sitting*. More and more of us spend more and more of our waking time in seated and recumbent positions. The implications for metabolic health have become a staple of science journalism, but there's something more going on here. When we sit, when we immobilize the trunk and lower limbs, we attenuate the flow of locomotor zeitgeber from our body to other bodies nearby—and we become less receptive to the motoric presence of others, physically less able to reenact observed movements in our own body. Standing, squatting, and even slouching preserve freedom of movement in the abdomen and thoracic cage, enabling us to incorporate body-to-body motor resonance into the coupling between moving and breathing in our own bodies. Sitting, by contrast, damps our capacity to take rhythms of movement from the nonself world into our own pattern of locomotor-respiratory coupling, rendering us less aware of movement in the world and less responsive to it.

Freerunning

At twenty-three, I had my first episode of major depression. This had a number of lasting consequences. For one thing I lost the ability to experience pleasure and desire. I write *lost the ability* but that suggests that the experience of pleasure and desire normally demands concentration. What I lost was simply the experience of pleasure and desire. For another I stopped sleeping through the night. At the end of eight years pleasure and desire had come back, and they have stayed, even through a second episode. But sleep—it has been fifteen years now—has never been the same. Unless I am profoundly jet-lagged, I never sleep through the boundary between two consecutive sleep cycles. Every ninety or a hundred minutes, at the conclusion of REM sleep, the period we associate with dreaming, and twitching of the eyes, and the immobilization of the body by an endogenous inhibition of skeletal motoneurons, I wake up. Often—I know I'm not alone in this—I awake before the GABA has cleared my bloodstream and find myself paralyzed.[25] Invariably when this happens I have rolled over onto my back, and I lie there for a minute or two, motor pathways spiking impotently, struggling to lift my chest.

A profound shift is underway in the economy of vigilance, the network of recurring gestures by which we ascribe value to arousal, alertness, motoric presence, desire. The sum of these gestures is a motoric metrical structure, a hierarchy of rhythmic pulses in the stream of movements that carry us through the day. This is (provisionally, problematically) *internal* vigilance we're talking about, motor vigilance. I have chosen vigilance as opposed to other terms (arousal, activity, wakefulness) to highlight its relationship, as yet poorly understood, to vigilance in the more common usage, collective vigilance, attunement to signs of incipient disruption (environmental, technological, political) in the fabric of social space.

Our rhythms of vigilance unfold over a range of temporal horizons. There is the moment-to-moment motor resonance—you move, I move—of the morning train. There is the stimulation of social contact, work and play, caring for and hanging out, along with timed energetic events, meals and exercise—these play out over hours, though of course they form the basis for registers of recurring social-somatic presence, a regime of periodic heightened responsiveness to particular mixes of stimuli, that coalesce and dissolve over weeks, seasons, years, and generations. And there is the 24-hour day with its alternation of light and dark. These *zeitgebers*, timing cues, are social *and* material in character, all of them—sensory experience is itself shaped by socialization—and I will not try to sort experience into the social and the merely sensory. (It's worth noting, though, that the transcription-translation feedback loops that govern circadian entrainment to light, both at the cellular level and, in vertebrates, via populations of dedicated pacemaker neurons in the central nervous system, are remarkably well conserved across the eukaryotes.)[26]

When I say a profound shift, what I have in mind is something more than a simple attenuation of the role of environmental zeitgeber, specifically the alternation of light and dark, in shaping our rhythms of activity and rest. What I have in mind is a change in the metrical architecture of human experience at every scale of its organization, from the 10–11 Hz physiological tremor that governs motor readiness up to the seasonality of our moods and habits. The problem, for me, is to develop a synoptic picture of how the changes in these nested oscillations fit together.

The laboratory studies alluded to earlier—the ones that confirmed Ekirch's "segmented sleep" hypothesis, the ones that have failed to disconfirm Puredoxyk's hypothesis that polyphasic sleeping, done carefully, is safe— go back to 1901, when Simpson and Galbraith, physiologists at Edinburgh, noticed that the body temperature of the macaque monkeys in their lab varied depending on what time of day it was measured and conceived an experiment to see how continuous light, continuous dark, and the inversion of light and dark from the natural day would affect the readings.[27] Not long after, Wesleyan University physiologist Francis Benedict, a pioneer in the measurement of metabolism in large mammals, devised a flexible rectal thermometer that could be worn for days on end, allowing the subject "to sleep normally, sit in any position, walk about the room . . . or even ride a stationary bicycle or ergometer," and used it to record the effects of schedule inversion on human core temperature, working with a seasoned night watchman.[28] In the 1920s and thirties, University of Chicago physiologist Nathaniel Kleitman experimented with forced desynchrony protocols, putting small numbers of research participants on 21- and 28-hour schedules for periods of weeks at a time so as to observe temperature rhythms free of the influence of the 24-hour activity day. In June 1938, Kleitman had two men spend five weeks on 28-hour rhythms while living in specially constructed quarters in Mammoth Cave, Kentucky.[29]

In 1962, physicist Rütger Wever and physiologist Jürgen Aschoff established a zeitgeber-free living environment in a Second World War–era surgical bunker in Andechs, outside Munich, and embarked on a series of isolation experiments that would run until 1989.[30] About half these experiments were designed to elicit *freerunning* behavior, that is, participants were given no special light-dark protocol but were free to set their own rhythms of activity and rest. Similar facilities were later constructed in the United States. The French speleologist Michel Siffre, meanwhile, preferred to carry out his freerunning experiments, on himself and others, in caves, first in the southern Alps,[31] later, in 1972 at the invitation of NASA, in Del Rio, Texas. The bunker-and-cave era of clinical chronobiology peaked in the 1970s, and by 1989, when NASA sponsored

Stefania Follini, a 27-year-old woman from Ancona, to spend 130 days in a cave in Carlsbad, New Mexico, the N-of-1 freerunning paradigm carried a tinge of steampunk defiance. As if you needed to descend into a cave to pry yourself loose from the alternation of night and day.

Catching the beat

In 2009, at thirty-four, I experienced a second episode of major depression. This time I was prepared. It was nowhere near as painful. It did not feel like my skin was on fire. I did not lose my hedonic drive. But when I recovered, something new happened: I become prone to manias. Two nights running of restricted sleep, or even just sleep shifted forward 3 hours, could set me off for a week or two. My whole personality took on a hypomanic cast, a mild fizziness, an undercurrent of euphoria and grandiosity that, for all its complications, beats depression with a stick.

Most astonishing of all, I became highly entrainable. Practically anything could provoke me to dance. Suddenly I wanted to listen to electronic dance music. I spent a year with LCD Soundsystem's *This Is Happening* (2010) on repeat.

Not long after all this began, I started using a lightbox. It made the Berlin winter less oppressive. But it also helped with the summer, when, bathed in light, my gestures grow exaggerated, threatening to jump the groove. The lightbox gives off a glow the color of a midday sky. It is tuned to 480 nm, the peak sensitivity wavelength of melanopsin, the photopigment found in the intrinsically photosensitive retinal ganglion cells responsible for encoding light into a nervous signal to be transmitted from the eyes to the central circadian pacemaker in the suprachiasmatic nuclei of the hypothalamus.[32] It acts as a supplementary zeitgeber, correcting for the deficits and surpluses of naturally occurring sunlight. Not unlike the driving pulse in dance music, keeping you in sync with your social environment when all else is chaos and noise.

In 1982, researchers at the Oregon Health Sciences University, Portland, and the U.S. National Institute of Mental Health reported the case of a 63-year-old man with rapid-cycling bipolarism who had noticed a distinct seasonal pattern to his mood cycles and whose winter depression responded to an improvised regime of bright fluorescent light, three hours in the morning and three in the evening for ten days.[33] Two years later the same network of researchers offered a preliminary description of seasonal affective disorder along with a light-based treatment.[34] Earlier, psychiatrists at the University Neurological Clinic in Tübingen had demonstrated the effectiveness of sleep deprivation as a treatment for depression.[35] Light therapy and the rebranded wake therapy began to coalesce into chronotherapeutics.[36] Acceptance has been slow, despite repeated confirmations that "the effects of light therapy are comparable to those found in many antidepressant pharmacotherapy trials" for nonseasonal as well as seasonal mood disorders.[37] Part of the problem is experimental design—how do you formulate a control for bright light? There's also the fact that, unlike drugs, you can't patent light.[38]

I began to read about entrainment, the coordination of activity through the active maintenance of a constant relationship of phase and period. As in dancing or making music or turn-taking in conversation, three distinctly human forms of behavior that exemplify our capacities—not unique, but uniquely elaborated—for empathy and shared attention.[39] As we discussed in Chapter 2, you don't need an innate "theory of mind" to get cooperation between moving beings. You do need motor resonance, a predisposition to take other social presences for zeitgeber, along with a sensitivity to rhythmic hierarchy.[40] You need a facility for coordinating pulsatile transient gain increases in one's own sensitivity to movement in the environment with perceived attentiveness pulses in others. At the base of social life stands a shared experience of *kinesthetic empathy*. Rhythmic elevation in vigilance is the currency of kinesthetic empathy.

In 1986 a case report from the Ghent University Medical Center described "marked sleep latency reduction and diminished vigilance" in two individuals admitted to the hospital during manic episodes. In one, "EEG showed prominent, regular, and sustained sleep spindles within 190–200 sec following eye closure"; in the other, it took just 60–70 seconds.[41] This report was ignored for two decades until, sometime after 2000, researchers in Germany and the United States independently began to comment on overlaps in the phenomenology of disturbances of mood, attention, and arousal, and the implications of circadian entrainment in all of them.[42] One group described mania as an effort on the part of the individual to create a more stimulating environment so as to offset the risks posed by diminished endogenous vigilance.[43]

The impetus for this renewed attention to the regulation of arousal and rest was a dramatic increase in the diagnosis of mood, attention, and arousal disorders in young people. Attention Deficit Hyperactivity Disorder is the best-known facet of this story, but it is not the whole story. Between 1994 and 2003, annual outpatient diagnoses of bipolar phenomenon in people under twenty in the United States grew *forty*fold.[44] Among the causes was an unofficial relaxation of diagnostic criteria for episodicity in recurring, socially disruptive irritability in young people. Bipolar disorder had become a diagnostic receptacle for surplus vigilance, prompting researchers at the National Institute of Mental Health to formulate a new nosology of nonepisodic severe irritability. The phenomenology, physiology, and trajectory of this new syndrome turn out to diverge from bipolar phenomenon as it presents in adults. Irritability, surplus arousal, had become "a pressing problem for clinical neuroscience" in young people.[45]

From chronotherapeutics to chronoactivism

> In many ways, light can be considered a drug, having the potential for both beneficial and deleterious effects.[46]

In 2012, I came across the Valkee, a light stimulation device that differs from my own beloved Philips goLite and every other light device on the market in two ways: (1) it delivers light through the ears, not the eyes; (2) it is very clearly designed to resemble an iPod. *Out of the clinic, into the Apple Store.*

Once you enter the world of consumer chronotherapeutics it does not take long before you encounter accelerometer bracelets. Soon, with two device categories to work with, my unformed thinking about entrainment had found a material scaffolding.

These days, accelerometer bracelets are the emblematic device in a rapidly expanding market dedicated to supporting personal management of rhythms of activity and rest. Vigilance is becoming a focal object of self-care. This, you will say, is not news. The vast majority of us have been self-administering a certain purine alkaloid known to enhance vigilance since the day we started making our own choices about what to eat and drink.[47] Stimulant alkaloids have been with us since long before talk of social acceleration and the nocturnalization of labor—in Mesoamerica for at least 3,000 years, on the Arabian Peninsula and in adjoining parts of Africa for 1,000, in China for perhaps more than 2,500. Isn't activity monitoring just more of the same?

Yes and no. It is one thing to know that if you drink a cup of coffee you will, some twenty minutes later, experience the onset of a short-lived episode of elevated clarity, enhanced capacity for sustained attention, reduced hunger, reduced perceived effort in physical exertion, and so on. It is another to receive hourly updates on how active you have been over the preceding hour, where you stand in relation to your goals for activity, and how today compares to yesterday, last week, and the day your friends have been having.

It is another thing again to drink a cup of coffee and then go to sleep with the expectation of waking in exactly nineteen minutes when the caffeine kicks in—indeed, to organize your life around sleeping in nineteen-minute naps so that you may dispense with consolidated nighttime sleep altogether. Polyphasic sleeping represents an extreme form of what we could call chronoactivism, but not that extreme. More and more people are devoting more and more energy to actively intervening in the architecture of their rhythms of sleep and wakefulness.

It's become easy to dismiss these things—modafinil, DIY transcranial direct current stimulation, polyphasic sleeping, nontherapeutic use of light stimulation, accelerometer bracelets, listening to dance music all day, practically any strategy of ergogenesis-as-personal-enhancement—as expressions of capitalism in its insatiable drive to produce.[48] There's something to this view. Refined sugar and tea were key ingredients in the making of the industrial working class.[49] But there's something deeper going on, the creation of a novel *somatic niche*, a new value schema for how we hold and move our bodies, one that, for all its continuity with the 500-year trajectory of capitalism,

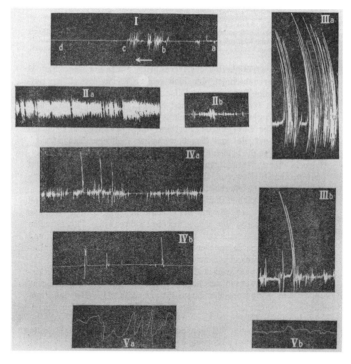

FIGURE 6.1 *"Varying intensities of activity over the course of a 24-hour cycle"— the first appearance of actigraphy, Szymanski's Aktograph (Szymanski 1920, 139, Figure 5). Szymanski devised a range of seismograph-like apparatuses to measure the activity-rest rhythms of different animals, including human children. The plots in this figure were generated, inter alia, by a canary, mice and a worm. Szymanski's observation that many animals experienced multiple activity-rest cycles in a single 24-hour day led him to coin the term* polyphasic.

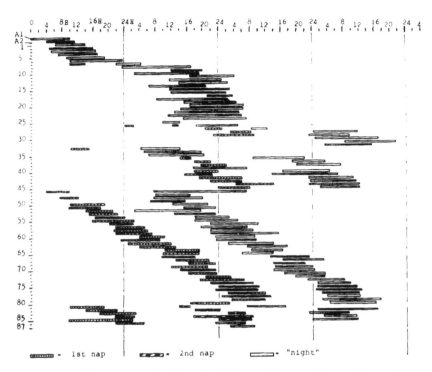

FIGURE 6.2 *Sleep-activity rhythms for 23-year-old research participant "JPM" during 174 days living underground (June–November 1966; Chouvet et al. 1974, 370, Figure 3). Note the radical change in JPM's activity pattern starting twenty-five days following his release from synchronization with surface time.*

represents a divergence from the tempo of human motor readiness over a longer horizon.

Bracelet actigraphy participates in a history of self-measurement that stretches back at least to William Ogle's observations "on the diurnal variations in the temperature of the human body in health."[50] It also participates in a more recent history of efforts to characterize the relationship between wakefulness and mood (Figures 6.1–6.2). The first use of a device recognizably like those marketed today for sleep and fitness tracking was in the study of activity rhythms in individuals with rapid-cycling bipolar phenomenon. Researchers from the same group at the U.S. National Institute of Mental Health as would later propose a diagnostic category for severe mood dysregulation identified a 48-hour rhythm of sleep-wake behavior, consistent with reports of recurring 48-hour sleep-wake cycles in individuals who had spent more than thirty days in freerunning environments.[51]

These bicircadian rhythms tend to occur under conditions of internal desynchrony, when the body's core temperature and plasma cortisol rhythms get disentrained from the activity-rest rhythm, promoting an alternating short day—long day pattern that in some individuals can stretch to as long as 48 hours.[52] This kind of internal desynchrony is similar to what happens in jet lag.

Delamination

We need a phenomenology of jet lag. Prolonged seated immobilization in a dim, noisy environment followed by a sudden resetting of the phase of environmental and social zeitgeber has a number of consequences, of which the decoupling of the body's rhythms of movement, core temperature, and corticosteroid expression is just one.[53] "Under jet lag," writes travel essayist Pico Iyer, "something deeper is dissolved. I get off a plane, 17 hours out of joint, and tell naked secrets to a person I know I don't trust. A friend starts talking about her days—her plans, her friends, the things she wants to do—and tears start welling in my eyes."[54] Jet lag is not unlike depression. You must fight the tendency toward social withdrawal, toward sleeping at inappropriate hours, toward inanition.[55]

More and more, the architect Keller Easterling has proposed, we move in an environment of *spatial products*, extents of built space whose architectonic and social features are conditioned not by geographic context but by the interests manifest in spatially dispersed organs of capital accumulation.[56] These are spaces shaped not by proximity but by nonlocal simultaneity.

Something similar is true of our bodies. Zeitgebers stream to us from well beyond perisomatic space, and we in turn project our social presences, plural, out into the new space of nonlocal simultaneity. Built space, of course, has always shaped how we hold and move our bodies, and habitual movement marks us in enduring ways. Some of these marks are anatomically salient: the lengths of limbs, the curvature of the spine, the wearing away of connective tissue. But habitual movement also shapes body schema, the constellation of pre-reflective expectancies about the proprioceptive, vestibular, and visual consequences of moving in particular ways by which we monitor the interface between self and world. When we extend our bodies in space we extend our awareness too, as when a tool comes to feel like an extension of your hand. When we become more or less continuously present at a distance something new happens. The *thereness*, the manifest quality of other presences (people, but not just people), impinges on us in a way that is more urgent, even (especially?) when those presences are low-fidelity—and at the same time less specific in its sensuous qualities. We start to attend less to what is going on in the field of experience defined by the space around our bodies and more to what is unfolding in the larger space of distant presence. We start to experience the spontaneous coordination, transient phase locking, and cascading of behavior among large numbers of individuals over great distances—human movement starts to exhibit criticality.[57]

There is something more: just as in jet lag our endogenous oscillators become delaminated from one another, in synchronization-at-a-distance social personae start to become delaminated from bodily presence—from bodily *desire*, from the very specific limbic sensations afforded by movement, rest, eye contact, skin-to-skin touch. Whatever else synchronization-over-distance is, it is a condition of *asymbolia*,[58] a damping down of the emotional resonance of sensory experience—or, in a more positive light, of *pratyahara*, the withdrawal from the moment-to-moment flux of sensory experience that is a prerequisite of the boundarylessness we associate with "flow states."[59]

One person's desynchrony is another's polyrhythmicity.

You are waiting for me to say something like *Vigilance becomes a scarce resource*. But actually, I think it's the other way around. Vigilance is something we create on demand, just as banks create money.[60]

How we distribute it is another matter.

Trance. Splitting

[Although m]y body was before my master,
I left Your Majesty in my dream;
My body before my master faced the unfinished game,
With dim eyes fully closed;
I left Your Majesty in my dream to ride the blessed cloud,
With spirit most eager and alert.
That dragon on the dragon execution block
Was bound up there by celestial hosts.
Your subject said,
'For breaking Heaven's law,
You are worthy of death.
Now by Heaven's command,
I end your wretched life.'
. . .
Your subjected bestirred his spirit,
Lifting robe and taking step to hold high his blade.
With one loud crack the knife descended;
And thus the head of the dragon fell from the sky.[61]

With depersonalization and flow states, we return to where we started—
"creatures neither of day nor night but of some new temporality whose totems

come from electronic dance music." There are few ethnographic studies of electronic dance music, or EDM, and those available tend to focus less on EDM phenomenology than on the social dynamics of the subcultures that have grown up around it.[62] When I was writing this chapter I was asked to give a lecture on the anthropology of sleep and dreaming. This was to form part of a workshop on collective dreaming. I found myself returning, after ten years away, to the literature in the anthropology of trance, possession, and altered states of consciousness. In the past thirty years the questions anthropologists ask about these states have shifted away from what physiological features might underlie commonalities in states of altered presence observed in different places to how these states provide disenfranchised actors a way to comment on political injustices they are not in a position to confront directly.[63]

We read that trance is a state of "parasympathetic domination," of heightened suggestibility, that it may proceed, via an ecstatic (shamanic) or contemplative (meditation-based) route, to reintegration—"a nondistorted recrystalization [sic] of the ego"—or to psychosis.[64] What if this process of creative ego destruction started to seep out of the tightly delimited bounds of ritual contexts (whether shamanic interventions or electronic dance music festivals) and into everyday life? What if we started to experience a surplus of motoric gain, of bodily vigilance?

Pursuing reports of these states among polyphasic sleepers, I found myself blocked by indifference on the part of my principal research partner. Over and over, Puredoxyk and I had some version of the following conversation:

Josh: So when you're on Uberman, when you're doing all-nap, no core sleep.

Puredoxyk: Yes.

J: In your book you talk about a state you refer to, with reservations, as "euphoria":

> I wasn't high, just very awake. I didn't have trouble relaxing, or feel jittery (unless I had coffee, which affected me more than usual when I was on Uberman). I simply felt on the razor's edge of completely-awake most of the time. It was an exceptionally pleasant experience, feeling like that, so then again maybe "euphoria" doesn't completely miss the mark. I would normally be willing to write off this feeling as not related to the sleep schedule itself, simply because it seems so subjective and so subjectable [sic] to any number of factors. But the fact is, besides my partner at the time who reported the same feelings, almost every successful adapter to Uberman that I've ever spoken to has reported the same thing, even if they claimed not to know that I'd experienced it.[65]

Pd: Yes.

J: I wonder if we could talk more about this state, what it felt like—

Pd: Everyone seems to get it, everyone seems to enjoy it, no big deal.

J: But—

Pd: 's just not that interesting.

The fizziness, the feeling of heightened motor gain, of being on the razor's edge, that Puredoxyk describes is remarkably similar to what many people experience in the first couple days of a mania, or even after simply being up all night (with or without the driving bass of electronic dance music). In my case it is usually linked to a sensation of intermodal slippage in the sense I have of where and how I am situated in space, a deregistration of visual, proprioceptive, and vestibular cues that offer an invitation to autoscopy. Puredoxyk's characterization of this razors'-edge state as "euphoria" is accurate.

Polyphasic sleeping is not the only new technique of vigilance management to induce alterations in motor presence. Many who have undergone eye movement desensitization and reprocessing (EMDR)—a therapeutic technique in which the therapist introduces a rhythmic pulse into the patient's visual or tactile sensorium and then guides the patient through the re-experiencing of traumatic events—report transient sensations of depersonalization and trance. It does not take much in the way of rhythmic entrainment to induce a softening of the boundaries of the self, and a short-lived state of depersonalization or autoscopy—imagining the remembered event as if one had been an observer looking on for somewhere else in the scene—could be integral to therapeutic effects of the exercise.[66]

Pedersen, writing both as an anthropologist of northern Asian shamanism and as an enthusiastic proponent of the integration of mobile instrumentation into the ethnography of social networks, cautions against mistaking connectedness for an unalloyed good, something we can never get too much of. In his work with "halfway shamans" among the Darhad of northern Mongolia, women and men struggling, on the basis of limited information, to revive a shamanic tradition that had been partly interrupted by the Soviet era, he observed that many of his shamanizing interlocutors seemed remarkably accident-prone. They tended to attribute their mishaps to leakage of the personages and characteristics of the world of shamanic flight into the workaday world of splitting firewood and butchering livestock. With the collapse of state socialism, Darhad Mongols "found themselves exposed to a violent intrusion of invisible spirit souls, energies and forces, which, for seventy years of socialism, had hovered only in the shadowy margins of self, household, community and nation. . . . [I]t was only by identifying ways of cutting, curtailing and severing a perceived overabundance of occult connections" that the Darhad could begin to formulate anew a productive way of relating to the spirit world.[67]

We are prone, these days, to minimizing the creative qualities of division.[68] We don't all regularly split firewood or butcher livestock—division is not, perhaps, salient as a genre of everyday productive labor for most readers of this book (save the polyphasic sleepers) as it would be for steppe dwellers. But we all sleep, we all dream, we all experience dissociative states. We all have moments when we turn our face away from the camera.

7

Faces

This chapter includes photographs of Indigenous Australian individuals who are no longer living. These photographs were likely made in circumstances that many today would consider coercive, and the subjects could not have known how their images would later be circulated. Those who might find these images painful are advised.

Persona

In a 2011 essay entitled "It's Not Your Face, It's Ours," the design ethnographer Jan Chipchase speculates on the implications of a coming revolution in face recognition technology:

> For a while people will want an awareness of how much it costs to place advertising next to their face—monitoring spikes and dips in cost depending on context—a popularity index of sorts. For most the novelty will wear off (especially once they figure out how little they are worth) but for a certain demographic the cost of placing an advert next to their face will be[come] part of their personal identity. . . . Whilst some careers will be destroyed by real time [face] recognition, others will be enabled—there will literally be a new army of people that will be the "faces of the brand."[1]

The date of this essay is October 30, 2011, and though he does not mention Halloween Chipchase is talking here about the evolution of *persona* in its original sense, that is, a type of mask donned for a performance. He is concerned, and in this chapter I am concerned, with the Janus-faced nature of facial display, the tension between two roles the face plays: that which we make up according to context and that which reveals our inner states in spite of our will to conceal them.

It was early 2012 when I came across Chipchase's "It's Not Your Face, It's Ours," when I was laid up with a broken foot as described in the Preface. But I'd been thinking about the convergence of persona and brand for five years. Never once did it occur to me that this convergence was a phenomenon of computing power, of the availability of face recognition technology, as Chipchase puts it, "in the palm of the hand." In that five years I was working on what became *Topology and Surveillance*, the unpublished ghost text that informs the book you are reading. I was writing about language documentation in the deserts of central and northwestern Australia. In Indigenous Australia, as in many parts of the world, languages, defined and delimited on the basis of a standard set of fieldwork artifacts—dictionaries, grammars, corpora of elicited utterances—have come to stand in for the communities whose habits of speech serve as the basis for these artifacts. These communities, in turn, struggle to present themselves—to courts and land claims commissions, to mining companies, to the liberal political order writ large, and to one another— as exponents of the personae embodied in these fieldwork artifacts.[2] How did research artifacts, specifically the artifacts of ethnographic observation, come to be both diagnostic and constitutive of membership in particular social formations, above all the politically marginalized but culturally charismatic communities that were long anthropology's *raison d'être*? When you ask this question, you find yourself pulled into the history of modern commercial branding, where images of colonized "primitives" have featured prominently, serving both as a form of *appelation d'origine contrôlée*, an assurance of place of origin, and as a marker of the fidelity of the specimen to its commodity form. Primitives, Durkheim was not alone in noting, seemed to have a remarkable gift for mimesis.[3] Again, none of this seemed to have anything to do with computability or instrumentation.

A couple years before I read Chipchase's essay on face recognition, I'd spent a week hanging around a community-based language documentation center in the Pilbara, on the northwestern coast of Australia. One day the manager, who was white, told me she'd once been slated to give a presentation on the center's work with the chairman of the center's board of directors, an Indigenous man. At the last minute he'd had to cancel. The manager felt uncomfortable representing an Indigenous organization without her Indigenous counterpart on hand, so she put a photo of him at the top of her slide deck. His image alone, she said, had a powerful effect on the audience. I knew what she meant. The chairman's role in the community, his success, over a thirty-year career in language documentation and cultural revitalization, in defending Indigenous interests against the state and the mining companies, depended in part on the skillful management of appearances. When, say, he went to court to interpret for another member of the community, he had to look the part.

A year later, writing up that conversation and others from that week, I experienced an episode of acute anxiety unlike any I'd had before. For about eight weeks from late May through mid-July 2011 I had a recurring sensation that I described by saying *it feels as if my body were being erased*. At the time I had no name for this sensation. Later I recognized it as a mild episode of depersonalization, a condition, mentioned in passing toward the end of the last chapter, in which one's body, and, in some cases, the world around it, loses a certain texture of tactile and affective presence. Things feel less vivid. The world appears, in the accounts of some sufferers, as if through a mist—or a camera.[4] At a number of points in this book I have used depersonalization and other conditions with overlapping features—autoscopic phenomena, dissociation, dreaming—as models to stimulate our thinking about the bodily implications of pervasive instrumentation, of becoming computable.[5] These conditions unwork our everyday understanding of bodies as things with fixed extension in time and space, things that can be in exactly one place a time.[6] They help us think about bodies as *configurational phenomena* like languages and cities (recall Chapter 1).

Of course, there *is* a dimension of bodily presence for which we've long since abandoned any pretense of the fixity and unity of the body: the photographic.

In this chapter we turn from how we hold and move our bodies to how we *display* them, in particular to how we display our faces. The new entente I've pointed to between surveillance and self-awareness bears more than passing resemblance to the forms of self-awareness experienced by marginalized but charismatic communities like those I was writing about when I had the episode of depersonalization. This is a self-awareness born of having one's gestures transcribed, cataloged, archived, and circulated for commentary. What pervasive instrumentation is creating is not just new spaces of remote copresence and new kinds of self-scrutiny but a scene in which we are all subject to the kinds of intense data collection once reserved for people like my Indigenous interlocutors in the Pilbara—and where, in turn, anyone can project, indeed many of us feel compelled to project, the vivid corporeal presence once ascribed exclusively to charismatic others. Instrumentation invites a kind of self-estrangement, a becoming-other.

This becoming-other has two dimensions. One, just described, has elements of ethnographic surveillance. The other has elements of depersonalization. It is a feeling of distance from one's thoughts, emotional states, and somatosensory experiences, a feeling of distance from the *world*, as if one were looking at it through a camera.

I want to examine the processes of dissociation and modality selection entailed in mediation, in the transmission of some mark of awareness from a body to others and from a body to itself. How does it happen that we get comfortable taking a limited repertoire of the observable features of somatic presence as metonyms of that presence? How is pervasive presence-at-a-distance engendering new registers of bodily display? How do these new registers of display feed back into the (phenomenal, social) experience of the self?

We discussed modality selection in Chapter 3, when we looked at how instrumentation enacts a raster—a rake, a screen, a sieve that limits both the granularity and the dimensionality of what is salient. There, I was concerned to set modality selection in the context of how we have learned to think of data as a constitutive dimension of bodily presence. I argued that Data, as a category, as a conceptual attractor, is itself body-centric. Here I want to approach modality selection from a different angle, one given by the history of the human field sciences. This history will lead us back to face recognition technology. The new registers of bodily display I want to pick out are not the *product* of face recognition technology in the strong sense suggested by Chipchase, but face recognition technology is channeling them and accelerating their formation. This will be clearer when we come to social signal processing—the machine classification of bodily display.

Frontality

On September 7, 2012 a fifteen-year-old young woman from British Columbia, Amanda Todd, posted to YouTube a nine-minute video in which she used a deck of handwritten cards, each inscribed with a few phrases or a sentence, to describe a series of events from the preceding two years. These included sexual extortion—systematic, serial, at one point her tormentor creating a Facebook profile expressly to communicate to her school circle the outcomes of his having induced her to flash her breasts over video chat—along with ongoing harassment and shunning from peers at a succession of schools, physical assault, attempted suicide, and further harassment. The video concluded with a plea for help (Figure 7.1).

Five weeks later, Amanda Todd was dead at her own hand.

Todd's was just one in a series of high-profile cases, predominantly in North America, of sexual extortion of young women. At least two others ended in suicide. These cases unfolded alongside growing awareness of *revenge porn*, a new genre of imagemaking practiced by resentful young men and facilitated by a handful of professional extortionists who make a living charging women targeted for humiliation to have their images removed from key nodes of distribution.[7]

What distinguishes Todd's case is her screen charisma and her masterful, really extraordinary understanding of the expressive parameters of fixed-camera video.

In the video, Todd's face is partly occluded by the top edge of the frame. Often she is cut off at the eyes. Her mouth and nose provide a running commentary on the cards below: tentative now, as if waiting to see how you will react to what she's telling you, punctuated by a frown when the card announces another setback in her effort to rebuild her life.

Amanda Todd haunts me. Her video is emblematic of the emerging register of bodily display I alluded to above. What stands out for me in Todd's video and works that resemble it in some particular or another is *frontality*, the fact of facing directly into the camera.

We are becoming more frontal. In confessional videos and selfies, a reorientation is underway, especially among young people, away from the conventions of documentary cinema, in which subject and interviewer have tended to be shown in three-quarter view, toward something that resembles older conventions of portraiture whose roots extend, in the North Atlantic, back to late Medieval iconography. These conventions found their most condensed expression in the anthropometric photography of the late colonial era. The full-frontal is a stance of intimacy and confrontation—and surveillance. It is where the gaze dominates other modalities of dyadic coordination.[8] It has, until recently, been understood as something put on: artifice, persona, submission to measurement. Here is Cambridge anthropologist A. C. Haddon, writing in 1912, advising would-be anthropologists—most in their early twenties[9]—on how to make photographs of their ethnographic subjects: "Besides the stiff profiles required by the anatomist, some portraits should be taken in three-quarter view or in any position that gives a more natural and characteristic pose."[10] For Haddon the full-frontal view, like the profile, was the antithesis of the "natural and characteristic pose."

FIGURE 7.1 Intimacy and confrontation. *Frontality in Amanda Todd's "My Story" and Lorde's "Tennis Court" (Todd 2012; Kefali and Yelich-O'Connor 2013).*

Perianthropometric

The history of ethnographic imagemaking is extensive and diverse and defies neat summary.[11] As a rule, when we imagine the images anthropologists and other fieldworkers have made of their local interlocutors in the field, we imagine anthropometric photographs, those made to document characteristic racial features of the people in question. But *anthropometric* does not capture the modes of bodily display I am gesturing at. With one exception that we'll come to presently, the images that offer the strongest case for the resurgence of an older aesthetics of surveillance in the habits of representation Chipchase associates with pervasive face recognition technology were not anthropometric. That is, they were not made with the purpose of eliciting a typology of racial difference implicating, among other things, thickness of lips, breadth of the nasal alae, presence of epicanthic folds, reflectance of the skin, or frizziness of the hair. The images that concern us were *peri*anthropometric: they were made alongside anthropometric images, either as a break from the tedium of exact morphological measurement, with its insistence on achieving standardized poses, backgrounds, and exposures so as to make bodies and faces comparable across individuals, photographic sessions, and communities. These were portraits, but they borrowed the pose conventions of anthropometry, above all frontality. These images carried, they carry today, an erotic charge. Often they were deliberately eroticized, for the colonial frontier was nothing if not a zone of erotic experimentation, a space where metropolitan constraints on desire were suspended or transformed. Always these portraits were stylized, stripped of details of setting—signs of poverty or displacement, or, alternately, of modernity or any kind of familiarity with the ethnographer's material culture, including photography itself—that did not align with the photographer's vision. Sometimes subjects were furnished with props to suggest a favored historical comparison, say to Greek antiquity.

Often—and this tends to go unremarked—there is a kinship between the way natives are depicted in posed portraits and the way explorers are depicted, specifically in the portraits used as frontispieces for travelers' accounts, in particular after around 1910. The thousand-mile-stare we associate with T. E. Lawrence, that intimate, confrontational frontality, is not so different from the frank, if less aggressive, frontality of ethnographic portraits. Both kinds index remoteness geographic, cultural, and attitudinal, a remoteness of mindset, of worldview.

Images like these are no longer common, even in the pages of *National Geographic*,[12] but they cast a long shadow over our habits of representing otherness, something face recognition and other technologies of pervasive instrumentation are making clear.

Sometime after 1940 these images became marked, that is, jarring and a bit uncomfortable. Around 1968 they started to appear in a new context, the public awareness campaigns on behalf of Indigenous emancipation mounted by new organizations such as Survival International and the International Work Group for Indigenous Affairs. The change, the moment when it became no longer appropriate to fetishize cultural remoteness in the name of science but only in the name of justice, was swift, but it came at different times in different places. In Australia, for instance, there is a clear register boundary, in the archives that pertain to what was once called native welfare, around 1975.[13] As late as 1967 it was, apparently, acceptable to publish extended series of photographs of Indigenous Australians for the express purpose of illustrating a hypothesis on the divergent racial origins of the people found in different parts of the continent (Figure 7.2)—complete with clinical commentary: "Clearly Negritoid in appearance. . . . Note lesions of dermal leprosy and generally infantile features. . . . Full-blooded in spite of very Caucasoid appearance. . . . An over-sized, masculinized type whose beard requires shaving. . . . Again, observe cephalo-facial relations and non-European look."[14]

Face recognition

Just at the moment when it became unacceptable to depict members of marginalized communities as exemplars of racial types, the nascent science of machine pattern recognition turned its attention to the characterization of typicality and difference in the human face.

The earliest approaches to machine face recognition focused on identifying key facial features and comparing the shapes of those features in a test image to the shapes of corresponding features identified from individuals in a reference archive. Takeo Kanade's 1973 doctoral dissertation at Kyoto University is the exemplary work in this literature. In Kanade's system, individuals' faces are acquired via television camera and transformed into contour images, using gradients in image brightness to detect edges in the surfaces of the face.[15] Next, the contour image is subjected to a process of local summarization that uses basic assumptions about the topography of the human face to identify distinct features in the input image. A series of summarization windows—in Kanade's description, "slits"—is moved across the contour image, horizontal slits from top to bottom, vertical slits from side to side. The width of the slit is adjusted according to the type of facial feature sought with an eye toward balancing the competing desiderata of maximizing information capture for the face in question while filtering out contour elements that represent noise—artifacts of the scanning process, along with contours such as wrinkles or

FIGURE 7.2 Scientific frontality, 1967. *These two individuals appear in a series of eighteen chosen from approximately 800 photographed in 1938–9 for a study of the "tribal" geography of Australia (Birdsell 1967, Plates II and III). I include these images with hesitation. Of the eighteen individuals included in the source, I chose the two oldest (her age is given as sixty-nine, his as seventy-five) to minimize the risk that the recirculation of their likenesses might cause pain in their communities. Even setting aside that risk, I remain concerned that it is exploitative to include these images when the subjects had no way of consenting to this use and, perhaps, sat for the portraits under coercion. Ultimately I concluded that there is no way to convey similarities in the aesthetics of facial display between this kind of surveillance and the kind implicated in contemporary face recognition without actually showing the pictures.*

eyeglass frames that could be mistaken for targeted facial features. Within the slit, the contour is summarized via "integral projection"—the slit serves as a frame, allowing a series of contour elements within the sliding window to be treated as a differentiable curve that can be matched to a library of standard curve types for the facial feature category in question. Nose, mouth, and chin are treated as a unit for the purpose of identifying the vertical disposition of features over the lower half of the face. The library curves are parameterized, that is, they allow variation in the realized shape of the curve according to the relative positions of curve elements (peaks and troughs) associated with facial features within the slit. If more than one standard curve matches the integral projected from the slit, the matching criteria are tightened. If no curves from the library match the curve observed in the test image, the matching criteria are relaxed, and if there is still no match, the sliding window, the slit, is moved. Here is how Kanade describes the procedure:

A vertical slit of width LR/4 is placed at the center of L and R as shown in Figure 2-14. A nose, mouth and a chin are probably in it if L and R are approximately correct and if the face does not tilt or turn a great deal. It is observed that in the integral projection curves of the slit the peaks appear which correspond to the nose, mouth and chin. . . . In a word, each standard type [of the nine curves stored in advance] specifies mutual positional relations of the nose, mouth and chin. The table can be extended simply by adding [*sic*] the new types. The integral projection of the input picture is compared with the standard types. If it matches with only one type, the vertical positions of the lower end of the nose N, the upper lip M and the point of the chin C are obtained. . . . In case there is no match, the matching criteria are slightly relaxed, or the vertical slit is shifted a little. . . . If there is no match even then, this step is a failure, and the backup procedure will work to reactivate the step 2).[16]

"Once the location of eyes, mouth, nose, etc. are known, at least approximately, one can return to the original picture to extract more accurate information by confining the processing to smaller regions and scanning with higher resolution."[17] Kanade's procedure entails a second pass, using a smaller flying-spot scanner to produce finer-grained images the facial features identified in the first pass. These finger-grained scans are analyzed to identify the corners of the eyes, the location and shape of the nostrils, and the extrema of the mouth—sixteen parameters in total.

It should be noted that the flying-spot scanner here was applied to *photographs* of the test participants. Participants—"all young people, 17 males and 3 females, without glasses, mustache or beard"—each sat for two photographs, one month apart. One photograph of each participant was included in the reference set, the other in the test set.[18]

The comparison between reference and test images involved simply computing a distance metric between facial feature parameter vectors for the test image and each image in the reference set. In Kanade's tests, the algorithm correctly matched test and reference images for fifteen of the twenty participants.

In another demonstration of Kanade's approach, 668 visitors to the 1970 World's Fair in Osaka participated in an attraction dubbed Computer Physiognomy: "A person sits before a TV camera, the picture of his face is digitized and fed into the computer, a simple program extracts lines and locates a few feature points . . . and, finally, his face is classified into one of seven categories, each of which is represented by a very famous person." Kanade adds,

Though the program was not very reliable, the attraction itself was very successful. A lot of people participated in it, a number of whose faces were stored on ten magnetic tapes. They include faces of young and old, males and females, with glasses and hats, and faces with a turn, tilt or inclination to a slight degree. It is of great interest to see how the program works with them.[19]

That is, to see how the program copes with deviations from standards of display designed to facilitate face acquisition.

Kanade's work presents a number of possible points of entry for commentary. We could, for instance, start with his emphasis on the technical apparatus of image acquisition—the television camera, the flying-spot scanner, by means of which the source signal (a seated individual in the case of the camera, photographic print in the case of the flying-spot scanner) "is converted to a digital array of 140 x 208 picture elements, each having a gray level of 5 bits."[20] This language echoes the concern with photographic technics, not to say the anxieties about getting delicate imagemaking equipment to work in remote field settings, that we find in earlier accounts of ethnographic photography.[21] These concerns have all but dropped out of view today.[22]

But a more interesting starting point is how *little* stress Kanade puts on the technical tradecraft of pattern recognition—for example, choice of edge detection algorithm and vector distance metric. This is only partly due to the constraints on algorithm design imposed by the hardware of the era. It also reflects the guiding role in face recognition technology of a tacit theory of the human face, a theory of what is socially salient about faces, what it is in faces that allows us to become present to one another. The ordinary human faculty of face recognition and discrimination was and remains the standard against which machine face recognition systems are judged.[23]

The tacit anthropology at work in machine face recognition technology is a theory not just of how we recognize one another but of what makes a face recognizable. That is, it is a theory of how we *typify* one another. This is the case not just for feature-based approaches to face recognition such as Kanade's but for the subsequent wave of approaches that relied on global dimensions of variance among faces, even though these global features "may or may not be directly related to our intuitive notion of face features such as the eyes, nose, lips, and hair."[24] These global-feature approaches involve taking the principal components or eigenvectors of the covariance among faces in a reference pool, where the pixelwise difference between two images in the pool, scaled and translated to make them comparable, is given by some basic property of the image data, for example, brightness. These eigenvectors—eigen*faces* in Turk and Pentland's coinage—"can be thought of as a set of features that together characterize the variation between face images"—*full-frontal* face images.[25] Any face presented for recognition, whether from the reference pool used to generate the eigenfaces or from novel test data, can be approximated as a weighted linear combination of eigenfaces. Of course, to get eigenfaces that allow for the supple approximation of new faces, you need the reference pool to encompass enough of the variance in facial appearance that you expect to encounter in test scenarios. How much is enough? Here is where a tacit theory of typical faces comes in, as Kirby and Sirovich explain for their own eigenvector-based approach: "The ensemble was deliberately chosen to be homogeneous, i.e., it consists of Caucasian males with no facial hair and eyeglasses removed. Otherwise, it is a fairly random selection of Brown University students and faculty who were passing through the Engineering Building, possibly a little too slowly."[26] Most linear decomposition approaches to face recognition today are not constrained in this way, but algorithms and testing imagesets continue to target the tightly framed frontal face (Figure 7.3).

In tests in airport settings—where subjects cannot be relied upon to hold still, strike a neutral expression, maintain a consistent distance from the camera, or refrain from wearing glasses, headscarves, or decorative facial hair—these approaches proved disappointing. The past fifteen years have seen renewed interest in approaches based on cognitively and socially salient facial features, sometimes using separate eigenvector series for eyes, nose, and mouth.[27]

The frontal niche

Of the conditions in which the twenty individuals who participated in the test of face recognition system were photographed, Kanade remarks, "No special arrangements [sic] on lighting and other photographic conditions were made, except for asking the subject to turn a full face."[28] Pose remains a major

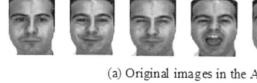

(a) Original images in the AR Database

(b) Corrupted images of (a) with 30% pixels replaced by random noises

(c) Recovered low-rank images of (b) by Robust PCA

FIGURE 7.3 Intimacy, confrontation, and noise. *Recent variants on principal component analysis afford eigenvector ensembles that ignore occlusive noise. The third row consists of faces recomposed from eigenfaces to undo the masking effect of the introduced noise (Hou et al. 2014, Figure 9).*

challenge for machine face recognition. The fact that the great majority of distance functions used to gauge similarity among images would fail a cross-pose recognition test that would be trivial for human observers is part of what has motivated the return to feature-based approaches, though feature-based principal component analysis ("eigenfeatures") has proved of little use in cross-pose recognition.[29] The return to feature-based approaches has revived the problem, focal for Kanade, of identifying facial features in the first place.[30]

In the pursuit of an unmixed frontality, designers of face recognition technologies have largely ignored repeated demonstrations of the role of "external facial features"—hair, jawline, glasses—in how face recognition works in humans.[31] Contemporary face recognition technology cleaves largely to the register of facial display enunciated by Haddon in his 1912 injunction to young ethnographers heading to the field for the first time. Here is the passage that precedes the one quoted earlier: "A certain number of typical individuals should always be taken as large [i.e., photographed] as large possible, full face and exact side view; the lens should be on a level with the face, and the eyes of the subject should be directed to a mark fixed at their own height from the ground, or to the horizon"; the background should be chosen to provide adequate contrast with "yellow and brown skins."[32]

Haddon here is not inventing a new register of face display so much as distilling elements of one that had taken form over the previous eighty years,[33] though of course his instructions, in their concision and specificity, shaped the imagemaking practice of a large number of ethnographers and, by extension, how all of us, in some degree or another, who inhabit the world created by the colonial enterprise, experience photographic images of human faces.[34] Haddon's instructions exemplify the phenomenon sociologists of science have come to refer to as epistemic purification, or, in James Scott's term, making things *legible*: the iterative simplification of our schemas for making sense of some phenomenon, be it microbial life, or forest ecosystems, or human faces, until these schemas conform to the limitations of our apparatus of measurement.[35] In time, these simplified schemas form the basis for new registers of social action—that is, our models start to eclipse what we experience.

Is there something intrinsic to the somatic and ecological parameters of copresence that would lead us, in certain circumstances, to prefer full-frontal images to other forms of face display? There could be, but such a predisposition, if it exists, is certainly not strong enough to drive frontality to "fixation," that is, to cause us to prefer frontal images to the exclusion of all others. There is, in any case, no predisposition in us to prefer *static* images of human faces, such as those demanded by almost all face recognition systems, over moving images. To the contrary, as we saw in Chapters 1 and 2 and as we'll discuss in the next section, movement is central to how we experience the presence of others.[36]

Rather, as Chipchase intuited, face recognition technologies provide one stream of signals in a broader process of somatic niche construction by which, among other things, we are constructing our environment to favor full-frontal display of more-or-less static faces. Face recognition technologies represent a continuation of the process of making human behavior transcribable that we looked at in Chapter 4. What is new is that the category of individuals who are immune to this ongoing transcription of behavior has shrunk dramatically.

Thin slices

In the same years as Kanade was conducting his experiments in face recognition, a young psychologist named Paul Ekman was conducting face recognition experiments of a different sort. In 1965, with a windfall from the U.S. Department of Defense and the injunction that it had to be spent on something uncontroversial, Ekman and collaborators decamped for the South East Highlands of New Guinea to test a hypothesis about the universality of facial expressions of emotion. The New Guinea Highlands afforded a pool of potential research participants whose behavior, it was believed, had not yet been contaminated by contact with the outside world.[37] Ekman concluded, contrary to his own initial expectations, that the facial expression of emotion follows universal patterns, as in fact does emotion itself. In the years since, Ekman's conclusions, that there exists a set of six or seven basic emotions, anger, fear, disgust, happiness, sadness, and surprise—contempt was later appended to the list—and that these emotions surface in a universal repertoire of facial expressions, has enjoyed tremendous success both in cognitive science and in broader publics.[38]

The criticisms of Ekman's basic emotions research program are many. Recent work has called into doubt a central premise of work on the facial expression of emotion, to wit, that emotions are "natural kinds" in which autonomic and behavioral (including facial expressive) features reliably co-occur with self-reports of specific emotions.[39] This recent work has been predominantly laboratory-based, but Ekman's field method is problematic too. These problems did not originate with Ekman. Like Ekman, Darwin, whom Ekman claimed as an intellectual progenitor, was faced, in *The Expression of the Emotions in Man and Animal* (1872), with the problem of assembling an archive of facial and bodily expressions. As we saw in Chapters 1 and 2, these are phenomena of movement, and, even more than with the botanical and zoological specimens Darwin had worked with earlier in his career, reducing corporeal gestures, facial and otherwise, to photographic representations that could be inspected at leisure and reproduced for publication entailed an epistemic flattening-out, a kinematic and kinesthetic decontextualization. The limits of the photographic technology available to Darwin required that all the images he used be of *posed* facial expressions, which is to say, of individuals acting with full awareness of being observed—a situation not so different from the everyday experience of people of Amanda Todd's generation.[40]

A hundred years later, Ekman made a virtue of working with posed images, arguing that in reducing facial expressions to cartoons, posed images cast in relief quanta of behavior that ordinarily appear only in combination, either with other facial expressions of emotion or with "display rules" that mask the open expression of emotion in conformance with community norms. Careful observation of individuals presented with stimuli designed to elicit particular basic emotions, in situations where they had no awareness they were being observed—that is, when their guard was down—would reveal the true, universal facial expressions of emotion normally muted or transformed by display rules.

Armed with a basic vocabulary of facial expressions, each emblematic of a particular basic emotion, Ekman and colleagues proceeded, in the decade following his revelatory fieldwork in New Guinea, to decompose naturally occurring facial expressions according to the emotions expressed by the different facial features. They observed that we are limited in our capacity to sustain display rules, especially in stressful circumstances such as when we are lying. "Nonverbal leakage" in the form of split-second "microexpressions" of one's true emotional state allows observers to detect deception, even when they are not consciously aware of having witnessed the microexpressions.[41] Detection of deception by observation of facial expressions, it turns out is a skill that can be cultivated, and Ekman's research has attracted a considerable following in law enforcement, where Ekman's Facial Action Coding System offers the promise of spotting individuals trying to conceal their true intentions, say, at an airport security checkpoint.[42]

Of significance for our discussion, the posed images for "unmixed" emotions that form the basis for the Facial Action Coding System are, without exception, tightly framed full-frontal images of a type that, modulo the mask-like facial expressions, would be familiar both to Haddon and his students and to designers of face recognition technologies.[43]

Microexpressions were first observed in clinical interviews, but it was through Ekman and Friesen's work on deception that they achieved broader reception.[44] Ekman and Friesen stress that, for a combination of "neuroanatomical and sociocultural reasons most individuals in Western cultures grow up subject to more commentary, instruction, and reinforcement on their facial activity than on their body movement during conversation."[45] In practicing deception, most people will give more attention to concealing facial expressions of true emotion, making the *body* a better source of information about the speaker's verdicality. By the same token, the face is where incongruencies between the deceiver's actual state of being and the state of being he or she wishes to project out into the world are more likely to slip through. To the trained observer, these incongruencies or "deception cues," along with "leakages" in the form of microexpressions of true emotion, provide a rich base of evidence for spotting deception.

In the past twenty years, Ekman's work on deception and microexpressions has been joined by a newer stream of research on the predictive value of "thin slices" of behavior, samples of posture, facial expression, or vocalization of thirty seconds or less that afford observers with no special training enough evidence to characterize an individual's intent or personality as accurately as if they'd had five minutes to observe their target. Nalini Ambady, the formulator of thin-slice theory, has pushed the slice metaphor to its tomographic conclusion, characterizing thin-slice judgments as a step toward "a histology of social behavior."[46]

Some within the social cognition community remain unconvinced.[47] But thin-slice theory has been enthusiastically received in the machine vision community, where, together with Ekman's theory of the facial expression of emotions and his work on the use of microexpressions to detect deception, it has inspired an ambitious new field of research, *social signal processing*. Social signal processing aspires to "provid[e] computers with the ability to sense and understand human social signals,"[48] including affective and attitudinal states ("e.g., fear, joy, stress, disagreement, ambivalence, and inattention"[49]), acts of tool manipulation, and nonverbal dimensions of conversation like pointing and eye engagement.

Among the challenges faced by social signal processing is that of making microexpressions computable. Yan and colleagues, describing the motivation for the Chinese Academy of Sciences Micro-Expression Database II, list the methodological subtleties. Past efforts to build microexpression databases have relied on posed microexpressions, which do not resemble those documented in spontaneous behavior. Others have captured spontaneous microexpressions but have not controlled for extraneous movements of the face and head as occur when the participant-model is speaking as she emotes. Some have been careless with duration, including expressions that last longer than the commonly accepted limit of 500 ms. As Yan and colleagues themselves discovered in previous work, video quality is a concern: a useful microexpression database should store video at 200 frames/second or higher (Figures 7.4–7.6).[50]

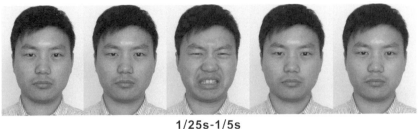

1/25s-1/5s

FIGURE 7.4 *"Synthesized" (i.e.,* posed*) disgust microexpression, created according to guidelines in Ekman's Micro-Expression Training Tool (Zhang et al. 2014, Figure 1).*

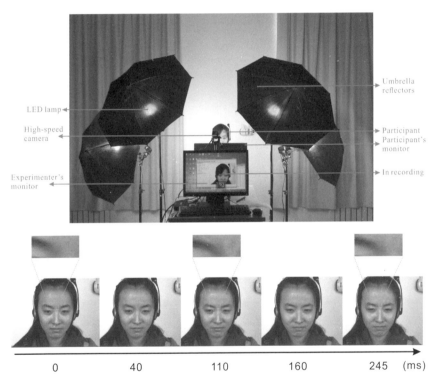

0   40   110   160   245   (ms)

FIGURE 7.5 *"Acquisition setup for elicitation and recording of micro-expressions" and "A demonstration of the frame sequence in a micro-expression" (Yan et al. 2014b, Figures 1 and 2). "Video episodes with high emotional valence proved to be effective materials for eliciting micro-expressions." The nineteen videos, each between fifty-one seconds and three minutes long, included "Larva (animation)," "Jokes on stool," "Tooth extraction," "A girl killed by cars," "Torturing a dog," and "Beating a pregnant woman." The modal emotion observed in elicited microexpressions was disgust.*

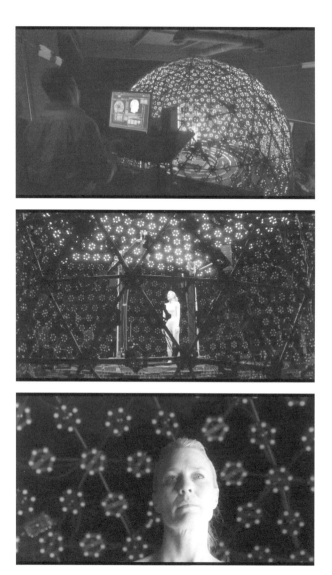

FIGURE 7.6 "Once we've scanned you, there's no going back." *Robin Wright as "Robin Wright" in* The Congress *(Folman 2013).*

By now my concern should be pretty clear. In acclimating to the forms of surveillance enacted by face recognition technologies and social signal processing, we are doing something more than learning the skillful management of appearances, the strategic essentialism familiar to communities long accustomed to ethnographic surveillance.[51] We are fashioning a new somatic niche characterized by registers of bodily display that match the constraints of the technologies by which we make our selves computable. These are registers defined, above all, by the slice, the frame, the close-cropped full-frontal face.

Indeed, the full-frontal register is starting to feed back into the science of human vision, providing a key class of test images for experiments in reconstructing sensory input from evoked functional brain imaging data (Figure 7.7).[52]

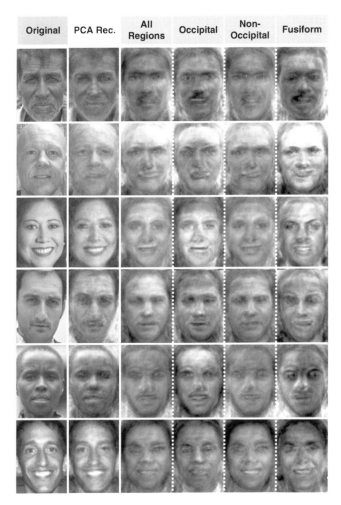

FIGURE 7.7 *"Reconstructions, averaged across participants, from various ROIs [regions of interest, i.e., aspects of the cerebral cortex used as sources of blood oxygenation data for the reconstructions in that column]" (Cowen et al. 2014, 15, Figure 2). "PCA Rec." refers to reconstructions from eigenfaces derived from a set of 300 training faces using Turk and Pentland's (1991) method. Note, the original version of this matrix is in color.*

The big We

"So that's how it is!" said Pilgrim. "Why don't you all run away and be done with it?" "Father, we can't!" said the monks. "Those immortal elders have obtained permission from the king to have our portraits painted and hung up in all four quarters of the kingdom. Although the territory of this Cart Slow Kingdom is quite large, there is a picture of monks displayed in the marketplace of every village, town, county, and province. It bears on top the royal inscription that any official who catches a monk will be elevated three grades, and any private citizen who does so will receive a reward of fifty taels of white silver. That's why we can never escape. Let's not say monks—but even those who have cut their hair short or are getting bald will find it difficult to get past the officials. They are everywhere, the detectives and the runners! No matter what you do, you simply can't flee. We have no alternative but to remain here and suffer."[53]

In *Schein der Person*, art historian Valentin Groebner documents the emergence of passports and other identity documents in early modern Europe. This was a time, Groebner points out, when the German word *Schein* took on an ambiguous set of meanings. A *Schein* was a *certificate* or a *pass*, a token of validation. But it was also an *appearance* in the sense of an *illusion* or *surface*, that which is contrasted to reality and substance. As a projection of social persona, the Schein was a sham, a fake, a poor substitute. It was the delamination of the Schein from the somatic presence of the individual it referred to that allowed it to achieve a social currency of its own.

Today, of course, we are accustomed to the fact that appearances, images, take on lives independent of the personages with which, in some approximate sense, they originate (Figure 7.8). *In some approximate sense*. I want to be careful here to avoid the pretense that the image is a projection, a slice, however thin, of a unitary social presence. An image is more like a transect, encompassing slices of the behavior, the movement, of a number of bodies arrayed over space and time. If we are inclined, with Benjamin, to lament the loss of the "aura" of the unique image, it is because we have been committed to an ideology of authentic representation that was untenable long before the passport or the selfie.

If this is the case, where is the depersonalization, the dissociation, the delamination? What is coming loose as we learn to present ourselves to cameras in a way that makes it easy to extract facial features and—whatever their relationship to inner state—microexpressions?

To be sure, there is something new in the ubiquity of the phenomenon of becoming alienated from one's image and the speed with which it happens.

FIGURE 7.8 *"Our database uses a set of images that was originally gathered from news articles on the web."—from Yahoo! News in 2002–3, to be more precise. The first six matching pairs of faces in the development (algorithm training) aspect of the database Labeled Faces in the Wild (Huang et al. 2007, 2, Figure 1; again, the originals are in color). This was the database that, in testing, provided the designers of Facebook's DeepFace algorithm with the claim to near "human-level performance" in face matching (Taigman et al. 2014).*

But there is also something deeper happening: social presence is getting delaminated from the kinesthetic context in which it unfolds.

Even as it gets easier to make and transmit moving images, we are learning to make ourselves legible in ever thinner slices, slices that can be reliably tagged with discrete qualities of sensing-feeling-moving. *How could things be otherwise when machine vision is itself frame-based?* But that too was a choice, and not an obvious one if our goal is to simulate the human faculties of social signal apperception. We can equally imagine a frameless image sensor in which individual pixels in the acquisition array signaled changes in illumination asynchronously.[54] This would yield a sparser representation, and one that made it easier to detect motion.

There are strong limits to how much I can speak of what *we* can imagine and the pressures to conform to certain registers of display that *we* face. The surveillance burden landscape is uneven in every imaginable dimension. Women, poorer people, people whose skin color and facial features do not match local prototypes, the gender-nonconforming, the neuroatypical (or somatoatypical), those who exhibit any kind of difference, any spark of charisma—for what the history of ethnographic imagemaking shows is that alterity *is* charisma, whether it manifests as attraction or repulsion is secondary—all are subject to heightened scrutiny, all internalize the sense of being observed in ways that belie platitudes about trading privacy for convenience.

But if, as I proposed at the outset, the skillful management of appearances, a knack for looking the part, is becoming a more general feature of what it means to enact social presence, then an awareness of the shared assumptions that join early anthropometric photography and contemporary face recognition can help us respond to the world foreseen in "It's Not Your Face, It's Ours," whatever surveillance burden we face as individuals. If pervasive face recognition technologies and social signal processing are guiding us toward a world in which, as Chipchase predicts, "a new generation of business leaders . . . will specialize in closing cross cultural deals, knowing that every micro-expression will be recorded and played back," this reflects not the inexorable tomographic logic of machine vision itself but the way machine vision has channeled a register of bodily display that was incipient in our earliest photographic experiences of surveillance at a distance.

.

8

Plenum

What does a world saturated by human data feel like? Does it have a distinct somesthetic and kinesthetic character, does it foster distinct habits of movement, posture, and display? What changes in the interface between body and world as we become instrumented, as the processes of sensorimotor calibration by which bodies fit their expectations to the world and the world to their expectations come to be modulated by streams of data—streams of information machinic in their precision and reliability, truncated in their modal dimensionality?

These are the questions this book started with, but of course it is too soon for definitive statements about what instrumentation does to us, what instrumentation *wants*.

You must find it impossible, friends say, *to keep up.* Meaning, every week sees the announcement of some new device or algorithm that threatens to render this book obsolescent before it is even finished. But that is a more general feature of social acceleration, and not something specific to writing about technology, or even "personal wellness" technology. Actually, keeping up with technology has been the least of my concerns. Devices of the kind that provide the basis for much of the discussion at a Quantified Self meetup—or, increasingly, at a planning meeting for a major health research initiative, something I'll come back to—represent a crude vehicle for the expression of the will of the communities that make and use them. This is *not* to say that technology is inert, that instruments do not "want" anything. They certainly do want something in that they exert a strong channeling effect on our desires and actions, making some features of behavior and modes of quantification more visible and others less so, enabling certain strategies of action and frustrating others. But if you were to write a history of humanity from the devices' perspective—not a history of technology but a history that portrayed humans and other living things as the instruments by which devices spread themselves through the world—it would have a static quality. This is because devices lack the presence, the responsiveness, the *animacy*—again, something we'll come back to—of, say, sentient things. Devices can be charismatic, but they are not bodies.

The problem has not been keeping up with technology. No, the problem has been keeping up with people, with the new registers of movement and of ethical action, which is to say *political* action, that emerge in response to, though not determined by, technology.

So let's conclude with a new set of questions: How is instrumentation changing us as *people*, as political presences? Does instrumentation guide us toward a particular *ethos*? How does instrumentation change what kinds of *moral* entities we imagine the world to contain?

Reduction

The question of what instrumentation wants, what pressures it exerts on our ethical niche, crystallized for me early on in this project when, one night in February 2013, I gave a talk to the Munich chapter of the Interaction Design Association.[1] My theme was "Circadian Selves." The talk I gave represented an early sketch for what became Chapters 3, 4, and 6 of this book. Things had been moving quickly: it was late October 2012 when I came across the Valkee, the bright-light therapy device designed to resemble an iPod. The same week, a friend mentioned in passing a movement called the Quantified Self. Four weeks later I was at a seminar in Berlin, holding up the Valkee as an exemplary artifact of the Anthropocene.[2] Now, in February, I was talking about "chronoplasticity" and "activity rhythms as a focal object of self-care" in front of a room full of people who designed things like bright-light therapy devices and accelerometer bracelets for a living.

Not quite full. Some weeks before the event the organizer wrote to me to say the local Quantified Self community was interested in cosponsoring the event. In fact, the Quantified Self people had the venue, so their participation was essential. Would I mind?

At the talk modest confusion arose as participants from the two camps, interaction designers on one side, self-trackers on the other, wondered who all these other people were. During the question-and-answer period, a difference in worldviews emerged. The designers had questions about historical developments in rhythms of activity and rest—the emergence of consolidated nighttime sleep, changes in diagnostic criteria for bipolar phenomenon in kids. The Quantified Self contingent had questions of a different type: Would I switch on my lightbox so we could see how it glowed blue? How long did I use it each day? At what hour and at what brightness setting? Had the Valkee worked for me?

As I got to know people in the Quantified Self—those who gave show-and-tell talks at regular meetups, those who kept a blog detailing the devices they'd tried, those who simply came to meetups and listened—I found that for most people, the aims of the exercise were exquisitely practical and surprisingly modest: How can I stand up straighter, get in a little more walking each day, better avoid distraction when I'm working?

It was not long before people started asking me what I thought of one device or another and which vital signs one should monitor to achieve flow state. I felt uncomfortable responding, even when I had something useful to share: these questions ran orthogonal, if not counter, to the ones that interested me. The questions that interested me were epistemological: How does "flow state" take form as an object of desire? How do we come to value certain rubrics of self-reflection over others? How do certain kinds of behavior modification come to seem virtuous? The bemusement I'd felt during the Q&A session that evening in Munich turned to disquiet and, occasionally, frustration. Rather than asking how the information provided by new sensor montages fit—or failed to fit—with other ways of experiencing one's presence in the world, some of the most enthusiastic self-trackers seemed content to let instrumentation define a new register of experience all its own. This new register bore the imprimatur of objectivity, of a "ground truth." More disturbing, it sometimes seemed to trace out a world that ended at the edge of the individual's perisomatic space. The Quantified Self was a more focally autonomous self, a self that took on a more saturated hue, becoming more distinct from its surroundings, more self-like.

What, people asked me, are you tracking?

I track a lot of things: what I eat, how long I sit in the mornings, how much weight I can deadlift under various combinations of sets, repetitions, and intervals. But I had learned, years earlier, that I was better off not keeping too close track, that the numbers had an insidious effect on me, blotting out all those things I did not have numbers for but that equally played a role in my performance—in fact, narrowing experience *to* performance, imparting an instrumentality to action that threatened the fragile peace with the day I had spent my twenties and thirties building. It was important, I had learned, to set limits on how driven I allowed myself to be. And how focused on the self.

So when a couple colleagues got wind of what I was working on and asked if I would design a "Quantified Self"–type study for a grant they were putting together, I was conflicted. The Wellcome Trust, among the world's largest private funders of health research, was launching a new kind of grants program. They wanted to inject the energy of the tech start-up world into biomedical research. They were looking for proposals that crossed too many disciplinary, methodological, and epistemological lines to get funded through other channels. Wellcome would create a kind of research incubator, the Hub, a space in central London where the funded project would have two years to prove its viability. My friends were competing to be the first occupants of the Hub. The theme of their proposal was "rest and busyness."[3] And they desperately wanted the project to include a self-tracking component.

What gave me mixed feelings was not the prospect of designing a study involving mobile body-borne instrumentation. I was thinking then—this was the summer of 2013—about the problems with how mobile instrumentation had been used in previous studies, and the thought of having the resources to try out something new was exciting. No, what left me feeling a little queasy was how everyone else involved in the proposal consistently referred to the part I was responsible for as the "Quantified Self" experiment. This continued after we won the Hub grant and moved in to newly finished open-plan offices on the fifth floor of the Wellcome Collection building. That first week, I was introduced—to Wellcome Trust and Collection staff, to other members of our research network—with variations on, "This is Josh. He's running the Quantified Self parts of the study."

This made me uncomfortable for two reasons. First, it did not feel right to be borrowing the Quantified Self brand like this. I was not officially associated with the Quantified Self, which had its own research vehicle, QS Labs, and had, just months earlier, staged a workshop, with support from the Robert Wood Johnson Foundation and the U.S. National Institutes of Health, to discuss how QS methods and a QS outlook might be incorporated into public health monitoring and research.[4] I was in touch with the Quantified Self leadership, and they were supportive and asked to be kept up to date—but this was not a QS project in the sense of having originated under the aegis of the movement or any of its key exponents.

At the same time as I wanted to avoid a kind of unsanctioned appropriation of the QS brand, with the substantial cultural currency attached to that brand, I also wanted to maintain a certain distance from the Quantified Self for concern that to call what we were doing Quantified Self would be to foreclose on ways of thinking about self-tracking data that did not align with the things typically heard at QS meetups. For me, the most stimulating and challenging thing about the Quantified Self was something that most participants gave little attention to, something that many would reject if you proposed it: *the Quantified Self created a space for epistemological pluralism, for multiple ways of measuring and thinking about what it means to flourish.* Some in the movement recognized this dimension of self-tracking and embraced it. But for many QSers just the opposite was true: quantification provided an incontrovertible ground truth, facts about one's behavior that left no room for differences of interpretation. For some, not all QSers, self-tracking was a vehicle of what one interlocutor, commenting not on the Quantified Self but on the overlapping world of liquid nutrition substitution, described to me as "quantified reductionis[m]."[5]

The first week in London, my colleague Daniel and I sat down to plan the mobile tracking study, which we'd dubbed "Cartographies of Rest." Daniel is a neuroscientist. What, he asked, did I want to use as the primary measure? Could we get reliable data on heart rate variability from carpal photoplethysmography (optical pulse sensing with a wrist bracelet)?

Possibly, I allowed. *Tell you the truth, Daniel, I care less about what we measure than about how we design the visualizations.* I wanted, I said, the research participants to be the people we designed the visualizations for. *So they can come in here and stand in front of that wall with me, and we'll have a big screen and a gesture interface. And we'll be able to pull up a set of heat maps showing the principal components of their heart rate variability and whatever else*—I favored a form of experience sampling, directly asking participants how they were feeling, the challenge being to design an interface minimized the disruption to participants' lives—*as they make their way around London. "Here's your data from last week. Here's the data from everyone else in the study.* You *tell* me *what's going on, what the maps show about what's been happening in your life."*

And what they don't show.

Above all I was interested in how playing with the data would change how participants experienced their own rhythms of activity and rest. And those of other participants.

I wanted to use instrumentation to open up new space for differences of interpretation. I wanted to get the cognitive scientists, and the Quantified Self, asking the question posed to me by the Grinberg trainer on the flight to Berlin fifteen months before: *What is a body?*[6]

Gamification

The same week as Daniel and I sat down in London to hash out a roadmap for Cartographies of Rest, I had lunch with my editor. Could I, he wondered, include something on gamification?

The day before, catching up with my friend J, a historian of public health then making a transition to something like design consulting, I'd described a conversation I'd been having with the organizers of a large music festival. *Every year*, they told me, *we have 130,000 visitors camping on our eighty-hectare site for eight days. We spend nearly €2 million every July just to clean up the site. Our number one question is:* How can we get people to put their trash in the bins?

Simple, J said. *People get to check in at the bin with a QR code or something and post a photo of tossing something in. The bin logs disposal events. You turn it into a competition: who can throw rubbish in the most bins over the greatest extent of the festival site?*

Why was I so resistant to this way of thinking?

I nodded at my editor. *Of course. I know exactly where the section on gamification should go.*

Not for the first time I was rescued by my main interlocutor in the polyphasic sleeping community, Puredoxyk, when, the following evening, she posted an announcement to the Slack channel she had set up for experienced polyphasers looking to experiment with ever-more-challenging sleep/wake schedules. This announcement had nothing to do with sleep schedules per se. Puredoxyk was forming a party on HabitRPG: who wanted to join?

HabitRPG?

HabitRPG, it transpired, was a cross between Dungeons and Dragons and Getting Things Done, a vaguely late Medieval-themed platform, replete with guilds and a tavern, for sharing one's to-do lists and aspirational habits. You earn experience points for crossing off to-do items, which can be keyed to rewards (watching an episode of Game of Thrones, to take an example provided by the game's creators). When you fail to complete your to-dos, you "take damage," losing vitality and jeopardizing the health of your avatar. Plays can form parties to undertake quests against "bosses," monster adversaries that threaten party members' productivity. During questions, everyone in the party takes damage when any member fails to meet her goals or stick to her good habits.

I was no stranger to role-playing games, but I found HabitRPG baffling. Others in our polyphasic sleeping discussion circle took to it, though, rapidly leveling up and crowing about what a boon to productivity it was—and how helpful for sticking to the rigorous schedule of twenty-minute naps required under core-free polyphasic sleeping.

It turned out my interlocutors were not the only polyphasers on HabitRPG. Soon I found myself welcomed into a guild known as "Naps of Power".

Early on in our encounter with HabitRPG, a brief debate unfolded on Slack over design strategy for gamification—the transformation of possibly tedious forms of everyday behavior (binning one's trash, taking one's 4:00 a.m. nap) into competitive games. At question was the appropriate role of *flow*, a quality of being immersed in something often identified with statements of the form, "I looked up and six hours had passed." Since the work of Czikszentmihaly and collaborators in the 1980s flow states have become a cornerstone of positive psychology.[7] The conversation started with a comment by z:

z [10:09 P.M.] [Responding to my comment that I'd been asked to include a section on gamification in this book] my 2 cents on gamification: the real thing would be addressing the hard problem of matching skill level to challenge level to foster a flow state, and on meaningful and practical rewards/achievements, while most things i've seen focus on point-score and/or social-networking driven motives, which are only of limited efficacy to a limited subset of the population.

z [10:09 P.M.] habitrpg looks like it can facilitate either, but the former still seems to be largely up to the user to leverage through it

puredoxyk [10:10 P.M.] my 2 cents on "flow-state"—I think it's a red herring, to be honest.

z [10:10 P.M.] (from what i've seen so far, which isn't much)

puredoxyk [10:11 P.M.] I guess let's test it and find out!:smile:

z [10:11 P.M.] hehe

z [10:26 P.M.] i'm curious about the red herring thing . . . flow state seems to be a central factor in effective game design, but i could also see it not being something sustainable/applicable in the kind of contexts people are trying to gamify . . . so just wondering what you mean by it and why

. . .

z [11:27 P.M.] well a main central feature of flow-states, as i understand it, is a well matched challenge level, which is also good for learning, and i've heard it claimed that flow states also are great for learning . . .

puredoxyk [11:28 P.M.] Maybe

puredoxyk [11:29 P.M.] The problem comes in when we feel like they're NEEDED for learning, or to look at it another way, the promise or possibility of them distracts us from the need to PRACTICE ANYWAY

puredoxyk [11:29 P.M.] And that, I think, is DEFINITELY applicable to polyphasic sleep

z [11:29 P.M.] ah

puredoxyk [11:30 P.M.] If I waited for, or quit when I wasn't feeling, flowy while doing taiji, I'd practice maybe once a week, instead of the every day I need, whether I feel like it or not

puredoxyk [11:30 P.M.] And also, flow state often comes about FROM practicing, and comes more often the more often you just dig in and fucking do it anyway, heh

z [11:30 P.M.] interesting points, something i could definitely learn from . . .

puredoxyk [11:31 P.M.] So while it's nice to experience, I get >.> when people get hung up on "creating" or encouraging it, because that's a short step to relying on it, and therefore not practicing

z [11:32 P.M.] i have a really hard time doing things i don't feel like doing, and have often had it seem to go too disastrously when trying to force it for me to have gone that route much . . . which leaves me in a rather problematic state with some things. . . .

A few weeks earlier I had heard comments similar in spirit to z's at the regular Quantified Self meetup in Berlin, when one of the organizers of the Berlin QS community gave a talk on tracking when one is in flow state and increasing the proportion of one's time in flow, irrespective of task. The theme of that evening's discussion was "How to reach your goals."[8] That evening I had found myself put off for the same reasons as Puredoxyk.[9] Operationalizing and targeting states of frictionless fusion with one's work seemed to me to be corrosive of exactly the awareness of where one's body ends and the nonself world begins that arises through steady, deliberate practice, with its awkwardnesses and frustrations, the failures to predict how the world (or one's model of it) will respond to action originating, to a rough approximation, from within the self.[10] Boundarylessness, I sensed, works best as a limit case, a marker of a kind of transient, but with practice recurring, pitch harmonization between world and body. When you try to turn it into a default state, it becomes a form of anesthesis. This is what the anthropologist Natasha Schüll discovered in her work with machine gambling addicts, many of whom use antianxiolytics, antidepressants, and dopaminergic stimulants such as Ritalin or Adderall to speed access to a state of self-exit they call *the zone*.[11]

Critics of gamification point to a similar phenomenon at work in the injection of game mechanics into every life: gamification strips away everything that makes games *playful*—the surprise, the narrative intricacy, the world-building dimension—retaining just the repetitive punishment-reward dynamics—the grinding, the "treadmilling," the unimaginative labor involved in leveling up. Most of the people decrying gamification along these lines come from within the serious games movement, a community of activists and researchers committed to promoting games as potential vehicles of well-being, as technologies for exploring alternate realities, configurations of social life that diverge from the actual. To proponents of serious games, gamification represents a hijacking of this potential, a rechanneling of game mechanics in the service of a distinctly capitalist instrumentalism.[12]

The animate

It is not that games, or even massively multiplayer online role-playing games, *must*, by their nature, be devoted to the gratification of a "lust for power,"[13] though it is instructive the degree to which, as a category, they are. There are degrees of instrumentalism. HabitRPG, for instance, for all that its appeal is selective, more than anything feels like a modest effort to inject a measure of play into those parts of everyday life that so many people find at once overwhelming and boring. The to-do list has become the emblem of social acceleration.[14] The playfulness of HabitRPG has nothing to do with the game mechanics. The playfulness is, rather, the playfulness, of cosplay, of *otaku*, of putting on a *character*.[15] It is the tropic play of code-switching, of adopting, with knowing exaggeration and infidelity, the superficial marks of an unfamiliar register. It is—to bring us back to our passing discussion of puppets in Chapter 1—a kind of *animation*.[16]

I'll double down. Animation is the semiotic kernel of all play: the nonfunctional exaggeration of movements that in other contexts *would be* functional, that is, oriented toward the satisfaction of basic drives. The exaggeration in play serves at least two purposes. Motor learning is one, where exaggeration offers a way to break down a complex motor cascade into its coordinate parts.[17] But in social play—play in dyads and groups—exaggeration serves an *indexical*, a pointing-out role too. It is a way of saying, "Look at what we're doing. This is how we move. This is how we would move if we were moving for real. This is how we'd signal one another."[18]

Humans are far from the only kind of living thing to play like this, to use movement to test the limits of motoric copresence, to figure out which forms of movement in the nonself world point to the presence of an intentional other, a being, an awareness sink guided by hidden states, like oneself. This is the deepest challenge posed by instrumentation to how we make the world and make our way through it: instrumentation is changing how we encounter animacy, indeed, what it means to be animate.

Modernity has been a project of evacuating the world of hidden sources of intention—of ghosts, of spirits, of totemic Ancestors and Masters of the Hunt (Figure 8.1).[19] We were left with a single invisible hand to satisfy our need for mystery, but at the same time we were assured that the hand was nothing more than the working out of a massively multiplayer game whose reward matrix was known to all.[20]

FIGURE 8.1 *Detail, Untitled* (Hungry Ghosts Scroll), *late twelfth-century CE, depicting monks setting out food and drink for the ghosts. From the seventh section of the* Hungry Ghosts Scroll *held in the Kyoto National Museum. Courtesy Wikimedia Commons. In many times and places people have been inclined to view the world as a plenum, populated by a wide range of but faintly discernible animate presences (Picone 1991).*

Modernity has failed. We share our world, we share our perisomatic space, with a proliferating array of partly autonomous animate copresences evincing fractional dimensions of that elusive quality—responsiveness, rhythm, intent—we are forever looking for when we move through the world. These new presences shape our habits of movement, shape how we shape the world, in ways the experiments of self-tracking activists have barely begun to make clear. We inhabit, as have so many communities before us, a plenum, and we need a somatic anthropology that takes this plenum's other-than-human—other-than-living—inhabitants seriously. The hungry ghosts are back, with gifts and a vengeance.[21]

Postscript: Precarity

L's question

In June 2013, when I was writing the proposal that became this book, I had a problem: I did not know where I would be living come July. I had to be in New York at the end of July—where I had the encounter that provided the question we started with in Chapter 1—but the first half of July was a blank. As was August and, to a degree, the rest of the year. My friend L had an apartment in Paris that she rented out. It would be empty in July—there was a problem with the plumbing. Would I like to spend part or all of July in Paris? I would.

So I decamped for Paris on an overnight train from Munich, relieved at least to have secured a quiet place to finish the book proposal. One day L and I took a walk. She asked what I was working on.

"But what," she asked, "should your reader *do* about the things you are describing? You have to conclude with some sort of prescription, a way to cope." L is a psychologist. Some years earlier she had been my first meditation student. She had gone on to found an organization to promote mind-body psychotherapy in France.

"It's not that kind of book," I said. "Prescriptive." But the question stuck with me. Paris was a respite from the precarity that had dogged me the better part of a year. That precarity would get worse in the year that followed—the stress of having no regular income, living in borrowed rooms, forever in doubt as to my legal status. My penultimate night in Paris my friend Elaine took me to the Arlequin, a cinema near her home, to see a new print of *Plein Soleil*, René Clément's 1960 adaptation of Patricia Highsmith's *The Talented Mr. Ripley*, starring Alain Delon as Tom Ripley. As the afternoon light off the Tyrrhenian Sea washed over me, Elaine produced a jam jar with two shots of Suntory lapping against the bottom. A scent like vanilla extract filled the room. Sitting in a darkened cinema passing a jar of Japanese whiskey back and forth, watching Ripley negotiate murder, identity theft, seduction, and the need to shift hotels daily, I could not but see a resemblance to my own life, modulo the sociopathic elements. It was exhausting just to watch.

This was a modest precarity. I was not responsible for children or aging parents. I was not burdened by debilitating injury or chronic disease. I was not subject to racial discrimination. I had no debt. I had few possessions, but by the same token I had not lost a home. Still, it was humbling.[1] It led me, in a moment of frustration and terror one night the following January, to send off an abstract for the upcoming annual Quantified Self Europe meeting in Amsterdam denouncing the movement's fixation on the self—a product, I argued, of an unquestioning commitment to the corrosive individualism that characterized our time.

Friends, other anthropologists working with self-trackers, told me my abstract would be rejected out of hand. It is a tribute to the Quantified Self leadership, Gary Wolf and Ernesto Ramirez in particular, that five months later I found myself on a plenary discussion panel at QS Europe with a platform to rail about "neoliberal fantasies of behavioral autarky" and to call for a Quantified *We*. I mentioned observations by Jane Costello and colleagues on the effects a supplementary stipend, provided by casino income, had on the lives of children in the poorest households among the Eastern Band Cherokee in North Carolina, with strikingly lower incidence of mental health disorders and substance abuse among those who had grown up with the stipends.[2] I pointed to an emerging anthropology of precarity that had sprouted up in the aftermath of Hurricane Katrina.[3] I pointed to signs of precarity's new salience for a much broader public than those with direct experience of displacement: the success of David Graeber's *Debt* and the visibility of the movement it helped launch, Occupy. The fact that, to general astonishment, Thomas Piketty's *Capital in the Twenty-first Century* had become a bestseller in the United States.[4]

I said it sometimes feels as if we have forgotten how to talk about how individual behavior change might be guided more by a desire to improve the lives of *others*, socially distant others, than by a desire to improve our own well-being.[5]

Above all I stressed that the factors that account for most of the variance in individual health and well-being are things that are beyond the individual's capacity to control with behavior change, quantified or otherwise. And I asked how the practices of self-instrumentation that the Quantified Self had done so much to develop and bring to wider awareness might be used to produce data on the social dimensions of well-being, on the health of communities.

Reaction was mixed. Some in the audience expressed the feeling that it was about time someone had said what I'd said. Others were unclear about what I *had* said: was the Quantified Self somehow responsible for the suffering of the communities I'd described? To this question, at least, I had a succinct response: responsible for *causing* it, perhaps not. Responsible for helping *fix* it, *yes*. We are *all* responsible for creating a world more conducive to collective flourishing.

By and large the response was much more positive than I'd expected. But I was shaking when the panel ended. I felt I had violated a community norm.

The technologies of instrumentation that have so changed our environment, and our bodies, and how we construct our somatic niche, have also made our world more precarious, even for those who in the recent past were insulated—by education, and professional status, and the possession of land and other difficult-to-commodify resources—from the vagaries of the business and climate cycles. Speed, mobility, and connectedness engender a new kind of volatility in day-to-day social and economic life. Among the causes of the global financial meltdown of 2008 was the unending demand, among the investment banks that facilitate the accelerating circulation of credit through capital markets, for new sources of *maturity conversion*, longer-term assets to buffer the uncertainty of the short-term commercial paper and overnight repurchase agreements that provide these banks with most of their day-to-day operating cash. Asset-backed securities—above all, repackaged low-grade consumer debt—provided a volatility sink, a highly rated form of collateral that allowed banks to take massively leveraged positions with their short-term debt.[6] The collateralized debt obligations at the heart of the meltdown arose in part as a kind of ballast to allow banks to capitalize on the speed provided by pervasive computing.

The acceleration of everyday life, including markets, is a topic of common commentary. We pay less attention to a different dimension of social acceleration: the acceleration in the turnover of cultural registers—professional identities, skillsets, living arrangements. This too contributes to precarity, to an inability to convert effort at one point in one's life—say, to master a craft—into a source of economic security and a stable social network over the longer run.[7]

Economic sociologists Marion Fourcade and Kieren Healy have proposed that the technologies of consumer behavior tracking that we have come to take for granted, above all credit scoring, have created a new landscape of people classification. "[W]hat makes the new market instruments so interesting is that they seem so much more democratic. . . . Rather than protecting certain groups through the creation of rents and monopolies, they thrive on the market's competitive logic, demanding that people be measured against one another, and then separating and recombining them into groups for efficiency and profit." These new groups embody *classification situations*, "positions in the credit market . . . that are associated with distinctive experiences of debt." Fourcade and Healy stress that creditworthiness classification situations do not simply reinscribe prior class relations. "Rather, they are independently, even 'artificially' generated classifications that can come to have distinctive and consequential class-like effects on life-chances and social identities. . . . By enabling and facilitating the differential pricing of people, [credit] scoring has expanded the reach of the market while opening the door to new forms of classification with powerful stratifying effects."[8]

Fourcade and Healy are talking about the application of actuarial analysis to credit histories, but it does not take much to imagine an extension of the logic of credit scoring to other kinds of human data, be it through sentiment analysis of social media output (classifying people according to how happy they appear to be) or activity classification of accelerometric data (classifying people according to how vigorous they are).

I wrote this book as a protest against the conceit—widespread in some segments of the self-tracking world—that there is nothing political about how we hold and move our bodies and about how technologies of self-instrumentation are reconfiguring our habits of posture, movement, and display. I wrote this book as a protest against the premise of L's question, which is also the premise of so much of what is said and done under the sign of the instrumentation of bodies: that these are, in the end, technologies of the *self*.[9] For if, as I have argued, the self, the phenomenal, *bodily* self no less than the social self, is an emergent property of the community, then the question is not, *How should we as individuals respond to the novel pressures of instrumentation?* but *How might we use instrumentation to expand the circle of those who feel at home in their skin?*

Surveillance, as I suggested in Chapter 3, is an apparatus not just of observation but of intervention—of prescription, of correction. Just as we can understand body schema as a network of learned expectancies for discrepancies between the predicted and experienced effects of moving, so we can understand the surveillance enacted by technologies of personal instrumentation as a network of (machine) learned expectancies for discrepancies between optimal and observed behavior. Classification situations for bodily behavior parallel—and often, as the cases discussed above suggest, are continuous with—classification situations for economic behavior. Most of the time, the expectancies folded into self-tracking technologies—assumptions about what is an appropriate, a *fit* way of holding, moving, and

FIGURE POSTSCRIPT 1 Classification situations. *Whose algorithm determines what the better version of you looks like? Jawbone Up Move promotional video, late 2014. jawbone.com/store/buy/upmove.*

displaying the body—remain opaque even to the most sophisticated users (Figure Postscript 1). In fact, the term *user* is misleading: increasingly, whether or not to participate in instrumented life is not something we, as individuals and communities, have a choice about. All the more reason to ask where instrumentation comes from and how it gets produced. By asking these questions we can begin to unwork instrumentation's opacity and imagine ways it might be other than it is— more inclusive, less reductive, more just—and so create a more capacious somatic niche.

Notes

Preface: Registers

1 The term *body schema* was introduced by Head and Holmes (1911) in their work on central nervous causes of losses of cutaneous tactile sensation. It is not to be confused with *body image*, introduced by Schilder (1923, 1935) to describe the ensemble of impressions a person has about how her body looks and how much space it takes up. (In early work, Schilder used the term *Körperschema*—body schema—to refer to what would come to be known in English as body image.) De Vignemont (2010) argues that body schema and body image represent functional aspects of a single nervous representation essentially like what we mean by *body schema*.

2 Ferriss 2010.

3 Harvey 2011; Koolhaas 1994.

4 Humphrey 2007; cf. Llinás 2001. See the discussion of sensory substitution and new sensory modalities in Chapter 2.

5 Reas et al. 2010, 17; cf. Ingold's (2010) suggestive remarks on the erasure of what he calls *textility* (the elicitation of lines of growth immanent in a substance from its previous history) from design.

6 Schmidt and Richardson 2008; Shockley 2012.

7 See Keen 2006 on fire as a tool of cultivation in late Holocene Australia.

8 Agha 2007.

9 James 1901; Husserl 1900–1.

10 Sharf 2000, 267; Sharf 1995, 268.

11 Sharf 2014; Lopez 2008.

Chapter 1

1 Schroeder et al. 2010.

2 Thompson 2007, 157.

3 On play as a dimension of animal behavior, see Graham and Burghardt 2010.

4 For complementary discussion, Cosmelli and Thompson 2010.

5 Hillier 2007, 15.

6 *Pace* De Landa 1997, 27.

7 Hillier 2007, 67–8.

8 Thompson 2007, 103.

9 Salonen and de Vos 2014.

10 Auvray and Rohde 2012; Schmidt and Richardson 2008.

11 Though in fact plants do achieve something like dyadic or "real-time" signaling with pheromones (De Vos and Jander 2010).

12 McFarland 2001; Wilson and Wilson 2005.

13 Phillips-Silver and Keller 2012.

14 Noë 2004.

15 Blanke and Metzinger 2008; Gapenne 2010; cf. Feinberg 2013.

16 Frith and Frith 2010.

17 Froese and Fuchs 2012.

18 Hurley and Chater 2005.

19 Becchio et al. 2012.

20 Dael et al. 2013.

21 McGlone et al. 2014.

22 Gray and Wegner 2012; Rhee 2013; Tresch 2012.

23 Foucault 1963; Kuriyama 1999.

Chapter 2

1 Kelso 2010.

2 Ibid.

3 Moretti and Muñoz 2013.

4 Cosmelli and Thompson 2010.

5 Shepard 2008.

6 De Jaegher et al. 2010; Gallotti and Frith 2013.

7 Jola (2013) represents an exception. Cf. Reynolds and Reason 2012 and Sheets-Johnstone 2011.

8 Llinás 2001, 29–35; Goodman and Kelso 1983.

9 Llinás 2001, 34, emphasis added, 46–8.

10 Buzsáki et al. 2013, 755.

11 Calderone et al. 2014.

12 Kitzbichler et al. 2009, 2.

13 Buzsáki 2010.

14 Ibid., 377.

15 Central pattern generation of respiration is an area of active investigation. See, for instance, Ramirez et al. 2014; Richter and Smith 2014. The coupling between locomotion and respiration is less well characterized still. Larsson

(2014) proposes that locomotor-respiratory coupling within the individual and entrainment of locomotor-respiratory rhythms among individuals may serve to reduce the auditory masking effect of self-generated noise from moving and breathing—and that this in turn may have provided the basis for our tendency toward auditory entrainment and musicality.

16 See, e.g., Cole 2004.

17 Niemitz 2010; Roberts and Thorpe 2014.

18 Barra and Pérennou 2013.

19 Learning to hold oneself upright is also a form of acculturation—see Ingold 2005.

20 MacDougall and Moore 2005.

21 Dietz 2003.

22 Merker et al. 2009, 7.

23 Fitch 2013.

24 Hattori et al. 2013.

25 Becchio et al. 2012; Sebanz et al. 2006.

26 Hurley 2008.

27 Auvray and Rohde 2012, 3.

28 On the drive to cooperate, Tomasello et al. 2005.

29 At least 25 percent of the genes in our genome are expressed according to a circadian cycle, and we have gene transcription-translation feedback loops that are keyed to ambient light. See Möller-Levet et al. 2013.

30 Clark 2013.

Chapter 3

1 Cf. Tufte's (1997) discussion of *smallest effective differences*.

2 Bizley and Cohen 2013; Gilbert and Li 2013.

3 Bach y Rita and Kercel 2003.

4 Hanneton et al. 2010.

5 Striem-Amit et al. 2012. The Visual Word Form Area has been found to consistently emerge in the left fusiform gyrus, an aspect of the visual cortex focally implicated in the recognition of the faces of conspecifics, that is, humans. See Dehaene and Cohen 2007 for discussion of this phenomenon of exaptive reuse of preexisting patterns of nervous connectivity.

6 Hurley and Noë 2003; Auvray and Myin 2009.

7 Johnson (2007) uses *crossmodal*, but this seems to miss the fact that there is some component of sensory experience that is orthogonal to or beyond its modal realizations if not separable from them in experience. After coming up with *metamodal*, I discovered Pascual-Leone and Hamilton (2001) had used the same term.

8 On graviception, Barra and Pérennou 2013.

9 Kuriyama 1999, 48–9.

10 *Slippery—rough* would seem a strong candidate, but the strongest candidates for such universals would be not those image schemas arising from the recurrence dynamics of sensory information but those arising from course-grained spatial and temporal relations of the kind so often encoded in the thematic profiles and aspectual semantics of verbs: *inside—outside*, *path—goal*—those features of bodily movement and its semiotic realization that Talmy (2000, ch. 7) calls "force dynamics." Even here we see marked variation from place to place (Hanks 2009; Levinson and Burenhult 2009).

11 Agha 2007.

12 *Shared history*: Auvray and Myin 2009, esp. 1049–50.

13 The durability of comparisons to kettles and tape hiss is another matter. On the affective dimension of pain, Grahek 2011.

14 Ward and Meijer 2010, 496.

15 Ibid., 497. Newer auditory-visual sensory substitution systems encode color into the sonification (Levy-Tzedek et al. 2012).

16 On the filling-in of color from memory, Bannert and Bartels 2013. The so-called "binding problem," that is, how we bind colored extents of the visual field to patterns of motion to pick out distinct colored objects, remains an object of intense research (Seymour et al. 2009).

17 Sahlins 1995.

18 Pentland et al. 2009; personal communication, Alex Pentland, February 2014. On personal sensing, Westerink et al. 2011.

19 And yet we tend to overestimate how deep these grooves need to be, the efficiencies gained by institutional canalization. On the suppleness of economies that flourish in the absence of this kind of canalization, see Nordstrom (2004) and the work of the Institute for Money, Technology & Financial Inclusion (www.imtfi.uci.edu; e.g., Chipchase et al. 2014).

20 Classically, Foucault 1975.

21 Deleuze 1992, 3–4.

22 Baumann and Lyon 2013; Marwick 2012.

23 Koomey et al. 2013, 332.

24 Defining a unit of computation turns out not to be so straightforward. In particular, measures of instructions per unit time performed on a processor core are problematic, both because modern instruction sets, even in reduced instruction set architectures, comprise operations that vary considerably in their energetic needs—a single instruction might read from memory, perform a series of calculations, and write the result back to memory—and because computing phenomena vary in the degree to which they are amenable to being run across multiple cores operating in parallel. So a unit of computing must be defined with respect to an *instruction mix*, a pattern of recurring instruction sequences typical of a particular kind of computing activity. In the case of pervasive sensing, the picture is further complicated by the growing use of application-specific integrated circuits (ASICs), computing elements designed with a specific end in mind.

25 Koomey et al. 2013, 327.

26 Ibid., 328.

27 Tsydenova and Bengtsson 2011.

28 *Earliest uses*: Hunter 1778; Ogle 1866. Lusk 1928 and Sherman 1950 are good sources on the history of nutrition physiology. Moore-Ede et al. 1982 includes a comprehensive bibliography on the history of sleep and activity cycle measurement.

29 Only automation has been the object of thorough historical contextualization (Daston and Galison 2007). On portability and ubiquity, see Castells 2010.

Chapter 4

1 Hey et al. 2009.

2 On Lumosity and its relationship to the cognitive science research space, see Sternberg et al. 2013. 23andMe's conflict with the U.S. Food and Drug Administration has received news attention. At stake is the fact that in the absence of correction for multiple comparisons (e.g., Bonferroni correction), it is difficult for nonexpert consumers to interpret the results provided by 23andMe's testing kit, which encompasses disease-associated alleles at a large number of loci in the genome (Pachter 2013). This gets to the broader question of clinical expertise and diagnostic responsibility in personalized medicine, but clinical expertise is just one of the issues in play—see Pálsson 2012.

3 Dominguez-Bello and Blaser 2011; Karasov et al. 2011.

4 Nekrutenko and Taylor 2012, 669, emphasis added. Cf. Marder 2013 on unequal access to scientific resources.

5 Nekrutenko and Taylor 2012, 668.

6 Clarke et al. 2012, 1, emphasis added.

7 Gymrek et al. 2013; Mailman et al. 2007.

8 Homer et al. 2008.

9 Kaye and Hawkins 2014; Parker et al. 2009, 3. See also Kowal et al. 2013 on the tensions between source communities and investigators over the long-term disposition of genetic material collected in Indigenous communities.

10 A similar story can be told for immortalized cell lines (Landecker 2006).

11 Buerkle et al. 2011, 1576–7.

12 Tikka et al. (2012) exemplify a trend in task-based brain imaging studies, in which the stimulus (in this case a movie) adapts to the participant's physiological signal during the experiment.

13 Button et al. 2013; Carp 2012.

14 Resting-state scans—no task, just relax and hold still—can run fourteen minutes or longer; task-based setups, in particular those that involve watching movies, can be much longer. The noise from the magnet coils vibrating in the magnetic field is like a cross between a jackhammer and an alarm klaxon straight out of a science fiction movie, and it is *loud*, even with hearing protection. And of course lying on your back in the confined space of the magnet bore induces a strong urge to move, if not outright panic. The institute I was attached to while I was writing this book, the Max Planck Institute for Human Cognitive and Brain Sciences, maintains a database of experienced research participants who can be relied upon to hold still for long acquisitions.

15 Button et al. 2013.

16 Weiner 1992.

17 Coleman 2013.

18 Kaye and Hawkins 2014, 5.

19 In what follows I make no mention of social signal processing. On SSP, see Chapter 5.

20 These observations have benefited from a long series of conversations with empirically oriented linguists about changes in linguistics over the past ten years. Thanks in particular to Lise Dobrin and Martin Haspelmath.

21 Haxby 2012; Stephan and Roebroeck 2012. See also Manovich's (2013) discussion of how particular software packages have shaped work habits in architecture, design, and animation.

22 Atkinson 2011 is a good example—it appeared in *Science* and was reported in the *New York Times* (Wade 2011), but linguists' concerns about its theoretical assumptions were ignored during peer review. Contrast Atkinson 2011 with the sensitivity to language and the interpretive rigorcaution—"We do not know what the underlying causes of this correlation [between speaker population size and phonemic inventory size] are"—of the study that provided the theoretical inspiration for Atkinson's work (Hay and Bauer 2007, 398).

23 Michel et al. 2011. On the politics of doing ethnotaxonomy in the lexicon, Berson 2014a.

24 Brockmann et al. 2006; González et al. 2008; Roth et al. 2011. In the case of mobile phone location data, this is the same kind of data—call metadata, including cell location—that was at the heart of the first round of revelations about the U.S. National Security Agency's bulk collection program, Prism, made public in June 2013 through the work of Edward Snowden.

25 González et al. 2008. The results of this kind of research have undermined a tacit assumption, namely, that displacement behavior is *ergodic*—that the probability of a trip of distance r is independent of the distances of recent trips. It turns out displacement behavior is not ergodic (Wang et al. 2014).

26 So, for instance, a scaling law relating trip distance to frequency might hold over all the trips made by members of a population even if individuals' behavior were non-ergodic as described in the previous footnote.

27 But see De Montjoye et al. 2013, who show that the call metadata used in displacement studies make it easy to uniquely identify individuals. At the single-cell grain of spatial resolution (i.e., each cell in the network is counted as a distinct location), four call events (incoming or outgoing) uniquely identify a cell network user with 95 percent confidence. The resolving power of call metadata decays as the 0.1 power of the metadata spatial resolution—even spatially coarse data afford a powerful instrument of user identification.

28 Pentland 2006.

29 Eagle and Pentland 2009; Eagle et al. 2009.

30 To derive eigenbehaviors, time series are decomposed into binary vectors of discrete behaviors pairing times with sensor events (e.g., ±'at "at home with family at 5am," ±'at "at work with coworkers at 10am," ±'elsewhere "elsewhere with friends at 9pm"). Eigenbehaviors are extracted from the covariance data for these behavior vectors by principal component analysis.

31 The Social Fabric/Sensible DTU project (Copenhagen 2013–17) represents an effort to integrate ethnography and mobile sensing in the service of a suppler understanding of how social networks evolve. See Stopczynski et al. 2014.

32 Adams 2010; Eagle et al. 2010.

33 Dodds et al. 2011; Mitchell et al. 2013. The term "hedonometrics" comes from Edgeworth's (1881) vision of "hedonimetry."

34 Layard 2010.

35 Mislove et al. 2011.

36 Hedonometer's valence ratings were farmed out to Amazon Mechanical Turk, on which see Irani and Silberman 2013.

37 Kramer et al. 2014.

38 "Rapid" here—that is, under the diagnostic criteria used by Wehr and colleagues c.1980—means four or more episodes in the course of a year. Most commonly one form of mood intensification comes directly after the other. The swings, the shifts, say, from mania to depression, unfold over a period of hours to days, though the manias and depressions themselves may last weeks.

39 Wehr et al. 1982, 559. Exceptionally, fourteen of the fifteen participants in this study were women.

40 Colburn et al. 1982, col. 4–5. It was the eight most significant bits that were preserved, truncating the device's dynamic range on the low end—if fewer than thirty-two movement pulses registered for an epoch, the epoch as a whole would be marked in storage as "no movement."

41 Shiffrar 2011; Lee et al. 2014. The index paper for point-light paradigms is Johansson 1973.

42 The device used in Wehr et al. 1982 recorded linear acceleration in just one dimension. Contemporary actimeters record acceleration in three dimensions, and sometimes angular acceleration as well.

43 Sadeh 2011; Domingues et al. 2014; Ancoli-Israel et al. 2003. For a broader review of techniques for instrumenting sleep architecture, Roebuck et al. 2014. Mullaney et al. 1980 is the index paper for studies of sleep classification via bracelet actigraphy. The "gold standard" (to use a common actors' term) for sleep classification remains polysomnography—a combination of EEG, electromyography, and electrooculography (for measuring eye movement), in some cases together with strain-sensor measures of thoracic and abdominal movements and pulse oximetry.

44 Bonomi et al. 2009 offer one of the few detailed descriptions of the method used to develop an activity classifier. The study in question involved twenty participants, mean age twenty-nine, asked to perform twenty activities (e.g., walking, running, cycling).

45 My thanks to Raine Daston and Liz Nelson, whose feedback clarified these points for me.

46 Imagine a hammer: the shape of its handle and the distribution of mass between handle and head afford a grasping of its intended mode of use that, with modest practice, comes to feel transparent and inevitable. The term *affordance* comes from the psychologist of vision James Gibson. The dictum that the best interface is none at all is often attributed to usability consultant Donald Norman, a key figure in the history of human-computer interaction and user-centered design.

47 Cf. Payne 2014.

48 Some will argue that there's a straightforward technical solution to the chain of custody problem: subject the registration of data in aggregating repositories to a *blockchain* protocol like that made popular by BitCoin.

Chapter 5

1 Descola 2005; Latour 2013.

2 Hacking 2007, 105.

3 *A distinctly modern phenomenon*: The literature, as they say, is vast. Griffith 2000 and Kuriyama 2008 offer models of how to use textual sources to get at how diet and physical conditioning became things one must work at; Alter 2004 offers a key case study in how knowledge and technique travel; Feher et al. 1989 remains remarkably fresh after twenty-five years.

4 Feher et al. 1989.

5 Kendal et al. 2011.

6 *Candidate* exemplars because, within evolutionary biology, niche construction remains a hypothesis, in part because it is difficult to establish directionality in a causal chain when there is but a single evolutionary history to go on—see Buerkle et al. 2011.

7 O'Brien and Laland 2012. Whether dairy products played a "secondary" role in the domestication of ruminants, or whether they were exploited early on in the domestication process, is a matter of continuing debate in zooarchaeology—see Greenfield 2010. On the contemporary globalization of fresh dairy consumption, see Wiley 2011. Most research on niche construction in humans has focused on agricultural communities, but see Keen 2006 for discussion of the controlled use of fire in late Holocene Australia.

8 Leach 2003; note Zeder's (comment, 363) vigorous rejection of Leach's hypothesis.

9 Iriki and Taoka 2012.

10 Of course, if those who go barefoot were conducting the study, they might prefer to characterize walking shod as a form of sensory deprivation.

11 Bilimoria et al. 2012, citing Christakis et al. 2012. The children's shows the mice were forced to listen to included *Pokemon* and *The Powerpuff Girls*.

12 On the problems with an environment-indifferent checklist approach to behavioral modernity, see Davidson 2010 and Habgood and Franklin 2008.

13 Wynn and Coolidge 2010, S5; Gowlett et al. 2012, 693. Bloch (2012) offers a wider-ranging assessment.

14 Gowlett and colleagues attribute paleoanthropology's irrelevance to its practitioners' interpretive caution. Archaeological evidence as we encounter it today is the product of a long chain of processes of decay and transformation, of which the actions of the actors whose behavior is stipulated to represent the source of that evidence are just the first. What you leave behind is not the same as what others will find later on. Even in the absence of deliberate obfuscation (Harrison 2004), archaeological assemblages, particularly those of mobile foragers, can become interpretively illegible in a remarkably short space of time (Gould 1980).

15 Strathern 1988; cf. Luhrmann's discussion (2011, 78–9) of "porous" and "buffered" selves.

16 Guthman 2011 and Schüll 2012 offer exemplary accounts.

17 Adams 2013. The Postscript returns to this theme.

18 For example, Richerson and Boyd 2005; Mesoudi 2012; O'Brien and Shennan 2009.

19 Berson 2014a, b.

20 Genomicsts, as we saw in the last chapter, might say the same thing: to wit, that the "gene" is hopelessly coarse-grained as a unit for tracing the flow of information across evolutionary history.

21 Afer Devereux's "psychic unity of mankind." See Bourguignon 1989.

22 Levinson 2013; Legate et al. 2014; Haspelmath 2011.

23 Gowlett et al. 2012, 706; Rito et al. 2013.

24 *Chaîne operatoire*: Haidle 2010.

25 Pelegrin 2009.

26 Bresnan 2007.

27 Schacter et al. 2012.

28 Haraway 1989, 253.

29 Van Schaik 2013.

30 Seligman 2010.

31 Recall the discussion of saccadic movements and sensory priming in Chapter 1.

32 Craig 2009.

33 Roberts and Thorpe 2014. On the "implicit assumption . . . that the narrower male pelvis is better suited to the mechanical demands of bipedalism" (i.e., that giving birth to babies with large crania entails an evolutionary tradeoff in which women come out intrinsically less fit than men), see Roberts and Thorpe 2014, 283.

34 Ungar et al. 2006. I write as a longtime vegan and I am keenly aware of how ideologically charged the behavioral ecology of human diet has been— basically since behavioral ecology emerged as a discipline. See Lee and DeVore 1968, 4.

35 David et al. 2013.

36 Navarrete et al. 2011; Fonseca-Azevado and Herculano-Houzel 2012.

37 Wirth 1938.

38 Scott (2010, 45) offers a beautiful illustration of how transport and communication networks condition the emergence of political power in lowland agricultural centers, specifically by conditioning the accumulation of grain surpluses from surrounding areas.

39 See Sattherthwaite 2007, v–vii on relevant methodological concerns.

40 See, for example, Chipchase et al. 2014.

41 Ellis 2011.

42 Koolhaas 1994; Fuller and Harley 2005.

43 Koselleck 2008.

44 Compare Tresch 2012 on the moral characterization of technology in Restoration France.

45 Virilio [1977] 2006; Rushkoff 2013. Rosa 2013 presents acceleration as a force of social transformation on a plane with those identified by Marx (capitalism), Weber (disenchantment), and Durkheim (the shift from mechanical to organic solidarity). Fabian ([1983] 2014) and Robbins (2007) discuss biases in anthropology against taking actors' reported experience of social rupture at face value.

46 Guyer 2007.

47 Itself partly a function of social acceleration, in particular in the shadow banking system that was at the heart of the 2008 financial crisis (Stein 2010). I discuss this further in the Postscript.

48 Adams et al. 2009.

49 McClelland 2014. Apart from refugee camps, the exemplary spaces of this kind of social suspension are the *ad hoc* extraterritorial holding facilities governments establish at ports of entry to prevent would-be asylum seekers from legally entering national space (Makaremi 2009).

50 On production, Steinfeld et al. 2006 and Thornton 2010. On consumption, Kearney 2010, which notes, for example, that between 1963 and 2003 China saw an increase in meat consumption, in calories per capita, of 349 percent.

51 Alter 2007.

52 Chipchase 2013.

53 Chakrabarty 2009.

Chapter 6

1 Ekirch 2005.

2 Wehr 2001, 358.

3 Hollan 2013.

4 As with dairy consumption, debate continues among zooarchaeologists over the time lag between initial domestication and the deliberate keeping and breeding of animals for fiber. See Greenfield 2010.

5 Nadel et al. 2004; Vallverdú et al. 2010; cf. Gould 1980, 7–10.

6 Sahlins 1972, 38. Sahlins' point in "The Original Affluent Society" is to show that the leisurely pace of life so many North Atlantic travelers had observed in these communities reflected the fact that, contrary to our own basic economic assumption—"that man's wants are great, not to say infinite, whereas his means are limited, although improvable"—the societies in question had simply chosen "a Zen road to affluence": "Human material wants are finite and few, and technical means unchanging but on the whole adequate" (Sahlins 1972, 2).

7 Musharbash 2013.

8 Hollan 2013, 25. Vogler (2008) describes the efforts of Karenni refugees to reestablish similar patterns of collective sleeping in a refugee camp on the Thai side of the Thailand-Myanmar frontier. Worthman and Melby (2002) offer a summary of evidence on variation in the ecology of human sleep. This variation encompasses the demographics of cosleeping, the use of specialized built structure for sleeping, maintenance of fire during the night, degree of social enforcement of bedtimes, presence of domesticated animals, and presence of predators (other-than-human macrocarnivores and human outsiders).

9 Worthman 2011, 173.

10 Matricciani et al. 2013.

11 Möller-Levet et al. 2013; Scheer et al. 2009; Tasali et al. 2008. On time-in-bed trends, Matricciani et al. 2012.

12 Hollan 2013, 26.

13 Dove 1996.

14 Matricciani et al. 2013, 527.

15 Adan et al. 2012; Czeisler and Gooley 2007; Ferrara and De Gennaro 2001; of historical interest, Horne and Östberg 1977.

16 Worthman and Brown 2013 offer an example of how to study this process of niche construction.

17 Her chosen *nom d'écran*.

18 Scheer et al. 2009, 4457, describes a typical modern forced desynchrony protocol.

19 Broussard et al. 2012; Möller-Levet et al. 2013. On circadian dimensions of metabolism generally, see Bass and Takahashi 2010. It has become clear that a number of the body's pacemakers, both in the central nervous system and in the organ systems implicated in metabolism, are *food-entrainable*, but translational research on this topic is at an early stage.

20 Advisory Group for Aerospace Research and Development 1979; Stampi 1992. Today, as Crary (2013) notes, military research on sleep needs *is* oriented toward allowing soldiers to go indefinitely with little to no sleep.

21 Puredoxyk is the first to stress that "polyphasic sleeping is not (yet) science."

22 In Puredoxyk's notation, Everyman 3 includes a three-hour core sleep and three naps, Everyman 4.5 a four-and-a-half-hour core sleep and two naps, and Everyman 1.5 a ninety-minute core sleep and four to five naps. The Polyphasic Sleep Society has promoted an alternate notation for Everyman schedules where the number indicates the number of *naps*, not the length of the core sleep.

23 Puredoxyk 2013.

24 Moore-Ede et al. 1982, ch. 7.

25 Blumberg 2013.

26 Dalchau and Webb 2011; Masri and Sassone-Corsi 2013; cf. Edgar et al. 2012.

27 Simpson and Galbraith 1906.

28 Benedict 1904, 148.

29 Kleitman 1963, 178–82.

30 Wever 1979.

31 Chouvet et al. 1974.

32 Lucas et al. 2014.

33 Lewy et al. 1982.

34 Rosenthal et al. 1984.

35 Pflug and Tölle 1970.

36 Wirz-Justice et al. 2013.

37 Golden et al. 2005, 660; Tuunainen et al. 2009.

38 Wirz-Justice 2005.

39 Phillips-Silver and Keller 2012.

40 Auvray and Rohde 2012; Burger et al. 2013; Fitch 2013; Frith and Frith 2012.

41 Van Sweden 1986.

42 Harvey 2011; Heiler et al. 2011.

43 Hegerl et al. 2009; Hegerl et al. 2010.

44 Moreno et al. 2007.

45 Leibenluft 2011, 139

46 Lucas et al. 2014, 6.

47 And yet we know little about the developmental pharmacodynamics of caffeine: Porciúncula et al. 2013.

48 Crary 2013.

49 Mintz 1986.

50 Ogle 1866; Kuriyama (2008) sets this kind of self-experimentation in the context of a longer durée.

51 Wehr et al. 1982. See Chapter 4 for further context.

52 Chouvet et al. 1974; Czeisler et al. 1980.

53 Klein and Wegmann 1979.

54 Iyer 2004.

55 See suggestive remarks in Dantzer et al. 2008 on common mechanisms in the social withdrawal of depression and that of inflammatory processes.

56 Easterling 2005.

57 Kelso 2010; Malabou 2004. See the discussion of human displacement studies in Chapter 4.

58 Grahek 2011; cf. Sierra and David 2011 and discussion in Chapter 7.

59 We will have much to say about flow states in Chapter 8.

60 McLeary et al. 2014.

61 Yu 2006, 154–5. The speaker is Wei Zheng, prime minister to the Tang emperor Taizong. Wei had dozed off during a chess game with the emperor. Dreaming, he executed the Dragon of the River Jing, who had previously come to Taizong to beg clemency.

62 St. John 2013, dealing specifically with Psytrance; contrast Saldanha 2007. Of course phenomenology and social dynamics are continuous—the social dynamics of EDM are partly conditioned by participation in a shared experience of what Durkheim called *collective effervescence*, and the physiognomy of this experience is shaped by the music itself (e.g., determinism and entropy in its beat structure, timbral quality) and the settings in which it unfolds.

63 Pedersen 2011; Mueggler 2001. On the physiology and phenomenology of trance, see Locke and Kelly 1985 and the next note.

64 Peters and Price-Williams 1983, 30.

65 Puredoxyk 2013, 102–3.

66 Stein et al. 2004, esp. 16–17. It is not yet firmly established that the thera-peutic effects ascribed to EMDR reflect something specific to the rhythmic driving protocol, as opposed, say, to treatment-neutral contextual factors.

67 Pedersen 2013, 200.

68 And, by turns, of splicing—as in the composition of this chapter.

Chapter 7

1 Chipchase 2011.

2 Berson 2012, 2014b; Dobrin and Berson 2011; cf. Blommaert 2010.

3 Coombe 1998.

4 Sierra and David 2011, 102. The Cambridge Depersonalization Scale (Sierra and Berrios 2000) asks respondents to comment on the frequency and duration of experiences such as *Out of the blue I feel strange, as if I were not real or as if I were cut off from the world*, *Parts of my body feel as if they didn't belong to me*, and *My surroundings feel detached or unreal, as if there were a veil between me and the outside world*.

5 *Overlapping features*: On a possible physiological relationship between depersonalization and autoscopic phenomena, compare Sierra and David

2011, 104 with Blanke and Metzinger's (2008) discussion of the role of the temporoparietal junction in first-person perspective. For depersonalization, dissociation and dream states, compare Sierra and David 2011, 102 with Stein et al. 2004, esp. 16, on the experiencing of autobiographical memories from a third-person perspective.

6 Cf. Mialet 2003. I thank Jamie Sherman for our ongoing conversation on this theme.

7 Citron and Franks 2014.

8 Phillips-Silver and Keller 2012.

9 Stilgoe (2014) notes that while the most influential vernacular image-making tends to be done by young people, in particular young women, most photographic theory has been written by men in late middle age.

10 Haddon 1912, 270.

11 For starting points see Dias 2008 and Geismar 2006.

12 Lutz and Collins 1993.

13 Nineteen seventy-five was the year Papua New Guinea attained independence from Australia. On the Australian mainland, it was 1977 when the Central and Northern Land Commissions started hearings on the transfer of land title to Aboriginal communities in the Northern Territory.

14 Birdsell 1967, 150–2. See Berson 2014b for further context.

15 In technical terms, edge detection here entails the application of a convolution filter implementing a Laplacian operator with binary thresholding.

16 Kanade 1977, 24–5. LR/4 refers to the width of the face between its left and right edges divided by four. Step 2 entails identifying the edges of the cheeks and determining the width of the face.

17 Kanade 1977, 50.

18 Ibid., 49.

19 Ibid., 33–4.

20 Ibid., 12.

21 Geismar 2006, 539.

22 Mod 2014.

23 Sinha 2002; Zhao et al. 2003.

24 Turk and Pentland 1991, 73. The training images "were taken from a database of over 2,500 face images digitized under controlled conditions. Sixteen subjects were digitized at all combinations of three head orientations, three head sizes or scales, and three lighting conditions. A six level Gaussian pyramid was constructed for each image, resulting in image resolution from 512 × 512 down to 16 × 16 pixels" (Turk and Pentland 1991, 81).

25 Turk and Pentland 1991, 73. Recall the discussion of eigenbehaviors in Chapter 2.

26 Kirby and Sirovich 1990, 105. They continue: "In the present investigation, we consider an oval-shaped portion of the face containing essentially the eyes,

nose, and mouth. The oval picture fits into a square of dimensions 91 × 51. We eliminated most of the hair as it significantly reduced the accuracy of the expressions."

27 Sinha 2002, 1094. On test protocols for face recognition technologies, see Zhao et al. 2003, 433–40, and Phillips et al. 2000. Phillips and colleagues, in their account of FERET, the largest face recognition technology validation suite of its time (mid-1990s), indicate that the testing database included 14,126 images for 1,197 individuals, but they give no indication of the demographics of the database.

28 Kanade 1977, 49.

29 Sinha 2002, 1094, Figure 1; Zhang and Gao 2009, 2881.

30 On feature detection, Zhao et al. 2003, 406–11.

31 Sinha 2002, 1095; Knowles and Hay 2014.

32 Haddon 1912, 269–70, quoted in Geismar 2006, 541.

33 Lydon 2005.

34 On Haddon's influence and British social anthropology generally, Kuklick 2008.

35 Scott 1998.

36 On video-based face recognition systems, Zhao et al. 2003, 427–33.

37 For context, Berson 2014a; Bashkow 2006.

38 Ekman 1973.

39 Lindquist et al. 2012; Barrett 2014. Nummenma et al. 2014 introduces a novel approach to investigating cross-cultural correspondences in the bodily experience of discrete emotions.

40 On Darwin, Ekman, and the problem of posed expressions, see Leys 2010, 70–80.

41 Ekman and Friesen 1969; Ekman 1988.

42 Weinberger 2010. Hurley et al. 2014 offer more information on the U.S. Transportation Safety Administration's Screening of Passengers by Observational Techniques (SPOT) and Behavior Detection Officer (BDO) programs.

43 For versions of Ekman's posed facial expressions of basic emotions made with New Guinean interpreters, see Ekman Group 2014.

44 Both Haggard and Isaacs (1966) and Ekman and Friesen (1969; Ekman 2003) described microexpressions in the context of psychiatric clinical interviews. Haggard and Isaacs hypothesized that microexpressions are diagnostic of conflict—"anxi[ety] or ambivalen[ce] with respect to [the patient's] (conscious or preconcious) feelings and impulses and how he wishes to express them" (1966, 161). Ekman and Friesen, by contrast, stressed their value in diagnosing deliberate deception.

45 Ekman and Friesen 1974, 288.

46 Ambady and Rosenthal 1992; Ambady et al. 2000.

47 Bodenhausen and Todd 2010, 162: "Some kinds of personality inferences based on minimal cues ('thin slices' of behavior) have surprising accuracy, but the evidence for veridicality is far from consistent and suggests that these inferences are often overgeneralizations of rules that may have some kernel of truth (e.g., masculine faces go with dominant behavior), but which are far from universally valid."

48 Vinciarelli et al. 2009, 1744.

49 Ibid.

50 Yan et al. 2014a, b.

51 *Strategic essentialism*: Engle 2010.

52 Nishimoto et al. 2011; Cowen et al. 2014. Studies of this type require participants to lie perfectly still in the magnet bore for up to two hours, during which time the noise of the coil vibration is constant. For this reason, the investigators themselves often serve as participants.

53 Yu 2006, 311.

54 Benosman 2010.

Chapter 8

1 See lxda.org. Interaction design is the design of the interfaces and associated behavior patterns by which we transmit our desires to the instruments that populate our world—refrigerators, heart rate monitors, ATMs, water purifiers, automobiles, and, of course, handsets and other computing devices *sensu strictu*—and receive instructions from these instruments in turn.

2 Berson 2015.

3 For the project's origins, see Callard and Margulies 2010.

4 Wolf and Ramirez 2014.

5 On the liquid nutrition movement, specifically Soylent, see Mikanowski 2014. My interlocutor was describing his own interest in liquid nutrition by contrasting it with the "quantified reductionism" he saw among Soylent backers.

6 It was October 2014 when Daniel Margulies and I had this conversation. At this writing (April 2015), we are preparing to conduct pilot studies.

7 Czikszentmihaly 1990.

8 www.meetup.com/QS-Berlin/events/200724182/.

9 At the time of her comments downplaying flow, Puredoxyk had been practicing taiji for ten years, teaching for about a year, and sleeping polyphasically for the better part of fifteen years. See Puredoxyk 2013.

10 *Failures to predict*: See recent work on *predictive error coding* as a model for understanding the physiological instantiation of body schema and other dimensions of embodied awareness, that is, Clark 2013 and Koster-Hale and Saxe 2013, and the final section of Chapter 2.

11 Schüll 2012.

12 Jagoda 2013; cf. Golumbia 2009.

13 *Lust for power*: Golumbia 2009, channeling Nietzsche.

14 Schulte 2014.

15 Ito et al. 2012; Nozawa 2013.

16 On *animation* as a theoretical device in linguistic anthropology, see Manning and Gershon 2013.

17 Compare Csibra and Gergely 2009 on the exaggeration of gesture in *infant-directed speech* and other forms of pedagogically demonstrative movement.

18 On animal play, Graham and Burghardt 2010.

19 Other-than-human personhood has recently become a hot topic in anthropology again. For an overview of the "ontological turn" see Holbraad et al. 2014, Pedersen 2012, and Descola 2005. For accessible applications to field data, Sharp 2004 and Willerslev 2007.

20 Mackenzie 2006.

21 For a complementary perspective, Turkle 2011.

Postscript

1 On everyday precarity see, for example, Packer 2013.

2 Costello et al. 2010; Velasquez-Manoff 2014. The fact that the Eastern Band community lived in similar circumstances to the adjoining non-Native households afforded a natural experiment, since only Cherokee households received the stipend. Among children followed who had been youngest (twelve years old) when the stipends started in 1996, the lifetime prevalence of psychiatric illness at age twenty-one was around one-third less than among an age-matched cohort who had not received the stipends over the same period.

3 Adams 2013; Adams et al. 2009; Muehlebach 2013.

4 Graeber 2011; Piketty 2013.

5 Contrast, for instance, the arguments Sherman (1950) gives for why consumers in the developed world should eat less meat—"it is time for an awakening of the sense of social justice of those who have been responsible for the luxury-consumer demand that diverted an undue proportion of the grain crop into the fattening of meat animals in the hope of getting the higher prices of the conventional Choice and Prime grades" (Sherman 1950, 119–20)—with arguments offered for reduced meat consumption today. Guthman (2004, 2014) shows how since the rise of the alternative foods movement in the 1980s, social justice has almost completely dropped out of the public conversation on diet reform in favor of an emphasis on personal health.

6 Stein 2010; cf. Trejo-Mathys 2013.

7 Rosa (2013) helpfully distinguishes acceleration in the "pace of life" from acceleration in "social change".

8 Fourcade and Healy 2013, 560, 564. Fourcade and Healy stress that attitudes toward consumer debt vary significantly from place to place, and with them the classifying power of credit histories. Their argument applies principally to situations arising from "the American view of credit as an instrument of individual empowerment" (2013, 565).

9 For histories of liberalism in software development, see Coleman 2013, Johns 2010, and Turner 2006.

References

Adams, J. (2010), "Distant friends, close strangers? Inferring relationships from behavior," *Proceedings of the National Academy of Sciences* 107: E29–E30. www.pnas.org/content/107/9/E29.

Adams, V. (2013), *Markets of sorrow, labors of faith: New Orleans in the wake of Katrina*. Durham: Duke University Press.

Adams, V., Van Hattum, T., and English, D. (2009), "Chronic disaster syndrome: Displacement, disaster capitalism, and the eviction of the poor from New Orleans," *American Ethnologist* 36: 615–36.

Adan, A., Archer, S., Paz Hidalgo, M., Di Milia, L., Natale, V., and Randler, C. (2012), "Circadian typology: A comprehensive review," *Chronobiology International* 29: 1153–75.

Advisory Group for Aerospace Research and Development (1979), *Sleep, wakefulness and circadian rhythm*. AGARD Lecture Series No. 105. London: North American Treaty Organization.

Agha, A. (2007), *Language and social relations*. Cambridge: Cambridge University Press.

Alter, J. (2004), *Yoga in modern India: The body between science and philosophy*. Princeton: Princeton University Press.

Alter, J. (2007), "The once and future 'Apeman': Chimeras, human evolution, and disciplinary coherence," *Current Anthropology* 48: 637–52.

Ambady, N. and Rosenthal, R. (1992), "Thin slices of expressive behavior as predictors of interpersonal consequences: A meta-analysis," *Psychological Bulletin* 111: 256–74.

Ambady, N., Bernieri, F., and Richeson, J. (2000), "Towards a histology of social behavior: Judgmental accuracy from thin slices of behavior," in M. Zanna (ed.), *Advances in experimental social psychology*, vol. 32, 201–72. San Diego: Academic Press.

Ancoli-Israel, S., Cole, R., Alessi, C., Chambers, M., Moorcroft, W., and Pollak, C. (2003), "The role of actigraphy in the study of sleep and circadian rhythms," *Sleep* 26: 342–92.

Atkinson, Q. (2011), "Phonemic diversity supports a serial founder effect model of language expansion from Africa," *Science* 332: 346–9.

Van Atteveldt, N., Murray, M., Thut, G., and Schroeder, C. (2014), "Multisensory integration: Flexible use of general operations," *Neuron* 81: 1240–53.

Auvray, M. and Myin, E. (2009), "Percepetion with compensatory devices: From sensory substitution to sensorimotor extension," *Cognitive Science* 33: 1036–58.

Auvray, M. and Rohde, M. (2012), "Perceptual crossing: The simplest online paradigm," *Frontiers in Human Neuroscience* 6: 181. http://journal.frontiersin.org/Journal/10.3389/fnhum.2012.00181/abstract.

Bach y Rita, P. and Kercel, S. (2003), "Sensory substitution and the human–machine interface," *Trends in Cognitive Sciences* 7: 541–6.

Bach y Rita, P., Collins, C., Saunders, F., White, B., and Scadden, L. (1969), "Vision substitution by tactile image projection," *Nature* 221: 963–4.

Bannert, M. and Bartels, A. (2013), "Decoding the yellow of a gray banana," *Current Biology* 23: 2268–72.

Barra, J. and Pérennou, D. (2013), "Le sens de verticalité est-il vestibulaire?" *Neurophysiologie Clinique/Clinical Neurophysiology* 43: 197–204.

Barrett, L. (2014), "What faces can't tell us," *New York Times*, February 28. http://www.nytimes.com/2014/03/02/opinion/sunday/what-faces-cant-tell-us.html.

Bashkow, I. (2006), *The meaning of Whitemen: Race and modernity in the Orokaiva*. Chicago: University of Chicago Press.

Bass, J. and Takahashi, J. (2010), "Circadian integration of metabolism and energetics," *Science* 330: 1349–54.

Baumann, Z. and Lyon, D. (2013), *Liquid surveillance: A conversation*. Cambridge: Polity.

Becchio, C., Cavallo, A., Begliomini, C., Sartori, L., Feltrin, G., and Castiello, U. (2012), "Social grasping: From mirroring to mentalizing," *NeuroImage* 61: 240–8.

Benedict, F. (1904), "Studies in body-temperature.—I. Influence of the inversion of the daily routine; the temperature of night-workers," *American Journal of Physiology* 11: 145–69.

Benosman, R. (2010), "Vision without frames: A semiotic paradigm of event based computer vision," *Biosemiotics* 3: 1–16.

Berson, J. (2012), "Ideologies of descent in linguistics and law," *Language & Communication* 32: 137–46.

Berson, J. (2014a), "Color primitive," *Cabinet* no. 52: 41–9.

Berson, J. (2014b), "The dialectal tribe and the doctrine of continuity," *Comparative Studies in Society and History* 56: 381–418.

Berson, J. (2015), "Forced desynchrony," in K. Klingan, A. Sepahvand, C. Rosol, and B. Scherer (eds), *Textures of the Anthropocene: Grain vapor ray*, 101–18. Cambridge, MA: MIT Press.

Bilimoria, P., Hensch, T., and Bavelier, D. (2012), "A mouse model for too much TV?" *Trends in Cognitive Sciences* 16: 529–31.

Birdsell, J. (1967), "Preliminary data on the trihybrid origin of the Australian Aborigines," *Archaeology & Physical Anthropology in Oceania* 2: 100–55.

Bizley, J. and Cohen, Y. (2013), "The what, where and how of auditory-object perception," *Nature Reviews Neuroscience* 14: 693–707.

Blanke, O. and Metzinger, T. (2008), "Full-body illusions and minimal phenomenal selfhood," *Trends in Cognitive Sciences* 13: 7–13.

Bloch, M. (2012), *Anthropology and the cognitive challenge*. Cambridge: Cambridge University Press.

Blommaert, J. (2010), *The sociolinguistics of globalization*. Cambridge: Cambridge University Press.

Blumberg, M. (2013), "Sleep physiology: Setting the right tone," *Current Biology* 23: R834–R836.

Bodenhausen, G., and Todd, A. (2010), "Social cognition," *WIREs Cognitive Science* 1: 160–71.

Bonomi, A., Goris, A., Yin, B., and Westerterp, K. (2009), "Detection of type, duration, and intensity of physical activity using an accelerometer," *Medicine & Science in Sports & Exercise* 41: 1770–7.

Bourguignon, E. (1989), "Multiple personality, possession trance, and the psychic unity of mankind," *Ethos* 17: 371–84.

Bresnan, J. (2007), "Is syntactic knowledge probabilistic? Experiments with the English dative alternation," in S. Featherson and W. Sternefeld (eds), *Roots: Linguistics in search of its evidential base*, 77–96. Berlin: Mouton de Gruyter.

Brockmann, D., Hufnagel, L., and Geisel, T. (2006), "The scaling laws of human travel," *Nature* 439: 462–5.

Broussard, J., Ehrmann, D., Van Cauter, E., Tasali, E., and Brady, M. (2012), "Impaired insulin signaling in human adipocytes after experimental sleep restriction", *Annals of Internal Medicine* 157: 549–57.

Buerkle, C., Gompert, Z., and Parchman, T. (2011), "The $n = 1$ constraint in population genomics", *Molecular Ecology* 20: 1575–81.

Burger, B., Thompson, M., Luck, G., Saarikallio, S., and Toiviainen, P. (2013), "Influences of rhythm- and timbre-related musical features on characteristics of music-induced movement", *Frontiers in Psychology* 4: 183. journal. frontiersin.org/Journal/10.3389/fpsyg.2013.00183/abstract.

Button, K., Ioannidis, J., Mokrysz, C., Nosek, B., Flint, J., Robinson, E., and Munafò, M. (2013), "Power failure: Why small sample size undermines the reliability of neuroscience", *Nature Reviews Neuroscience* 14: 365–76.

Buzsáki, G. (2010), "Neural syntax: Cell assemblies, synapsemblies, and readers", *Neuron* 68: 362–85.

Buzsáki, G., Logothetis, N., and Singer, W. (2013), "Scaling brain size, keeping timing: Evolutionary preservation of brain rhythms", *Neuron* 80: 751–64.

Calderone, D., Lakatos, P., Butler, P., and Castellanos, F. (2014), "Entrainment of neural oscillations as a modifiable substrate of attention", *Trends in Cognitive Sciences* 18: 300–9.

Callard, F., and Margulies, D. (2010), "The industrious subject: Cognitive neuroscience's revaluation of 'rest'," in D. Hauptmann and W. Neidich (eds), *Cognitive architecture: From bio-politics to noo-politics—architecture and mind in the age of communication and information*, 324–45. Rotterdam: 010 Publishers.

Carp, J. (2012), "On the plurality of (methodological) worlds: Estimating the analytic flexibility of fMRI experiments," *Frontiers in Neuroscience* 6: 149. journal.frontiersin.org/Journal/10.3389/fnins.2012.00149/abstract.

Castells, M. (2010), *The rise of the network society*, 2nd edn. Malden, MA: Wiley.

Chakrabarty, D. (2009), "The climate of history: Four theses," *Critical Inquiry* 35: 197–222.

Chipchase, J. (2011), "It's not your face, it's ours," *Future Perfect* (blog), 30 October. janchipchase.com/2011/10/its-not-your-face-its-ours.

Chipchase, J. (2013), "The viscosity of data," *Future Perfect* (blog), 12 October. janchipchase.com/2013/10/the-viscosity-of-data/.

Chipchase, J., Serota, L., Tay, V., Mon, S., Ko, A., Oo Yin, and Oo Ye (2014), *Afford two, eat one: Financial inclusion in rural Myanmar*. Self-distributed with support from the Institute for Money, Technology & Financial Inclusion

(University of California, Irvine). Available at www.studiodradiodurans.com/myanmar-money-project.

Chouvet, G., Mouret, J., Coindet, J., Siffre, M., and Jouvet, M. (1974), "Periodicité bicircadienne du cycle vielle–sommeil dans des conditions hors du temps. Étude polygraphique," *Electroencephalography and Clinical Neurophysiology* 37: 367–80.

Christakis, D., Ramirez, J. S. B., and Ramirez, J. M. (2012), "Overstimulation of newborn mice leads to behavioral differences and deficits in cognitive performance," *Scientific Reports* 2: 546. www.nature.com/srep/2012/120731/srep00546/full/srep00546.html.

Citron, D., and Franks, M. (2014), "Criminalizing revenge porn," *Wake Forest Law Review* 49: 345–91.

Clark, A. (2013), "Whatever next? Predictive brains, situated agents, and the future of cognitive science," *Behavioral and Brain Sciences* 36: 181–253.

Clarke, L., Zheng-Bradley, X., Smith, R., Kulesha, E., Xiao, C., Toneva, I., Vaughan, B., Preuss, D., Leinonen, R., Shumway, M., Sherry, S., Flicek, P., and 1000 Genomes Project Consortium (2012), "The 1000 Genomes Project: Data management and community access," *Nature Methods* 9(5).

Clément, R., dir. (1960), *Plein soleil*. Robert et Raymond Hakim, 35mm, 118min.

Colburn, T., and Smith, B. (1982), Activity monitor for ambulatory subjects. U.S. Patent no. 4,353,375.

Cole, J. (2004), *Still lives: Narratives of spinal cord injury*. Cambridge, MA: MIT Press.

Coleman, E. (2013), *Coding freedom: The ethics and aesthetics of hacking*. Princeton: Princeton University Press.

Coombe, R. (1998), *The cultural life of intellectual properties: Authorship, appropriation, and the law*. Durham: Duke University Press.

Cosmelli, D. and Thompson, E. (2010), "Embodiment or envatment? Reflections on the bodily basis of consciousness," in J. Stewart, O. Gapenne, and E. Di Paolo (eds), *Enaction: Toward a new paradigm for cognitive science*, 361–85. Cambridge, MA: MIT Press.

Costello, E., Erkanli, A., Copeland, W., and Angold, A. (2010), "Association of family income supplements in adolescence with development of psychiatric and substance use disorders in adulthood among an American Indian population," *Journal of the American Medical Association* 303: 1954–60.

Cowen, A., Chun, M., and Kuhl, B. (2014), "Neural portraits of perception: Reconstructing face images from evoked brain activity," *NeuroImage* 94: 12–22.

Craig, B. (2009), "How do you feel—now? The anterior insula and human awareness," *Nature Reviews Neuroscience* 10: 59–70.

Crary, J. (2013), *24/7: Late capitalism and the ends of sleep*. London: Verso.

Csibra, G. and Gergely, G. (2009), "Natural pedagogy," *Trends in Cognitive Sciences* 13: 148–53.

Czeisler, C. and Gooley, J. (2007), "Sleep and circadian rhythms in humans," *Cold Spring Harbor Symposia on Quantitative Biology* 72: *Clocks and rhythms*, 579–97. http://symposium.cshlp.org/content/72/579.abstract.

Czeisler, C., Weitzman, E., Moore-Ede, M., Zimmerman, J., and Knauer, R. (1980), "Human sleep: Its duration and organization depend on its circadian phase," *Science* 210: 1264–7.

Czikszentmihaly, M. (1990), *Flow: The psychology of optimal experience*. New York: Harper & Row.

Dael, N., Goudbeek, M., and Scherer, K. (2013), "Perceived gesture dynamics in nonverbal expressions of emotion," *Perception* 42: 642–57.

Dalchau, N. and Webb, A. (2011), "Ticking over: Circadian systems across the kingdoms of life," *Biochemist* 33: 12–15.

Dantzer, R., O'Connor, J., Freund, G., Johnson, R., and Kelley, K. (2008), "From inflammation to sickness and depression: When the immune system subjugates the brain," *Nature Reviews Neuroscience* 9: 46–57.

Daston, L. and Galison, P. (2007), *Objectivity*. New York: Zone.

David, L., Maurice, C., Carmody, R., Gootenberg, D., Button, J., Wolfe, B., Ling, A., Devlin, A., Varma, Y., Fischbach, M., Biddinger, S., Dutton, R., and Turnbaugh, P. (2013), "Diet rapidly and reproducibly alters the human gut microbiome," *Nature* 505: 559–63.

Davidson (2010), "The colonization of Australia and its adjacent islands and the evolution of modern cognition," *Current Anthropology* 51: S177–S189.

De Jaegher, H., Di Paolo, E., and Gallagher, S. (2010), "Can social interaction constitute social cognition?" *Trends in Cognitive Sciences* 14: 441–7.

Dehaene, S. and Cohen, L. (2007), "Cultural recycling of cortical maps," *Neuron* 56: 384–98.

Deleuze, G. (1992), "Postscript on the societies of control," *October* no. 59: 3–7.

Descola, P. (2005), *Par-delà nature et culture*. Paris: Gallimard.

Dias, N. (2008), "Double erasures: Rewriting the past at the Musée du quai Branly," *Social Anthropology* 16: 300–11.

Dietz, V. (2003), "Spinal cord pattern generators for locomotion," *Clinical Neurophysiology* 114: 1379–89.

Dobrin, L. and Berson, J. (2011), "Speakers and language documentation," in P. Austin and J. Sallabank (eds), *The Cambridge handbook of endangered languages*, 187–211. Cambridge: Cambridge University Press.

Dodds, P., Harris, K., Kloumann, I., Bliss, C., and Danforth, C. (2011), "Temporal patterns of happiness and information in a global social network: Hedonometrics and Twitter," *PLOS ONE* 6: e26752. www.plosone.org/article/info%3Adoi%2F10.1371%2Fjournal.pone.0026752.

Domingues, A., Paiva, T., and Sanches, J. (2014), "Sleep and wakefulness state detection in nocturnal actigraphy based on movement information," *IEEE Transactions on Biomedical Engineering* 61: 426–34.

Dominguez-Bello, M., and Blaser, M. (2011), "The human microbiota as a marker for migrations of individuals and populations," *Annual Review of Anthropology* 40: 451–74.

Dove, M. (1996), "Rice-eating rubber and people-eating governments: Peasant versus state critiques of rubber development in colonial Borneo," *Ethnohistory* 43: 33–63.

Eagle, N., and Pentland, A. (2009), "Eigenbehaviors: Identifying structure in routine," *Behavioral Ecology and Sociobiology* 63: 1057–66.

Eagle, N., Pentland, A., and Lazer, D. (2009), "Inferring friendship network structure by using mobile phone data," *Proceedings of the National Academy of Sciences* 106: 15274–8.

Eagle, N., Clauset, A., Pentland, A., and Lazer, D. (2010), "Reply to adams: Multi-dimensional edge inference," *Proceedings of the National Academy of Sciences* 107: E31. www.pnas.org/content/107/9/E31.

Easterling, K. (2005), *Enduring innocence: Global architecture and its political masquerades.* Cambridge, MA: MIT Press.

Edgar, R., Green, E., Zhao, Y., van Ooijen, G., Olmedo, M., Qin, X., Xu, Y., Pan, M., Valekunja, U., Feeney, K., Maywood, E., Hastings, M., Baliga, N., Merrow, M., Millar, A., Johnson, C., Kyriacou, C., O'Neill, J., and Reddy, A. (2012), "Peroxiredoxins are conserved markers of circadian rhythms," *Nature* 485: 459–64.

Edgeworth, F. (1881), *Mathematical psychics: An essay on the application of mathematics to the moral sciences.* London: Kegan Paul.

Ekirch, A. (2005), *At day's close: Night in times past.* New York: Norton.

Ekman, P. (1973), *Darwin and facial emotion.* New York: Academic Press.

Ekman, P. (1988), "Lying and nonverbal behavior: Theoretical issues and new findings," *Journal of Nonverbal Behavior* 12: 163–75.

Ekman, P. (2003), "Darwin, deception, and facial expression," *Annals of the New York Academy of Sciences* 1000: 205–21.

Ekman, P. and Friesen, W. (1969), "Nonverbal leakage and clues to deception," *Psychiatry* 32: 88–106.

Ekman, P. and Friesen, W. (1974), "Detecting deception from the body or face," *Journal of Personality and Social Psychology* 29: 288–98.

Ekman Group [Paul Ekman Group] (2014), "Are there universal facial expressions?" www.paulekman.com/universal-facial-expressions.

Ellis, E. (2011), "Anthropogenic transformation of the terrestrial biosphere," *Philosophical Transactions of the Royal Society A* 369: 1010–35.

Engle, K. (2010), *The elusive promise of indigenous development: Rights, culture, strategy.* Durham: Duke University Press.

Fabian, J. [1983] (2014), *Time and the other: How anthropology makes its object.* New York: Columbia University Press.

Feher, M., Naddaf, R., and Tazi, N. (eds) (1989), *Fragments for a history of the human body*, Parts 1–3. New York: Zone.

Feinberg, T. (2013), "Neuropathologies of the self and the right hemisphere: A window into productive personal pathologies," *Frontiers in Human Neuroscience* 7: 472. journal.frontiersin.org/Journal/10.3389/fnhum.2013.00472/full.

Ferrara, M. and De Gennaro, L. (2001), *How much sleep do we need?* Sleep Medicine Reviews 5: 155–79.

Ferriss, T. (2010), *The 4-hour body: An uncommon guide to rapid fat-loss, incredible sex, and becoming superhuman.* New York: Crown.

Fitch, W. (2013), "Rhythmic cognition in humans and animals: Distinguishing meter and pulse perception," *Frontiers in Systems Neuroscience* 7: 68. journal.frontiersin.org/Journal/10.3389/fnsys.2013.00068/abstract.

Folman, A., dir. (2013), *The Congress.* Bridgit Folman Film Gang, 35mm/DCP, 122min.

Fonseca-Azevedo, K., and Herculano-Houzel, S. (2012), "Metabolic constraint imposes tradeoff between body size and number of brain neurons in human evolution," *Proceedings of the National Academy of Sciences* 109: 18571–6. www.pnas.org/content/109/45/18571.

Foucault, M. (1963), *Naissance de la clinique*. Paris: Presses Universitaires Françaises.

Foucault, M. (1975), *Surveiller et punir: Naissance de la prison*. Paris: Gallimard.

Fourcade, M. and Healy, K. (2013), "Classification situations: Life chances in the neoliberal era," *Accounting, Organizations and Society* 38: 559–72.

Frith, C. and Frith, U. (2010), "The social brain: Allowing humans to boldly go where no other species has been," *Philosophical Transactions of the Royal Society B* 365 no. 1537: 165–76.

Frith, C. and Frith, U. (2012), "Mechanisms of social cognition," *Annual Review of Psychology* 63: 287–313.

Froese, T. and Fuchs, T. (2012), "The extended body: A case study in the neurophenomenology of social interaction," *Phenomenology and the Cognitive Sciences* 11: 205–35.

Fuller, G. and Harley, R. (2005), *Aviopolis: A book about airports*. London: Black Dog.

Gallotti, M. and Frith, C. (2013), "Social cognition in the we-mode," *Trends in Cognitive Sciences* 17: 160–5.

Gapenne, O. (2010), "Kinesthesia and the construction of perceptual objects," in J. Stewart, O. Gapenne, and E. Di Paolo (eds), *Enaction: Toward a new paradigm for cognitive science*, 183–218. Cambridge, MA: MIT Press.

Geismar, H. (2006), "Malakula: A photographic collection," *Comparative Studies in Society and History* 48: 520–63.

Gilbert, C. and Li, W. (2013), "Top-down influences on visual processing," *Nature Reviews Neuroscience* 14: 350–63.

Golden, R., Gaynes, B., Ekstrom, R., Hamer, R., Jacobsen, F., Suppes, T., Wisner, K., and Nemeroff, C. (2005), "The efficacy of light therapy in the treatment of mood disorders: A review and meta-analysis of the evidence," *American Journal of Psychiatry* 162: 656–62.

Golumbia, D. (2009), "Games without play," *New Literary History* 40: 179–204.

González, M., Hidalgo, C., and Barabási A.-L. (2008), "Understanding individual human mobility patterns," *Nature* 453: 779–82.

Goodman, D., and Kelso, J. (1983), "Exploring the functional significance of physiological tremor: A biospectroscopic approach," *Experimental Brain Research* 49: 419–31.

Gould, R. (1980), *Living archaeology*. Cambridge: Cambridge University Press.

Gowlett, J., Gamble, C., and Dunbar, R. (2012), "Human evolution and the archaeology of the social brain," *Current Anthropology* 53: 693–722.

Graeber, D. (2011), *Debt: The first 5,000 years*. New York: Melville House.

Graham, K., and Burghardt, G. (2010), "Current perspectives on the biological study of play: Signs of progress," *Quarterly Review of Biology* 85: 393–418.

Grahek, N. (2011), *Feeling pain and being in pain*, 2nd edn. Cambridge, MA: MIT Press.

Gray, K., and Wegner, D. (2012), "Feeling robots and human zombies: Mind perception and the uncanny valley," *Cognition* 125: 125–30.

Greenfield, H. (2010), "The Secondary Products Revolution: The past, the present and the future," *World Archaeology* 42: 29–54.

Griffith, R. (2000), "Apostles of abstinence: Fasting and masculinity during the Progressive era," *American Quarterly* 52: 599–638.

Guthman, J. (2004), *Agrarian dreams: The paradox of organic farming in California*. Berkeley: University of California Press.

Guthman, J. (2011), *Weighing in: Obesity, food justice, and the limits of capitalism*. Berkeley: University of California Press.

Guyer, J. (2007), "Prophecy and the near future: Thoughts on macroeconomic, evangelical, and punctuated time," *American Ethnologist* 34: 409–21.

Gymrek, M., McGuine, A., Golan, D., Halperin, E., and Erlich, Y. (2013), "Identifying personal genomes by surname inference," *Science* 339: 321–4.

Habgood, P. and Franklin, N. (2008), "The revolution that didn't arrive: A review of Pleistocene Sahul," *Journal of Human Evolution* 55: 187–222.

Hacking, I. (2007), "Our neo-Cartesian bodies in parts," *Critical Inquiry* 34: 78–105.

Haddon, A. (1912), "Appendix on photography," in B. Freire-Marreco and J. Myres (eds), *Notes and Queries on Anthropology*, 4th edn, 269–77. London: Royal Anthropological Institute.

Haggard, E. and Isaacs, K. (1966), "Micromomentary facial expressions as indicators of ego mechanisms in psychotherapy," in L. Gottschalk and A. Auerbach (eds), *Methods of research in psychotherapy*, 154–65. New York: Appleton–Century–Crofts.

Haidle, M. (2010), "Working-memory capacity and the evolution of modern cognitive potential: Implications from animal and early human tool use," *Current Anthropology* 51: S149–S166.

Hanks, W. (2009), "Fieldwork on deixis," *Journal of Pragmatics* 41: 10–24.

Hanneton, S., Auvray, M., and Durette, B. (2010), "The Vibe: a versatile vision-to-audition sensory substitution device," *Applied Bionics and Biomechanics* 7: 269–76.

Haraway, D. (1989), *Primate visions: Gender, race, and nature in the world of modern science*. New York: Routledge.

Harrison, S. (2004), "Forgetful and memorious landscapes," *Social Anthropology* 12: 135–51.

Harvey, A. (2011), "Sleep and circadian functioning: Critical mechanisms in the mood disorders?" *Annual Review of Clinical Psychology* 7: 297–319.

Haspelmath, M. (2011), "The indeterminacy of word segmentation and the nature of morphology and syntax," *Folia Linguistica* 45: 31–80.

Hattori, Y., Tomonaga, M. and Matsuzawa, T. (2013), "Spontaneous synchronized tapping to an auditory rhythm in a chimpanzee," *Scientific Reports* 3: 1566.

Haxby, J. (2012), "Multivariate pattern analysis of fMRI: The early beginnings," *NeuroImage* 62: 852–5.

Hay, J. and Bauer, L. (2007), "Phoneme inventory size and population size," *Language* 83: 388–400.

Head, H. and Holmes, G. (1911), "Sensory disturbances from cerebral lesions," *Brain* 34: 102–254.

Hegerl, U., Sander, C., Olbrich, S., and Schoenknecht, P. (2009), "Are psychostimulants a treatment option in mania?" *Pharmacopsychiatry* 42: 169–74.

Hegerl, U., Himmerich, H., Engmann, B., and Hensch, T. (2010), "Mania and attention-deficit/hyperactivity disorder: Common symptomatology, common pathophysiology, and common treatment?" *Current Opinion in Psychiatry* 23: 1–7.

Heiler, S., Legenbauer, T., Bogen, T., Jensch, T., and Holtmann, M. (2011), "Severe mood dysregulation: In the 'light' of circadian functioning," *Medical Hypotheses* 77: 692–5.

Hey, T., Tansley, S., Tolle, K. (eds) (2009), *The fourth paradigm: Data-intensive scientific discovery*. Redmond, WA: Microsoft Research.

Hillier, B. (1996/2007), *Space is the machine: A configurational theory of architecture*, open access edition. London: Space Syntax. eprints.ucl. ac.uk/3881/.

Holbraad, M., Pedersen, M. and Viveiros de Castro, E. (2014), "The politics of ontology: Anthropological positions," *Cultural Anthropology Online*, 13 January. www.culanth.org/fieldsights/462-the-politics-of-ontology-anthropological-positions.

Hollan, D. (2013), "Sleeping, dreaming, and health in rural Indonesia and the urban U.S.: A cultural and experiential approach," *Social Science & Medicine* 79: 23–30.

Homer, N., Szelinger, S., Redman, M., Duggan, D., Tembe, W., Muehling, J., Pearson, J., Stephan, D., Nelson, S., and Craig, D. (2008), "Resolving individuals contributing trace amounts of DNA to highly complex mixtures using high-density SNP genotyping microarrays," *PLOS Genetics* 4: e1000167. www.plosgenetics.org/article/info%3Adoi%2F10.1371%2Fjournal. pgen.1000167.

Horne, J., and Östberg, O. (1977), "Individual differences in human circadian rhythms," *Biological Psychology* 5: 179–90.

Hou Y.-F., Sun Z.-L., Chong Y.-W., and Zheng C.-H. (2014), "Low-rank and eigenface based sparse representations for face recognition," *PLOS ONE* 9: e110318. www.plosone.org/article/info%3Adoi%2F10.1371%2Fjournal. pone.0110318.

Huang, G., Ramesh, M., Berg, T., and Learned-Miller, E. (2007), "Labeled Faces in the Wild: A database for studying face recognition in unconstrained environments." University of Massachusetts, Amherst, Technical Report 07-49, October. vis-www.cs.umass.edu/lfw/lfw.pdf.

Humphrey, N. (2007), "The society of selves," *Philosophical Transactions of the Royal Society B* 362: 745–54.

Hunter, J. (1778), "Of the heat, &c. of animals and vegetables," *Philosophical Transactions of the Royal Society of London* 68: 7–49.

Hurley, C., Anker, A., Frank, M., Matsumoto, D., and Hwang, H. (2014), "Background factors predicting accuracy and improvement in micro expression recognition," *Motivation and Emotion* 38: 700–14.

Hurley, S. (2008), "The shared circuits model (SCM): How control, mirroring, and simulation can enable imitation, deliberation, and mindreading," *Behavioral and Brain Sciences* 31: 1–58.

Hurley, S., and Chater, N. (eds) (2005), *Perspectives on imitation: From neuroscience to social science*, vol. 2: *Imitation, human development, and culture*. Cambridge, MA: MIT Press.

Hurley, S. and Noë, A. (2003), "Neural plasticity and consciousness," *Biology and Philosophy* 18: 131–68.

Husserl, E. (1900–1), *Logische Untersuchungen*. Halle: Niemeyer.

Ingold, T. (2005), "Culture on the ground: The world perceived through the feet," *Journal of Material Culture* 9: 315–40.

Ingold, T. (2010), "The textility of making," *Cambridge Journal of Economics* 34: 91–102.

Irani, L. and Silberman, M. (2013), "Turkopticon: Interrupting worker invisibility in Amazon Mechanical Turk," *CHI'13: Proceedings of the SIGCHI Conference on Human Factors in Computing Systems, Paris, 27 April–3 May*, 611–20. New York: Association for Computing Machinery.

Iriki, A., and Taoka, M. (2012), "Triadic (ecological, neural, cognitive) niche construction: A scenario of human brain evolution extrapolating tool use and language from the control of reaching actions," *Philosophical Transactions of the Royal Society B* 367: 10–23.

Ito, M., Okabe, D. and Tsuji, I. (eds) (2012), *Fandom unbound: Otaku culture in a connected world*. New Haven: Yale University Press.

Iyer, P. (2004), "In the realm of jet lag," *New York Times*, 7 March. www.nytimes.com/2004/03/07/magazine/in-the-realm-of-jet-lag.html (Reprinted as: Nightwalking. *Sun after dark: flights into the unknown*. New York: Knopf, 2004.)

Jagoda, P. (2013), "Gamification and other forms of play," *boundary 2* 40: 114–44.

James, W. (1901), *The varieties of religious experience: A study in human nature*. New York: Longmans, Green.

Johansson, G. (1973), "Visual perception of biological motion and a model for its analysis," *Perception & Psychophysics* 14: 201–11.

Johns, A. (2010), *Piracy: The intellectual property wars from Gutenberg to Gates*. Chicago: University of Chicago Press.

Johnson, M. (2007), *The meaning of the body: Aesthetics of human understanding*. Chicago: University of Chicago Press.

Jola, C. (2013), "Do you feel the same way too?" in G. Brandstetter, G. Egert, and S. Zubarik (eds), *Touching and being touched: Kinesthesia and empathy in dance and movement*, 181–210. Berlin: De Gruyter.

Kanade, T. (1977), *Computer recognition of human faces*. Basel: Birkhäuser.

Karasov, W., Martínez del Rio, C., and Caviedes-Vidal, E. (2011), "Ecological physiology of diet and digestive systems," *Annual Review of Physiology* 73: 69–93.

Kaye, J., and Hawkins, N. (2014), "Data sharing policy design for consortia: Challenges for sustainability," *Genome Medicine* 6: 4.

Kearney, J. (2010), "Food consumption trends and drivers," *Philosophical Transactions of the Royal Society B* 365: 2793–807.

Keen, I. (2006), "Constraints on the development of enduring inequalities in late Holocene Australia," *Current Anthropology* 47: 7–38.

Kefali, J. and E. Yelich-O'Connor (performing as Lorde) (2013), "Video for 'Tennis court'," digital video, 3'20". vimeo.com/68841186.

Kelso, J. (2010), "Metastable mind," in C. Hauptmann and W. Neidich (eds), *Cognitive architecture: From biopolitics to noopolitics: architecture & mind in the age of communication and information*, 117–38. Rotterdam: 010 Publishers.

Kendal, J., Tehrani, J., and Odling-Smee, J. (2011), "Human niche construction in interdisciplinary focus," *Philosophical Transactions of the Royal Society B* 366: 785–92.

Kirby, M. and Sirovich, L. (1990), "Application of the Karhunen–Loève procedure for the characterization of human faces," *IEEE Transactions on Pattern Analysis and Machine Intelligence* 12: 103–8.

Kitzbichler, M., Smith, M., Christensen, S., and Bullmore, E. (2009), "Broadband criticality of human brain network synchronization," *PLOS Computational Biology* 5: e1000314.

Klein, K. and Wegmann, H.-M. (1979), "Circadian rhythms in air operations," in A. Nicholson (ed.), *Sleep, wakefulness and circadian rhythm*. London: NATO Advisory Group for Aerospace Research and Development.

Kleitman, N. (1963), *Sleep and wakefulness*, rev. edn. Chicago: University of Chicago Press.

Knowles, M. and Hay, D. (2014), "The role of inner and outer face parts in holistic processing: A developmental study," *Acta Psychologica* 149: 106–16.

Koolhaas, R. (1994), "The generic city," in R. Koolhaas and B. Mau (eds), *S, M, L, XL*. 1248–62. New York: Monacelli.

Koomey, J., Matthews, H., and Williams, E. (2013), "Smart everything: Will intelligent systems reduce resource use?" *Annual Review of Environment and Resources* 38: 311–43.

Koselleck, R. (2008), "Is there an acceleration of history?" in H. Rosa and W. Schleuerman (eds), trans. J. Ingram, *High-speed society*, 113–34. University Park, PA: Pennsylvania State University Press.

Koster-Hale, J. and Saxe, R. (2013), "Theory of mind: A neural prediction problem," *Neuron* 79: 836–48.

Kowal, E., Radin, J., and Reardon, J. (2013), "Indigenous body parts, mutating temporalities, and the half-lives of postcolonial technoscience," *Social Studies of Science* 43: 465–83.

Kramer, A., Guillory, J., and Hancock, J. (2014), "Experimental evidence of massive-scale emotional contagion through social networks," *Proceedings of the National Academy of Sciences* 111: 8788–90. www.pnas.org/content/111/24/8788.

Kuklick, H. (2008), "The British tradition," in H. Kuklick (ed.), *A new history of anthropology*, 52–78 Oxford: Blackwell.

Kuriyama, S. (1999), *The expressiveness of the body and the divergence of Greek and Chinese medicine*. New York: Zone.

Kuriyama, S. (2008), "The forgotten fear of excrement," *Journal of Medieval and Early Modern Studies* 38: 413–42.

De Landa, M. (1997), *A thousand years of nonlinear history*. New York: Zone.

Landecker, H. (2006), *Culturing life: How cells became technologies*. Cambridge, MA: Harvard University Press.

Larsson, M. (2014), "Self-generated sounds of locomotion and ventilation and the evolution of human rhythmic abilities," *Animal Cognition* 17: 1–14.

Latour, B. (2013), *An inquiry into modes of existence*, trans. C. Power. Cambridge, MA: Harvard University Press.

Layard, R. (2010), "Measuring subjective well-being," *Science* 327: 534–5.

LCD Soundsystem (2010), *This is happening*. Musical recording. DFA 22501.

Leach, H. (2003), "Human domestication reconsidered," *Current Anthropology* 44: 349–68.

Lee, R. and De Vore, I. (1968), *Man the hunter*. Chicago: Aldine.

Lee, T., Belkhatir, M., and Sanei, S. (2014), "A comprehensive review of past and present vision-based techniques for gait recognition," *Multimedia Tools and Applications* 72: 2833–69.

Legate, J., Pesetsky, D., and Yang, C. (2014), "Recursive misrepresentations: A reply to Levinson," *Language* 90: 515–28.

Leibenluft, E. (2011), "Severe mood dysregulation, irritability, and the diagnostic boundaries of bipolar disorder in youths," *American Journal of Psychiatry* 168: 129–42.

Levinson, S. (2013), "Recursion in pragmatics," *Language* 89: 149–62.

Levinson, S. and Burenhult, N. (2009), "Semplates: A new concept in lexical semantics?" *Language* 85: 153–74.

Levy-Tzedek, S., Hanassy, S., Abboud, S., Maidenbaum, S. and Amedi, A. (2012), "Fast, accurate reaching movements with a visual-to-auditory sensory substitution device," *Restorative Neurology and Neuroscience* 30: 313–23.

Lewy, A., Kern, H., Rosenthal, N. and Wehr, T. (1982), "Bright artificial light treatment of a manic-depressive patient with a seasonal mood cycle," *American Journal of Psychiatry* 139: 1496–8.

Leys, R. (2010), "How did fear become a scientific object and what kind of object is it?" *Representations* 110: 66–104.

Lindquist, K., Wager, T., Kober, H., Bliss-Moreau, E., and Barrett, L. (2012), "The brain basis of emotion: A meta-analytic review," *Behavioral and Brain Sciences* 35: 121–202.

Llinás, R. (2001), *I of the vortex: from neurons to self*. Cambridge, MA: MIT Press.

Locke, R. and Kelly, E. (1985), "A preliminary model for the cross-cultural analysis of altered states of consciousness," *Ethos* 13: 3–55.

Lopez, R. (2008), *Buddhism and science: A guide for the perplexed*. Chicago: University of Chicago Press.

Lucas, R., Peirson, S., Berson, D., Brown, T., Cooper, H., Czeisler, C., Figueiro, M., Gamlin, P., Lockley, S., O'Hagan, J., Price, L., Provencio, I., Skene, D., and Brainhard, G. (2014), "Measuring and using light in the melanopsin age," *Trends in Neuroscience* 37: 1–9.

Luhrmann, T. (2011), "Hallucinations and sensory overrides," *Annual Review of Anthropology* 40: 71–85.

Lusk, G. (1928), *The science of nutrition*, 4th edn. Philadelphia: Saunders.

Lutz, C. and Collins, J. (1993), *Reading National Geographic*. Chicago: University of Chicago Press.

Lydon, J. (2005), *Eye contact: Photographing indigenous Australians*. Durham: Duke University Press.

McClelland, M., "How to build a perfect refugee camp," *New York Times*, 13 February 2014. www.nytimes.com/2014/02/16/magazine/how-to-build-a-perfect-refugee-camp.html.

MacDougall, H. and Moore, S. (2005), "Marching to the beat of the same drummer: The spontaneous tempo of human locomotion," *Journal of Applied Physiology* 99: 1164–73.

McFarland, D. (2001), "Respiratory markers of conversational interaction," *Journal of Speech, Language, and Hearing Research* 44: 128–43.

McGlone, F., Wessberg, J., and Olausson, H. (2014), "Discriminative and affective touch: Sensing and feeling," *Neuron* 82: 737–55.

Mackenzie, P. (2006), *An engine, not a camera: How financial models shape markets*. Cambridge, MA: MIT Press.

McLeary, M., Radia, A., and Thomas, R. (2014), "Money creation in the modern economy," *Quarterly Bulletin of the Bank of England* 2014(Q1). www.bankofengland.co.uk/publications/Documents/quarterlybulletin/2014/qb14q1prereleasemoneycreation.pdf.

Mailman, M., Feolo, M., Jin, Y., Kimura, M., Tryka, K., Bagoutdinov, R., Hao, L., Kiang, A., Paschall, J., Phan, L., Popova, N., Pretel, S., Ziyabari, L., Lee, M., Shao, Y., Wang, Z., Sirotkin, K., Ward, M., Kholodov, M., Zbicz, K., Beck, J., Kimelman, M., Shevelev, S., Preuss, D., Yaschenko, E., Graeff, A., Ostell, J., and Sherry, S. (2007), "The NCBI dbGaP database of genotypes and phenotypes," *Nature Genetics* 39: 1181–6.

Makaremi, C. (2009), "Governing borders in France: From extraterritorial to humanitarian confinement," *Canadian Journal of Law and Society* 24: 411–32.

Malabou, C. (2004), *Que faire de notre cerveau?* Paris: Fayard.

Manning, P. and Gershon, I. (2013), "Animating interaction," *HAU: Journal of Ethnographic Theory* 3(3): 107–37. www.haujournal.org/index.php/hau/article/view/hau3.3.006.

Manovich, L. (2013), *Software takes command.* London: Bloomsbury.

Marder, E. (2013), "Living science: the haves and the have nots," *eLife* 2: e01515. http://elifesciences.org/content/2/e01515 OA.

Marwick, A. (2012), "The public domain: Social surveillance in everyday life," *Surveillance & Society* 9: 378–93.

Masri, S. and Sassone-Corsi, P. (2013), "The circadian clock: A framework linking metabolism, epigenetics and neuronal function," *Nature Reviews Neuroscience* 14: 69–75.

Matricciani, L., Olds, T., and Petkov, J. (2012), "In search of lost sleep: secular trends in the sleep time of school-aged children and adolescents," *Sleep Medicine Reviews* 16: 203–11.

Matricciani, L., Blunden, S., Rigney, G., Williams, M., and Olds, T. (2013), "Children's sleep needs: Is there sufficient evidence to recommend optimal sleep for children?" *Sleep* 36: 527–34.

Maturana, H. and Varela, F. (1980), *Autopoiesis and cognition: The realization of the living.* Dordrecht: Reidel.

Meijer, P. (1992), "An experimental system for auditory image representations," *IEEE Transactions on Biomedical Engineering*, 39: 112–21.

Merker, B., Madison, G., and Eckerdal, P. (2009), "On the role and origin of isochrony in human rhythmic entrainment," *Cortex* 45: 4–17.

Mesoudi, A. (2012), *Cultural evolution: How Darwinian theory can explain human culture and synthesize the social sciences.* Chicago: University of Chicago Press.

Mialet, H. (2003), "Reading Hawking's presence: An interview with a self-effacing man," *Critical Inquiry* 29: 571–98.

Michel, J.-B., Shen, Y., Presser Aiden, A., Veres, A., Gray, M., The Google Books Team, Pickett, J., Hoiberg, D., Clancy, D., Norvig, P., Orwant, J., Pinker, S., Nowak, M., and Lieberman Aiden, E. (2011), "Quantitative analysis of culture using millions of digitized books," *Science* 331: 176–82.

Mikanowski, J. (2014), Noma. The Point. thepointmag.com/2014/criticism/noma.

Mintz, S. (1986), *Sweetness and power: The place of sugar in modern history.* London: Penguin.

Mislove, A., Lehmann Jøregensen, S., Ahn, Y.-Y., Onnela, J.-P., and Rosenquist, N. (2011), "Understanding the demographics of Twitter users," in *Proceedings of the Fifth International AAAI Conference on Weblogs and Social Media*, 554–7. Cambridge, MA: AAAI Press. See http://www.aaai.org/Library/ICWSM/icwsm11contents.php.

Mitchell, L., Frank, M., Harris, K., Dodds, P., and Danforth, C. (2013), "The geography of happiness: Connecting Twitter sentiment and expression, demographics, and objective characteristics of place," *PLOS ONE* 8: e64417. www.plosone.org/article/info%3Adoi%2F10.1371%2Fjournal.pone.0064417.

Mod, C. (2014), Photography, hello. craigmod.com/journal/photography_hello/.

Möller-Levet, C., Archer, S., Bucca, G., Laing, E., Slak, A., Kabiljo, R., Lo, J., Santhi, N., von Schantz, M., Smith, C., and Dijk, D.-J. (2013), "Effects of insufficient sleep on circadian rhythmicity and expression amplitude of the human blood transcriptome," *Proceedings of the National Academy of Sciences* 110: E1132–E1141. www.pnas.org/content/110/12/E1132.

De Montjoye, Y.-A., Hidalgo, C., Verleysen, M., and Blondel, V. (2013), "Unique in the crowd: The privacy bounds of human mobility," *Scientific Reports* 3: 1376.

Moore-Ede, M., Sulzman, F., and Fuller, C. (1982), *The clocks that time us: Physiology of the circadian timing system*. Cambridge, MA: Harvard University Press.

Moreno, C., Laje, G., Blanco, C., Jiang, H., Schmidt, A., and Olfson, M. (2007), "National trends in the outpatient diagnosis and treatment of bipolar disorder in youth," *Archives of General Psychiatry* 64: 1032–9.

Moretti, P., and Muñoz, M. (2013), "Griffiths phases and the stretching of criticality in brain networks," *Nature Communications* 4: 2521.

Mueggler, E. (2001), *The age of wild ghosts: Memory, violence, and place in southwest China*. Berkeley: University of California Press.

Muehlebach, A. (2013), "On precariousness and the ethical imagination: The year 2012 in sociocultural anthropology," *American Anthropologist* 115: 297–311.

Mullaney, D., Kripke, D., and Messin, S. (1980), "Wrist-actigraphic estimation of sleep time," *Sleep* 31: 83–92.

Musharbash, Y. (2013), "Night, sight, and feeling safe: An exploration of aspects of Warlpiri and Western sleep," *Australian Journal of Anthropology* 24: 48–63.

Nadel, D., Weiss, E., Simchoni, O., Tsatskin, A., Danin, A., and Kislev, M. (2004), "Stone age hut in Israel yields world's oldest evidence of bedding," *Proceedings of the National Academy of Sciences* 101: 6821–6. www.pnas.org/content/101/17/6821.

Navarrete, A., van Schaik, C., and Isler, K. (2011), "Energetics and the evolution of human brain size," *Nature* 480: 91–4.

Nekrutenko, A. and Taylor, J. (2012), "Next-generation sequencing data interpretation: enhancing reproducibility and accessibility," *Nature Reviews Genetics* 13: 667–72.

Niemitz, C. (2010), "The evolution of the upright posture and gait—a review and a new synthesis," *Naturwissenschaften* 97: 241–63.

Nishimoto, S., Vu, A., Naselaris, T., Benjamini, Y., Yu, B., and Gallant, J. (2011), "Reconstructing visual experiences from brain activity evoked by natural movies," *Current Biology* 21: 1641–6.

Noë, A. (2004), *Action in perception*. Cambridge, MA: MIT Press.

Nordstrom, C. (2004), *Shadows of war: Violence, power, and international profiteering in the twenty-first century*. Berkeley: University of California Press.

Nozawa, S. (2013), "Characterization," *Semiotic Review* 3. www.semioticreview. com/index.php/open-issues/issue-open-2013/21-characterization.html.

Nummenma, L., Glerean, E., Hari, R., and Hietanen, J. (2014), "Bodily maps of emotions," *Proceedings of the National Academy of Sciences* 111: 646–51. www.pnas.org/content/111/2/646.

O'Brien, M. and Laland, K. (2012), "Genes, culture, and agriculture: an example of human niche construction," *Current Anthropology* 53: 434–70.

O'Brien, M. and Shennan, S. (eds) (2009), *Innovation in cultural systems: Contributions from evolutionary anthropology*. Cambridge, MA: MIT Press.

Ogle, W. (1866), "On the diurnal variations in the temperature of the human body in health," *St. George's Hospital Reports* 1: 221–45.

Pachter, L. (2013), "23andMe genotypes are all wrong, *later updated to* Multiple testing an issue for 23andMe," *Bits of DNA: Reviews and Commentaries on Computational Biology* (blog), 30 November. liorpachter.wordpress. com/2013/11/30/23andme-genotypes-are-all-wrong/.

Packer, G. (2013), *The unwinding: An inner history of the new America*. New York: Farrar, Straus and Giroux.

Pálsson, G. (2012), "Decode me! Anthropology and personal genomics," *Current Anthropology* 53: S185–S195.

Parker, M. and Bull, S. (et al.) (2009), "Ethical data release in genome-wide association studies in developing countries," *PLOS Medicine* 6: e1000143. OA

Pascual-Leone, A. and Hamilton, R. (2001), "The metamodal organization of the brain," in C. Casanova and M. Ptito (eds), *Progress in Brain Research*, vol. 134, *Vision: from neurons to cognition*, 427–45. Amsterdam: Elsevier.

Payne, C. (2014), "How activity trackers remove our rights to our most intimate data," *Guardian*, 3 June. www.theguardian.com/technology/2014/jun/03/how-activity-trackers-remove-rights-personal-data.

Pedersen, M. (2011), *Not quite shamans: Spirit worlds and political lives in northern Mongolia*. Ithaca, NY: Cornell University Press.

Pedersen, M. (2012), "Common nonsense: A review of certain recent reviews of the 'ontological turn'," *Anthropology of This Century* 5. aotcpress.com/articles/common_nonsense/

Pedersen, M. (2013), "The fetish of connectivity," in P. Harvey, E. Casella, G. Evans, H. Knox, C. McLean, E. Silva, N. Thoburn, and K. Woodward, *Objects and materials: A Routledge companion*, 197–207. London: Routledge.

Pelegrin, J. (2009), "Cognition and the emergence of language: A contribution from lithic technology," in S. De Beaune, F. Coolidge, and T. Wynn (eds), *Cognitive archaeology and human evolution*, 95–108. Cambridge: Cambridge University Press.

Pentland, A. (2006), "Automatic mapping and modeling of human networks," *Physica A* 378: 59–67.

Pentland, A., Lazer, D., Brewer, D., and Heibeck, T. (2009), "Using reality mining to improve public health and medicine," *Studies in Health Technology and Informatics* 149: 93–102.

Peters, L., and Price-Williams, D. (1983), "A phenomenological overview of trance," *Transcultural Psychiatry* 20: 5–39.

Pflug, B. and Tölle, R. (1970), "Disturbances of the 24-hour rhythm in endogenous depression and the treatment of endogenous depression by sleep deprivation," *International Pharmacopsychiatry* 6: 187–96.

Phillips, P., Moon, H., Rizvi, S. and Rauss, P. (2000), "The FERET evaluation methodology for face-recognition algorithms," *IEEE Transactions on Pattern Analysis and Machine Intelligence* 22: 1090–104.

Phillips-Silver, J. and Keller, P. (2012), "Searching for roots of entrainment and joint action in early musical interactions," *Frontiers in Human Neuroscience* 6: 26 journal.frontiersin.org/Journal/10.3389/fnhum.2012.00026/abstract.

Picone, M. (1991), "Ombres japonaises: l'illusion dans les contes de revenants (1685–989)," *L'Homme* 117: 122–50.

Piketty, T. (2013), *Capital in the twenty-first century*, trans. A. Goldhammer. Cambridge, MA: Harvard University Press.

Porciúncula, L., Sallaberry, C., Mioranzza, S., Botton, P., and Rosemberg, D. (2013), "The Janus face of caffeine," *Neurochemistry International* 63: 594–609.

Puredoxyk (2013), *Ubersleep: Nap-based sleep schedules and the polyphasic lifestyle*, 2nd edn. Self-published.

Ramirez, J.-M., Anderson, T., and Garcia, A. (2014), "The ins and outs of breathing," *eLife* 3: e03375. elifesciences.org/content/3/e03375.

Reas, C., McWilliams, C., and LUST (2010), *Form + code in design, art, and architecture*. Princeton: Princeton Architectural Press.

Reynolds, D. and Reason, M. (eds) (2012), *Kinesthetic empathy in creative and cultural practices*. Bristol: Intellect.

Rhee, J. (2013), "Beyond the Uncanny Valley: Masahiro Mori and Philip K. Dick's *Do Androids Dream of Electric Sheep?*" *Configurations* 21: 301–29.

Richerson, P. and Boyd, R. (2005), *Not by genes alone: How culture transformed human evolution.* Chicago: University of Chicago Press.

Richter, D. and Smith, J. (2014), "Respiratory rhythm generation in vivo," *Physiology* 29: 58–71. physiologyonline.physiology.org/content/29/1/58.

Rito, T., Richards, M., Fernandes, V., Alshamali, F., Cerny, V., Pereira, L., and Soares, P. (2013), "The first modern human dispersals across Africa," *PLOS ONE* 8: e80031. www.plosone.org/article/info%3Adoi%2F10.1371%2Fjournal. pone.0080031.

Robbins, J. (2007), "Continuity thinking and the problem of Christian culture: Belief, time, and the anthropology of Christianity," *Current Anthropology* 48: 5–38.

Roberts, A. and Thorpe, S. (2014), "Challenges to human uniqueness: Bipedalism, birth and brains," *Journal of Zoology* 292: 281–9.

Roebuck, A., Monasterio, V., Gederi, E., Osipov, M., Behar, J., Malhotra, A., Penzel, T., and Clifford, C. (2014), "A review of signals used in sleep analysis," *Physiological Measurement* 35: R1–R57.

Rosa, H. (2013), *Social acceleration: A new theory of modernity*, trans. J. Trejo-Mathys. New York: Columbia University Press.

Rosenthal, N., Sack, D., Gillin, C., Lewy, A., Goodwin, F., Davenport, Y., Mueller, P., Newsome, D., and Wehr, T. (1984), "Seasonal affective disorder: a description of the syndrome and preliminary findings with light therapy," *Archives of General Psychiatry* 41: 72–80.

Roth, C., Kang, S., Batty, M., and Barthélemy, M. (2011), "Structure of urban movements: Polycentric activity and entangled hierarchical flows," *PLOS ONE* 6: e15923. www.plosone.org/article/info%3Adoi%2F10.1371%2Fjournal.pone.0015923.

Rushkoff, D. (2013), *Present shock: When everything happens now.* New York: Current.

Sadeh, A. (2011), "The role and validity of actigraphy in sleep medicine: An update," *Sleep Medicine Reviews* 15: 259–67.

Sahlins, M. (1972), *Stone age economics.* London: Tavistock.

Sahlins, M. (1995), *How 'natives' think: About Captain Cook, for example.* Chicago: University of Chicago Press.

Saldanha, A. (2007), *Psychedlic white: Goa Trance and the viscosity of race.* Minneapolis: University of Minnesota Press.

Salonen, A. and de Vos, W. (2014), "Impact of diet on human intestinal microbiota and health," *Annual Review of Food Science and Technology* 5: 239–62.

Sattherthwaite (2007), *The transition to a predominantly urban world and its underpinnings.* London: International Institute for Environment and Development.

Schacter, D., Addis, D., Hassabis, D., Martin, V., Spreng, N., and Szpunar, K. (2012), "The future of memory: Remembering, imagining, and the brain," *Neuron* 76: 677–94.

Van Schaik, C. (2013), "The costs and benefits of flexibility as an expression of behavioural plasticity: A primate perspective," *Philosophical Transactions of the Royal Society B* 368: 20120339.

Scheer, F., Hilton, M., Mantzoros, C., and Shea, S. (2009), "Adverse metabolic and cardiovascular consequences of circadian misalignment," *Proceedings of the National Academy of Sciences* 106: 4453–8.

Schilder, P. (1923), *Das Körperschema.* Berlin: Springer.

Schilder, P. (1935), *The image and appearance of the human body.* London: K. Paul, Trench, Trubner.

Schmidt, R. and Richardson, M. (2008), "Dynamics of interpersonal coordination," in A. Fuchs and V. Jirsa (eds), *Coordination: Neural, behavioral and social dynamics*, 281–308. Berlin: Springer.

Schroeder, C., Wilson, D., Radman, T., Scharfman, H., and Lakatos, P. (2010), "Dynamics of active sensing and perceptual selection," *Current Opinion in Neurobiology* 20: 172–6.

Schüll, N. (2012), *Addiction by design: Machine gambling in Las Vegas.* Princeton: Princeton University Press.

Schulte, B. (2014), *Overwhelmed: Work, love, and play when no one has the time.* New York: Farrar, Straus and Giroux.

Scott, J. (1998), *Seeing like a state: How certain schemes to improve the human condition have failed.* New Haven: Yale University Press.

Scott, J. (2010), *The art of not being governed: An anarchist history of upland Southeast Asia.* New Haven: Yale University Press.

Sebanz, N., Bekkering, H., and Knoblich, G. (2006), "Joint action: Bodies and minds moving together," *Trends in Cognitive Sciences* 10: 70–6.

Seligman, E. (2010), "The unmaking and making of self: Embodied suffering and mind-body healing in Brazilian Candomblé," *Ethos* 38: 297–320.

Seymour, K., Clifford, C., Logothetis, N., and Bartels, A. (2009), "The coding of color, motion, and their conjunction in the human visual cortex," *Current Biology* 19: 177–85.

Sharf, R. (1995), "Buddhist modernism and the rhetoric of experience," *Numen* 42: 228–83.

Sharf, R. (2000), "The rhetoric of experience and the study of religion," *Journal of Consciousness Studies* 7: 267–87.

Sharf, R. (2014), "Mindfulness and mindlessness in early Chan," *Philosophy East & West* 64: 933–64.

Sharp, H. (2004), *Loon: Memory, meaning, and reality in a Northern Dene community*. Lincoln: University of Nebraska Press.

Sheets-Johnstone, M. (2011), *The primacy of movement*, 2nd edn. Amsterdam: John Benjamins.

Shennan, S. (ed.) (2009), *Pattern and process in cultural evolution*. Berkeley: University of California Press.

Shepard, M. (ed.) (2008), *Sentient city: Ubiquitous computing, architecture, and the future of urban space*. Cambridge, MA: MIT Press.

Sherman, H. (1950), *The nutritional improvement of life*. New York: Columbia University Press.

Shiffrar, M. (2011), People watching: Visual, motor, and social processes in the perception of human movement. *WIREs Cognitive Science* 2: 68–78.

Shockley, K. (2012), "Cross recurrence quantification of interpersonal postural activity," in M. Riley and G. Van Orden (eds), *Tutorials in contemporary nonlinear methods for the behavioral sciences*, 142–77. Washingtong, DC: National Science Foundation. www.nsf.gov/sbe/bcs/pac/nmbs/nmbs.pdf.

Sierra, M. and Berrios, G. (2000), "The Cambridge Depersonalization Scale: A new instrument for the measurement of depersonalization," *Psychiatry Research* 93: 153–64.

Sierra, M. and David, A. (2011), "Depersonalization: A selective impairment of self-awareness," *Consciousness and Cognition* 20: 99–108.

Simpson, S. and Galbraith, J. (1906), "Observations on the normal temperature of the monkey and its diurnal variation, and on the effect of changes in the daily routine on this variation," *Transactions of the Royal Society of Edinburgh* 45: 65–106.

Sinha, P. (2002), "Recognizing complex patterns," *Nature Neuroscience* 5: 1093–7.

St. John, G. (2013), "The vibe of the exiles: Aliens, afropsychedelia and psyculture," *Dancecult* 5: 56–87.

Stampi, C. (ed.) (1992), *Why we nap: Evolution: Chronobiology, and the functions of polyphasic and ultrashort sleep*. Basel: Birkhäuser.

Stein, D., Rousseau, C., Lacroix, L. (2004), "Between innovation and tradition: The paradoxical relationship between Eye Movement Desensitization and Reprocessing and altered states of consciousness," *Transcultural Psychiatry* 41: 5–30.

Stein, J. (2010), "Securitization, shadow banking and financial fragility," *Daedalus* 139(4): 41–51.

Steinfeld, H., Gerber, P., Wassenaar, T., Castel, V., and de Haan, C. (2006), *Livestock's long shadow: Environmental issues and options*. Rome: Food and Agriculture Organization.

Stephan, K. and Roebroeck, A. (2012), "A short history of causal modeling of fMRI data," *NeuroImage* 62: 856–63.

Sternberg, D., Ballard, K., Hardy, J., Katz, B., Doraiswamy, P., and Scanlon, M. (2013), "The largest human cognitive performance dataset reveals insights into the effects of lifestyle factors and aging," *Frontiers in Human Neuroscience* 7: 292. OA

Stilgoe, J. (2014), *Old fields: Photography, glamour, and fantasy landscape.* Charlottesville: University of Virginia Press.

Stopczynski, A., Sekara, V., Sapienzynski, P., Cuttone, A., Madsen, M., Larsen, J., and Lehmann, S. (2014), "Measuring large-scale social networks with high resolution," *PLOS ONE* 9: e95978. www.plosone.org/article/info%3Adoi%2F10.1371%2Fjournal.pone.0095978.

Strathern, M. (1988), *The gender of the gift: Problems with women and problems with society in Melanesia.* Berkeley: University of California Press.

Striem-Amit, E., Cohen, L., Dehaene, S., and Amedi, A. (2012), "Reading with sounds: Sensory substitution selectively activates the visual word form area in the blind," *Neuron* 76: 640–52.

Van Sweden, B. (1986), "Disturbed vigilance in mania," *Biological Psychiatry* 21: 311–13.

Szymanski, J. (1920), Aktivität und Ruhe bei Tieren und Menschen.

Taigman, Y., Yang, M., Ranzato, M. A., and Wolf, L. (2014), "Deepface: Closing the gap to human-leel performance in face verification." IEEE Conference on Computer Vision and Pattern Recognition, Columbus, OH, 24–7 June. Open access version at www.cv-foundation.org/openaccess/content_cvpr_2014/papers/Taigman_DeepFace_Closing_the_2014_CVPR_paper.pdf.

Talmy, L. (2000), *Toward a cognitive semantics*, vol. 1. Cambridge, MA: MIT Press.

Tasali, E., Leproult, R., Ehrmann, D., and Van Cauter, E. (2008), "Slow-wave sleep and the risk of type 2 diabetes in humans," *Proceedings of the National Academy of Sciences* 105: 1044–9.

Thompson, E. (2007), *Mind in life: Biology, phenomenology, and the sciences of mind.* Cambridge, MA: Harvard University Press.

Thornton, P. (2010), "Livestock production: Recent trends, future prospects," *Philosophical Transactions of the Royal Society B* 365: 2853–67.

Tikka, P., Väljamäe, A., de Borst, A., Pugliese, R., Ravaja, N., Kaipainen, M., and Takala, T. (2012), "Enactive cinema paves the way for understanding complex real-time social interaction in neuroimaging experiments," *Frontiers in Human Neuroscience* 6: 298. journal.frontiersin.org/Journal/10.3389/fnhum.2012.00298/abstract.

Todd, A. (2012), "My story: Struggling, bullying, suicide, self harm." Self-produced, digital video, 8'54". www.youtube.com/watch?v=vOHXGNx-E7E.

Tomasello, M., Carpenter, M., Call, J., Behne, T., and Moll, H. (2005), "Understanding and sharing intentions: The origins of cultural cognition," *Behavioral and Brain Sciences* 28: 675–735.

Trejo-Mathys, J. (2013), "Translator's introduction: Modernity and time," in H. Rosa (ed.), *Social acceleration: A new theory of modernity*, xi–xxxii. New York: Columbia University Press.

Tresch, J. (2012), *The romantic machine: Utopian science and technology after Napoleon.* Chicago: University of Chicago Press.

Tsydenova, O. and Bengtsson, M. (2011), "Chemical hazards associated with treatment of waste electrical and electronic equipment," *Waste Management* 31: 45–58.

Tufte, E. (1997), *Visual explanations*. Cheshire, CT: Graphics Press.

Turk, M. and Pentland, A. (1991), "Eigenfaces for recognition," *Journal of Cognitive Neuroscience* 3: 71–86.

Turkle, S. (2011), *Alone together: Why we expect more from technology and less from each other*. New York: Basic Books.

Turner, F. (2006), *From counterculture to cyberculture: Stewart Brand, the Whole Earth Network, and the rise of digital utopianism*. Stanford: Stanford University Press.

Tuunainen, A., Kripke, D., and Endo, T. (2009), "Light therapy for non-seasonal depression (review)," *The Cochrane Library* 2009, Issue 3. Reprinted from *Cochrane Database of Systematic Reviews* 2004, Issue 2, Article No. CD004050.

Ungar, P., Grine, F., and Teaford, M. (2006), "Diet in early *Homo*: A review of the evidence and a new modal of adaptive versatility," *Annual Review of Anthropology* 35: 209–28.

Vallverdú, J., Vaquero, M., Cáceres, I., Allué, E., Rosell, J., Saladié, P., Chacón, G., Ollé, A., Canals, A., Sala, R., Courty, M., and Carbonell, E. (2010), "Sleeping activity area within the site structure of archaic human groups," *Current Anthropology* 51: 137–45.

Velasquez-Manoff, M. (2014), "What happens when the poor receive a stipend?" *New York Times*, 18 January. opinionator.blogs.nytimes.com/2014/01/18/what-happens-when-the-poor-receive-a-stipend/.

De Vignemont, V. (2010), "Body schema and body image—pros and cons," *Neuropsychologia* 48: 669–80.

Vinciarelli, A., Pantic, M., and Bourlard, H. (2009), "Social signal processing: Survey of an emerging domain," *Image and Vision Computing* 27: 1743–59.

Virilio, P. ([1977] 2006), *Speed and politics*, trans. M. Polizzotti. Los Angeles: Semiotext(e).

Vogler, P. (2008), "Sleeping as a a refuge? Embodied vulnerability and corporeal security during refugees' sleep at the Thai–Burma border," in L. Brunt and B. Stieger (eds), *Worlds of Sleep*, 193–210. Berlin: Franke and Timme.

De Vos, M. and Jander, G. (2010), "Volatile communication in plant–aphid interactions," *Current Opinion in Plant Biology* 13: 366–71.

Wade, N. (2011), "Phonetic clues hint language is Africa-born," *New York Times*, 14 April. www.nytimes.com/2011/04/15/science/15language.html.

Wang X.-W., Han X.-P., and Wang B.-H. (2014), "Correlations and scaling laws in human mobility," *PLOS ONE* 9: e84954. www.plosone.org/article/info%3Adoi%2F10.1371%2Fjournal.pone.0084954.

Ward, J. and Meijer, P. (2010), "Visual experiences in the blind induced by an auditory sensory substitution device," *Consciousness and Cognition* 19: 492–500.

Wehr, T. (2001), "Photoperiodism in humans and other primates: evidence and implications," *Journal of Biological Rhythms* 16: 348–64.

Wehr, T., Goodwin, F., Wirz-Justice, A., Breitmaier, J., and Craig, C. (1982), "48-hour sleep–wake cycles in manic–depressive illness," *Archives of General Psychiatry* 39: 559–65.

Weinberger, S. (2010), "Intent to deceive?" *Nature* 465: 412–15.

Weiner, A. (1992), *Inalienable possessions: The paradox of keeping-while-giving.* Berkeley: University of California Press.

Westerink, J., Krans, M., and Ouwekerk, M. (eds) (2011), *Sensing emotions: The impact of context on experience measurements.* Dordrecht: Springer.

Wever, R. (1979), *The circadian system of man: Results of experiments under temporal isolation.* Berlin: Springer.

Wiley, A. (2011), *Re-imagining milk.* London: Routledge.

Willerslev, R. (2007), *Soul hunters: Hunting, animism, and personhood among the Siberian Yukaghirs.* Berkeley: University of California Press.

Wilson, M. and Wilson, T. (2005), "An oscillator model of the timing of turn-taking," *Psychonomic Bulletin and Review* 12: 957–68.

Wirth, L. (1938), "Urbanism as a way of life," *American Journal of Sociology* 44: 1–24.

Wirz-Justice, A. (2005), "Chronotherapeutics (light and wake therapy) in affective disorders," *Psychological Medicine* 35: 939–44.

Wirz-Justice, A., Benedetti, F., and Terman, M. (2013), *Chronotherapeutics for affective disorders: A clinician's manual for light and wake therapy*, 2nd edn. Basel: Karger.

Wolf, G. and Ramirez, E. (2014), *Quantified Self/Public Health Symposium.* San Francisco: QS Labs. Available at quantifiedself.com/symposium/ Symposium-2014/QSPublicHealth2014_Report.pdf.

Worthman, C. (2011), "Developmental cultural ecology of sleep," in M. El-Sheikh (ed.), *Sleep and development: Familial and socio-cultural considerations*, 167–94. Oxford: Oxford University Press.

Worthman, C. and Brown, R. (2013), "Sleep budgets in a globalizing world: Biocultural interactions influence sleep sufficiency among Egyptian families," *Social Science & Medicine* 79: 31–9.

Worthman, C. and Melby, M. (2002), "Toward a comparative developmental ecology of human sleep," in M. Carskadon, *Adolescent sleep patterns: Biological, social, and psychological influences*, 69–117. Cambridge: Cambridge University Press.

Wynn and Coolidge (2010), "Beyond symbolism and language: An introduction to Supplement 1, Working memory," *Current Anthropology* 51: S5–S16.

Yan, W.-J., Wang, S.-J., Liu, Y.-J., Wu, Q., and Fu, X. (2014a), "For micro-expression recognition: Database and suggestions," *Neurocomputing* 136: 82–7.

Yan, W.-J., Li, X., Wang, S.-J., Zhao, G., Liu, Y.-J., Chen, Y.-H., and Fu, X. (2014b), "CASME II: an improved spontaneous micro-expression database and the baseline evaluation," *PLOS ONE* 9: e86041. www.plosone.org/article/ info%3Adoi%2F10.1371%2Fjournal.pone.0086041.

Yu, A. (2006), *The monkey and the monk: A revised abridgement of* The Journey to the West. Chicago: University of Chicago Press.

Zhang, M., Fu, Q., Chen, Y.-H., Fu, X. (2014), "Emotional context influences micro-expression recognition," *PLOS ONE* 9: e95018. www.plosone.org/ article/info%3Adoi%2F10.1371%2Fjournal.pone.0095018.

Zhang, X. and Gao, Y. (2009), "Face recognition across pose: A review," *Pattern Recognition* 42: 2876–96.

Zhao, W., Chellappa, R., Phillips. P., and Rosenfeld, A. (2003), "Face recognition: A literature survey," *ACM Computing Surveys* 35: 399–458.

Index